A Light to the Gentiles

A Light to the Gentiles

Jonathan Cope

The Christadelphian
404 Shaftmoor Lane, Hall Green, Birmingham B28 8SZ, UK

2015

First published 2015

© 2015 The Christadelphian Magazine and Publishing Association

ISBN 978 0 85189 296 2 (print edition)
ISBN 978 0 85189 297 9 (electronic edition)

Printed and bound in Malta by
Gutenberg Press Limited

Extracts from the Authorised Version of the Bible (The King James Bible), the rights in which are vested in the Crown, are reproduced by permission of the Crown's Patentee, Cambridge University Press.

Scripture quotations marked (NKJV) are from the New King James Version®. Copyright © 1982 by Thomas Nelson Inc. Used by permission. All rights reserved.

Contents

Preface vii
1. Introduction 1
2. Abraham 6
3. Tamar 12
4. Pharaoh's dealings with Joseph and his family 21
5. Pharaoh's daughter 29
6. A mixed multitude 34
7. Zipporah and her family 40
8. The kindness of the Kenites 51
9. Caleb the Kenezite 56
10. Rahab the harlot 65
11. The Gibeonites 75
12. Jael and Heber 87
13. Ruth the Moabitess 96
14. David's army 105
15. Uriah the Hittite 112
16. Shobi the Ammonite 121
17. Araunah the Jebusite 128
18. Obed-edom the Gittite 137
19. Hiram king of Tyre 145
20. The queen of Sheba 152
21. The widow of Zarephath 160

22. Naaman the Syrian 168
23. Elisha and the Syrian army 177
24. Jonah and the mariners 184
25. Jonah and the Ninevites 191
26. The Rechabites 199
27. Ebed-melech the Ethiopian 210
28. In the days of Daniel 219
29. In the days of Esther 231
30. The return from captivity 238
31. Wise men from the east 248
32. John the Baptist 257
33. The centurion at Capernaum 264
34. The Syrophenician woman 272
35. The Ethiopian eunuch 280
36. Cornelius 288
Scripture index 297

Preface

THE children of Israel were about to enter God's land, the land promised to Abraham. Prior to that momentous time, the challenge of the Father for His people was very clear: they were to avoid the practices of the Gentile nations at all costs. Worshipping the pagan deities of those people was punishable by death (Deuteronomy 13:6-11). Separation was absolutely vital (12:10-31). In this they would be emulating the example of their forefather Abraham who, at the instruction of God, had come out of Ur of the Chaldees (Genesis 12:1-3).

However, this did not mean that there was no hope for any of those from the nations. Right throughout the Old Testament, and at the commencement of the New, we read of faithful men and women who came to Israel from surrounding lands. They embraced Israel's hope; they worshipped Israel's God. Their lives cry out to us of courage, faith and sacrifice. In seeking to become associated with the only true and living God, many of these people would have turned their backs on everything and everyone they knew and loved. Family allegiances would have been severed; friendships would have come to an end. Jesus spoke of one who followed him suffering at the hands of his relations and losing his life to find it (Matthew 10:36,39). We see a wonderful manifestation of this practice in the lives of these faithful Gentiles.

Truly these giants of faith are both a challenge and a source of great encouragement to any seeking to serve the God of Israel in these last days.

"Arise, shine; for thy light is come, and the glory of the LORD is risen upon thee. For, behold, the darkness shall cover the earth, and gross darkness the people: but the LORD shall arise upon thee, and his glory shall be seen upon thee. And the Gentiles shall come to thy light, and kings to the brightness of thy rising." (Isaiah 60:1-3)

Jonathan Cope
Coventry
March 2015

1 |

Introduction

THE largest proportion of the word of God, the Old Testament especially, revolves around the nation of Israel. From the days of Abraham, Isaac and Jacob, the historical record of the lives of the natural descendants of these wonderful men fill the pages of much of God's word. Jacob was renamed Israel after his encounter with the angel at Penuel (Genesis 32:28) and it is this one key nation whom the Father selected as His people, calling them, blessing them, chastening them and loving them (Deuteronomy 7:6-8).

The Old Testament describes Israel in times of strength and times of weakness. We encounter them in their own land and in captivity amongst the nations round about (Egypt, Assyria or Babylon). They are led by judges and kings. Sometimes we find them united; at other times they descend into civil war and virtual anarchy. And we learn of their attitude to the Lord God and His laws: from times when they manifested the greatest spirituality, to days of apathy or occasions when it appears they could barely have been any more godless.

"Salvation is of the Jews" said the Lord Jesus Christ when speaking with the Samaritan woman (John 4:22). The hope contained in scripture is "the hope of Israel" (Acts 28:20). Paul's earnest desire and prayer to God was that Israel might be saved (Romans 10:1). Are they cast away? Are they no longer God's people? Paul asks, and then answers, this question most forcibly: "God forbid" (11:1); literally (as the NKJV records it): "Certainly not!"

Is there any hope for the Gentiles?

Based upon passages such as those listed above, it would be logical for a Gentile man – one who has no association with the nation of Israel and unable to trace his ancestry back to the forefathers of the Jewish race – to conclude that there is no hope for him. If the God of the Bible is "the God of Israel" (a phrase used over two hundred times in scripture), what hope is there for someone *not* of this race?

The answer is very clear: just as the love of God was shown primarily to one nation in the days before the death and resurrection of the Master, that same love is poured out on any who will turn to Him in faith, believing and responding to His word.

The promise of salvation for faithful Gentiles

The command of the Master, immediately prior to his ascension to heaven was that the word of God should be preached:

> "... in Jerusalem, and in all Judaea, and in Samaria, and unto the uttermost part of the earth." (Acts 1:8)

The Apostle Peter, astounded that the gifts of the Holy Spirit were poured out upon Gentiles, stated:

> "... Of a truth I perceive that God is no respecter of persons: but in every nation he that feareth him, and worketh righteousness, is accepted with him." (10:34,35)

Upon his return to Jerusalem, Peter was asked about his actions. Having heard of that which had taken place, the disciples were moved to declare:

> "... Then hath God also to the Gentiles granted repentance unto life." (11:18)

Indeed, in numerous passages in the Old Testament, even in the days when the greatest proportion of Gentiles remained in total darkness, there was the promise of the time to come when those *not* of the house of Israel would be blessed:

> "And in that day there shall be a root of Jesse, which shall stand for an ensign of the people; to it shall the Gentiles seek: and his rest shall be glorious." (Isaiah 11:10)

"A light to the Gentiles"

Speaking of this great hope, made plain for any who will come to Him in faith, the Father speaks on a number of occasions of faithful Gentiles being blessed. Man's natural state is one of ignorance of the things of the truth. Only those whom the Father chooses to call are made aware of His glorious promises, and therefore have a hope of eternal life. Others, as the Psalmist teaches, live out their lives ignorant of the hope of Israel:

> "Like sheep they are laid in the grave; death shall feed on them ... He shall go to the generation of his fathers; they shall never see light." (Psalm 49:14,19)

However, throughout scripture the Father speaks of His chosen ones being caused to "see the light":

> "For with thee is the fountain of life: in thy light shall we see light." (36:9)

It should come as no surprise, therefore, that scripture speaks on a number of occasions of Gentiles being "enlightened". In two Messianic prophecies Isaiah was inspired to record the Lord Jesus being "a light to (or of) the Gentiles" (Isaiah 42:6; 49:6). This language is picked up by Simeon (Luke 2:32), and Paul (Acts 13:47; 26:23). Indeed when we examine Paul's words in Acts 13, referring to the promise of the Messiah in Isaiah 49, we see how he states that these words refer not simply to the Master, but also to himself and Barnabas, as preachers of the truth concerning Jesus:

> "For so hath the Lord commanded us, saying, I have set thee to be a light of the Gentiles, that thou shouldest be for salvation unto the ends of the earth." (Acts 13:47)

Paul and Barnabas are the "us" in this verse. They were the lights, shining as Jesus had shone, enlightening the darkness of the Gentiles' lives. This was literally true in the later case of the Philippian jailor. When Paul and Silas had been singing in jail at midnight, following the earthquake, the jailor "called for a light" (16:29).

What we see in the action of Paul and his companions is obedience to a command of the Master during his ministry. He

was, and is, "the light of the world" (John 8:12; 9:5). However he also said this of his disciples:
"Ye are the light of the world ..."   (Matthew 5:14)
The Master was instructing his followers that they should shine as he shines, reflecting the glory of the God they serve. Others, then, would see the light, and some would desire to know of the hope the 'light-bearers' possess. This is, surely, a challenge and an exhortation for every one of us. Is our light shining in the darkness of this age? Do people see that we are different? And if they ask why we behave as we do, are we "ready to give an answer" (1 Peter 3:15)?

Faithful Gentiles in Old Testament times
Even under the Old Covenant, when an adherence to the things of the Mosaic Law was required, there were a number of faithful Gentiles who embraced Israel's hope.

Although we know of the background to the lives of some of these great men and women (people such as Rahab and Ruth), in the case of others we are left to surmise. How did Caleb (or his parents) become associated with the Israelites? From whom did Uriah learn the truth? Why was Araunah the Jebusite spared when the men of his city were killed? How was it that Elijah was sustained by a widow from Zarephath (of all places, for Jezebel originated in that very area)? Much as we might like to know the answers to such questions the word of God is largely silent. All we know is that these were people of the utmost faith. Indeed, it is often on occasions of extreme faithlessness within Israel that we find Gentile believers manifesting and loving Israel's God in a manner which is an example to us all.

In this book we shall be considering a number of these faithful Gentiles. We shall note their responses to the truth, and the immense sacrifices made by so many of these remarkable men and women. Truly, if not by birth then in spirit, they were "Israelites indeed" (see John 1:47). While their own people served their pagan deities, these faithful few believed, loved and obeyed the truth, often rejecting their families and friends, to

become part of the nation of Israel. Although speaking primarily of the immortal bride of Christ, the words of Psalm 45 are a fitting description of the actions of these amazing people:
> "Hearken, O daughter, and consider, and incline thine ear; forget also thine own people, and thy father's house."
> (verse 10)

These few Gentile men and women surely stand as representatives of the greater number who were to respond to the truth after the ascension of the Lord Jesus into heaven, when God's word was preached throughout the Gentile world.

The ecclesia today: enlightened and blessed

Most members of the ecclesia today are, by birth, Gentiles. Therefore as we consider these faithful men and women who lived so long ago, we see in their actions a pattern of our own conversion. Their decision to associate themselves with the nation of Israel mirrors our response to the word of God. By grace, we have been enlightened and become part of a community – "spiritual Israel" – seeking to manifest Israel's God and His beloved Son in a world of gross darkness:

> "But ye are a chosen generation, a royal priesthood, an holy nation, a peculiar people; that ye should shew forth the praises of him who hath called you out of darkness into his marvellous light."
> (1 Peter 2:9)

Abraham

ABRAHAM is, without any question, one of the greatest men of all time. The events in his life are recorded in immense detail for us in the book of Genesis. Such is the importance of the man, he is mentioned in fifteen other books in the Old Testament, as well as in eleven books in the New. We learn of his calling, his journey to the Promised Land, his time spent in Egypt, his dealings with Lot and the Gentiles who lived in Canaan. We know of his family, how he married Sarah and later took Hagar, and the sons they bore. Most especially we are told of the promises made to him by God, and how they can apply to every one of us, if we are willing to respond in faith.

The promises to Abraham and the salvation of faithful Gentiles

As we have noted in chapter one, Abraham was the father of the nation of Israel. Although he had other children, only one (Isaac) was the child of promise (Romans 9:7; Galatians 4:28). The same can be said of Isaac's sons: in the foreknowledge of God, Esau was hated, whilst Jacob was loved (Malachi 1:2,3). It was through a son of Jacob that the promised seed should come: Jesus Christ was born of David's line, descended from Judah (Luke 1:32,33; Hebrews 7:14). Naturally speaking therefore, a man born to Gentile parents might read of Abraham, the events in his life and the promises made to him, and conclude that these things have little or no relevance to him. However nothing could be further from the truth.

Firstly, the promises to Abraham do not *exclude* those unable to trace their ancestry back to him; rather faithful Gentiles are *included* in the promises made to this great man. Secondly, there is a strong indication that some of the Gentiles who came into contact with Abraham after he had entered the land embraced the same hope.

Abram had been called to leave Ur. To those of his city, this may have been highly unusual. A man was rejecting the comfort and safety of city life, taking his family and servants, and choosing to live in tents. Doubtless they wondered, and maybe even laughed at, this apparently irrational act. Yet Abraham had been called by the Father, and departed in faith. However, despite turning his back upon the people of Ur, he received a promise which spoke, in part, of hope for Gentiles:

"Now the LORD had said unto Abram, Get thee out of thy country, and from thy kindred, and from thy father's house, unto a land that I will shew thee: and I will make of thee a great nation, and I will bless thee, and make thy name great; and thou shalt be a blessing: and I will bless them that bless thee, and curse him that curseth thee: and in thee shall all families of the earth be blessed." (Genesis 12:1-3)

Note the final words in this first recorded section of blessings: in him (i.e., through one of his line who would be born afterwards), all families – Jews and Gentiles – would be blessed. The final promises made to this man also include the same wonderful words (22:18). No wonder, then, that Abraham is called "the father of us all" in Romans 4:16. Indeed the hope of salvation is freely available to –

"... the Jew first, and also to the Greek (Gentile)."

(1:16; 2:9,10)

How appropriate it is, therefore, that throughout the Bible, and most especially after the ascension of the Master to heaven, we read of Gentiles who embraced the hope of Israel. We accept that the nation of Israel are God's witnesses (Isaiah 43:10,12), for the covenant cannot be broken (Jeremiah 33:20). Today they are, for the most part, ignorant of the truth regarding

Jesus, for they are "veiled" to these things (2 Corinthians 3:14-16). Nonetheless they remain God's people, witnesses of His existence. Despite this, all who come to God in faith are accepted of Him, so Paul was inspired to write:

> "For as many of you as have been baptized into Christ have put on Christ. There is neither Jew nor Greek, there is neither bond nor free, there is neither male nor female: for ye are all one in Christ Jesus. And if ye be Christ's, then are ye Abraham's seed, and heirs according to the promise."
> (Galatians 3:27-29)

What an honour is ours! We are, by grace, Christ's, and therefore heirs of the promises made to Abraham. The land, one day, will be ours, when the number of the elect is made up, and a multitude of redeemed ones are united with the immortal Son of God (Revelation 7:9), sharing his nature (1 John 3:2). We are, in the time of our probation, called upon to look away from the things of this world. We must do in symbol what Abraham did in reality, refusing the temptations of this present age, and looking in faith to the time when all the promises of God will be fulfilled.

Abraham and the men of the land

We do not know how the call came. Whether by vision, angelic manifestation, or even from the lips of a man (perhaps Melchizedek?), Abraham was called to leave Ur of the Chaldees. Upon hearing the words of the Father, he departed, without knowing precisely where he was going (Hebrews 11:8). In due course he entered the land of promise, then known as Canaan (Genesis 12:5), and was told that his seed would possess it one day (verse 7). Later he was told that, as well as his seed inheriting it, he himself would also be a possessor of the land when those great promises have their ultimate fulfilment (13:15).

The Gentiles who inhabited the land at that time, Canaanites and Perizzites (verse 7), along with eight other nations named in Genesis 15:18-21, had, according to these promises, no lasting right to do so. They were able to claim ownership in the time of their mortality, but eternally the land would never be theirs. One day, according to the promises of our Heavenly Father, Abraham and his seed will take possession of it.

However the Genesis record makes it clear that Abraham had a very close association with some of the men of the land. He was, to the men of the city later known as Hebron, a "mighty prince" (23:6). Such was the respect in which he was held, Ephron the Hittite, the owner of the area Abraham desired to use as a burial place for Sarah, offered him the land for free (verse 15). Indeed, prior to this, there is a strong indication that some Gentiles had come to embrace the promises made to him. Despite having no relationship or connection with him naturally, they became "Abraham's seed".

Faithful Gentiles, possessors of the covenant with Abraham

The cities of Sodom and Gomorrah had been attacked, and the people either slain or taken captive. Lot, Abraham's nephew, had been captured, and news of this event reached the ears Abraham:

> "And there came one that had escaped, and told Abram the Hebrew; for he dwelt in the plain of Mamre the Amorite, brother of Eshcol, and brother of Aner: and these were confederate with Abram." (14:13)

Abram is termed "the Hebrew". This may have reference to his crossing over of the Euphrates; some commentators suggest this means 'one from beyond'. Strong's Concordance says a Hebrew was "an Eberite or descendant of Eber". Eber was one of Abraham's ancestors, who, along with Shem, was still alive in Abraham's day (indeed, like Shem, he outlived Abraham, see Genesis 11:10,11,16,17; 25:7). Some of the men of the land embraced the promises and became Abraham's seed.

Being a Hebrew, therefore, made Abraham an outsider. He was a stranger, a sojourner, as we are called upon to be. Like him, all members of the ecclesia are termed "pilgrims" (see Hebrews 11:13; 1 Peter 2:11). Nonetheless we find Abraham dwelling amongst three Amorites: Mamre, Aner and Eshcol.

Was he simply living in the same area, or was this something more important? The fact that these men accompanied him and his own trained servants on the mission to rescue Lot (Genesis 14:24) gives us a hint that they had a very close association with Abraham. However the word used to describe their relationship leaves us in no doubt: they were "confederate" with him (verse 13).

This is a combination of two Hebrew words: *ba'al*, which means 'master', 'husband', 'owner'; and *beriyth*, which means 'a compact'. Other translations speak of these men being "allies of Abram" (see, for example, RSV, NKJV). Rotherham's Literal Translation goes further: "they also having a covenant with Abram." The same Hebrew word is used in the following chapter:

"In the same day the LORD made a covenant (as in "confederate", 14:13) with Abram, saying, Unto thy seed have I given this land …" (15:18)

So the Abrahamic covenant of chapter 15 was *preceded* by a covenant between him and faithful Gentiles in chapter 14. He had, we assume, made these men aware of the promises he had received and they, believing the things that he had relayed unto them, had desired to become allied with him, serving his God. Abraham, like Noah was a "preacher (herald) of righteousness" (2 Peter 2:5). When asked of the reason for his dwelling in tents in a land which was not his, he was, to paraphrase 1 Peter 3:15:

"… ready always to give an answer to every man that asked of him a reason of the hope that was in him with meekness and fear."

Indeed, in the meanings of the names of these three men there may well be an allusion to this wonderful spiritual relationship which existed between them:
- Aner: 'a boy, servant'
- Eshcol: 'a bunch of grapes'
- Mamre: 'lusty' (vigorous)

Is this a picture of an ecclesia? *Servants* can become *alive*, like *a bunch of grapes*, for many are bound together as one.

Within an ecclesia, all sorts of people, male and female, young and old, natural and spiritual Israel, dwell together in love. They work for the spiritual benefit of others, and dwell in covenant relationship, having embraced the same promises. How appropriate it is, therefore, that Abraham should enjoy this relationship, not simply with some of his natural descendants (Hebrews 11:9), but also with certain faithful Gentiles. These men had, doubtless, rejected the pagan deities and practices of their own people, to serve the living God in truth and holiness. As we journey towards the Promised Land in faith, like Abraham, 'rejoicing to see Christ's day' (John 8:56), these faithful men are an example for us all.

3

Tamar

JACOB'S family was growing. He had been blessed with twelve sons and many daughters. Only one daughter is named in scripture, Dinah (see Genesis 34), however the phrase "all his daughters" (37:35) tells us that his family was great in number. Having severed himself from Laban (31:52), he wrestled with, and spoke to, an angel of God (32:24-29). At this time he was renamed Israel, being assured by the angel that as a prince he had "power with God" (verse 28). After meeting with Esau (33:4), he journeyed through the land of promise, finally arriving at Succoth. Here he built a house for his family and booths for his cattle (verse 17). Later he moved on once more, returning to the practice of living in tents (see Hebrews 11:9):

"And Jacob came to Shalem, a city of Shechem, which is in the land of Canaan, when he came from Padan-aram; and pitched his tent before the city." (Genesis 33:18)

Why did he leave a place of shelter and safety to live in tents again? Maybe instruction to do so had come directly from the Father. Or was it the location which was of such importance to him? Shalem is elsewhere translated "Salem" (14:18; Psalm 76:2). It was the city of Melchizedek, which would later become known as Jebus, and later still, Jerusalem, or Zion.

However a great number of people need food and drink. Flocks have to be sustained, and Jacob's sons were shepherds (Genesis 46:32). Strangers and pilgrims are unable to avoid all association with those around about them, and Israel's children had much contact with the people of the land. Such times can be positive: those of the world can come to embrace the truth, having seen the light of the Gospel message manifested by God's people. We know what Jesus said about being "the light of the world", and perhaps more appropriately considering the location here, about "a city that is set on an hill" (Matthew 5:14-16). Of course it is also possible that people of the world can draw away those of the truth. The vile events of Genesis 34 commence with Dinah going out to see "the daughters of the land" (Genesis 34:1).

The actions of Judah

As sons grew, wives would be sought for them. In Old Testament times, it was not unusual for the faithful to marry their close relations. Abraham's wife, Sarai, was his half-sister (20:12). Isaac married his cousin Rebekah (24:15,67). Jacob's wives, Leah and Rachel, were his cousins (28:5; 29:16,23-28). Clearly the genetic problems which can arise when children are conceived by close relatives today did not affect the people of God. This was surely an example of the Father making provision for His children. There was no need for His chosen to look outside of the "household of faith" for companionship and love. Yet, despite the many relations who were surely available, we know that in at least two cases, Gentile brides were sought.

> "And it came to pass at that time, that Judah went down from his brethren, and turned in to a certain Adullamite, whose name was Hirah. And Judah saw there a daughter of a certain Canaanite, whose name was Shuah; and he took her, and went in unto her." (38:1,2)

Here we have the practice of Genesis 3:6,7 and 6:2 being repeated. The people of God look, lust and then take. In each case, the result was disaster. Adam and Eve became subject to the curse and were driven from the garden (3:24). The sons of God embraced the ways of a world which was "filled with violence" (6:11). Judah became embroiled in a family from the world. Such things were to have an amazing and far-reaching effect upon him and his household, as we shall see. Hiram's name means 'nobility, a noble race' (Gesenius' Lexicon). He was an Adullamite, a people of whom we know very little, except that the name means 'justice of the people' (Gesenius). Regardless of the meanings, these people were of the world, and such associations invariably bring problems for the people of God:

"Ye adulterers ... know ye not that the friendship of the world is enmity with God? whosoever therefore will be a friend of the world is the enemy of God." (James 4:4)

Why did Judah leave the 'ecclesia' of his day? The previous chapter describes the ten brothers' dealings with Joseph. They were planning to kill him; however moved by Judah, they sold him to slavery. Indeed it was Judah's declaration that such practice was entirely appropriate – "for he is our brother and our flesh" (Genesis 37:27) – that prompted the other eight brothers (in Reuben's absence) to act as they did. Was it remorse that caused Judah to leave the family home and seek solace in the world? Could he not bear to see the sorrow that he and his brothers had brought upon their father (verse 35)? His words and actions later, when appealing before Joseph for the life of Benjamin, show us the real character of this man (44:18-34). Here was not someone whose conscience was seared (see 1 Timothy 4:2), rather he was touched by the sorrow of others, and had a genuine desire to ease the suffering of his family.

Three sons were born to Judah and Shuah: Er, Onan and Shelah (Genesis 38:3-5). There is no indication that Judah had returned to Jacob's fold, for Shelah's birth took place at a town called Chezib, with no mention of any of the natural family of Israel being present.

Tamar

It is at this stage that we are introduced to a woman by the name of Tamar. She was chosen as a wife for Er by Judah (verse 6). As we shall see later, she had almost certainly come from outside the family of Israel. Tamar's name, interestingly, means 'palm tree' (Strong).

A palm tree is truly amazing, able to survive and produce fruit where other trees and plants perish. Palms are mentioned many times in the Bible: Jericho, the first city to be taken by Israel after the crossing of the Jordan (Joshua 6) was known as "the city of palm trees" (Deuteronomy 34:3; 2 Chronicles 28:15). In scripture a palm tree is a symbol of life:

"The righteous shall flourish like the palm tree: he shall grow like a cedar in Lebanon." (Psalm 92:12)

"After this I beheld, and, lo, a great multitude, which no man could number, of all nations, and kindreds, and people, and tongues, stood before the throne, and before the Lamb, clothed with white robes, and palms in their hands ..." (Revelation 7:9)

How remarkable that a woman of the world should be called after that which speaks of righteousness and life! As we consider her words and actions, we shall see how appropriate this is.

Er was slain by the Lord for his wickedness (Genesis 38:7). In a command which was to be repeated under the Mosaic Law (Deuteronomy 25:5,6), Judah commanded his brother Onan to marry Tamar, that seed might be raised up to his dead brother. However, in an act of immense selfishness, Onan took steps to ensure that Tamar did not conceive by him (Genesis 38:9). Such was the seriousness of this act, the judgements of the Father were once more poured out:

"And the thing which he did displeased the LORD: wherefore he slew him also." (verse 10)

We are reminded of the refusal of the unnamed kinsman in Ruth to raise up seed to his dead relation. Boaz gathered the elders of Bethlehem together, and in their presence offered the man the opportunity to perform all that the law required. The man of Israel, like Onan, refused to raise up seed to another by a Gentile woman (Ruth 4:1-11).

The phrase used above is an unusual one. The thing "displeased" the Lord: it sounds almost trivial, as we may be displeased today if we are unable to act in a particular way. However the KJV margin states that the Hebrew is better rendered "was evil in the eyes of the LORD". The same phrase appears on only two other occasions in the Old Testament. One is in Isaiah 59:15, where the inspired prophet laments the fact that truth and judgement had failed from the nation. The other describes one of the greatest tragedies in the whole of God's word, a time when seed *was* conceived:

> "And when the mourning was past, David sent and fetched her (Bathsheba) to his house, and she became his wife, and bare him a son. But the thing that David had done displeased the LORD." (2 Samuel 11:27)

Would David have been moved to dwell on the sin of his ancestor's sons, as he contemplated that which he had done with Uriah and his wife, and the horrendous and far-reaching consequences for him and his family?

Judah's dealings with Tamar

Having lost two sons, and still, it seems, without any other son to continue his family line (see Genesis 46:12), Judah then made a somewhat unusual request of Tamar:

> "Then said Judah to Tamar his daughter in law, Remain a widow at thy father's house, till Shelah my son be grown: for he said, Lest peradventure he die also, as his brethren did. And Tamar went and dwelt in her father's house." (38:11)

Much as his concern for the well-being of his surviving son was commendable, his actions towards Tamar were wrong. Did he regard Tamar as 'cursed'? Did he feel she was unable or too old to bear a child, and hence an unsuitable bride? Whatever his thinking, sending her away from the things of Israel, back into the world, was a reversal of what had happened before (in the life of Abraham), and would happen later (Rahab, Ruth, etc.). Such an act can never be right for a son or daughter of God.

Describing the actions of those who have known the truth and turned back to the things of this age, the Apostle Peter was inspired to use particularly powerful language:

> "But it is happened unto them according to the true proverb, The dog is turned to his own vomit again; and the sow that was washed to her wallowing in the mire." (2 Peter 2:22)

In time, the promises of Judah were shown to be empty. He had no intention of giving Tamar to Shelah, and she knew this. A further tragedy then befell Judah, for his wife died (Genesis 38:12). We also learn of the true relationship between him and Hirah, in whose company he had first met his wife:

"... Judah was comforted, and went up unto his sheepshearers to Timnath, he and his friend Hirah the Adullamite."

(verse 12)

So Judah had severed himself from the household of faith, was friends with the world (see above, James 4:4), and was neglecting his duties concerning his daughter-in-law as required by the law of God. Truly, here we see a man whose grip on the things of the truth was, at this stage, virtually non-existent.

Tamar's desire to bear the seed

Tamar was unable to marry another. She lived in her father's house in a state of perpetual widowhood, waiting the time when she should have been given to Judah's third son. However as the years passed, she could see exactly what his intentions were:

"... for she saw that Shelah was grown, and she was not given unto him to wife." (Genesis 38:14)

The word of God does not command us to do wrong that good might come. Nowhere are we told that the end justifies the means, if such an outcome requires us to sin. However, Tamar was unable to bear a child because of the sin of Judah, and there is a strong indication that she knew the promises. She wanted to conceive seed – a "seed of the woman" – who would be an ancestor of the one promised to Abraham, through whom all families of the earth could be blessed (12:3). She therefore removed her widow's garments, veiled her face, dressed as a harlot, and waited for Judah to pass, sitting by the side of the road that led to Timnath (38:14).

It was in this place, Timnath, that Samson saw a Philistine woman who he desired to marry. It was also in the vineyards of that town that he killed a lion, where a swarm of bees was later found in the carcase (Judges 14:1-6). In Genesis 38 we find the same elements: an inappropriate relationship between a man and a woman, death and life.

Judah saw Tamar and, without realising who she was, went in unto her. He promised to send a kid from his flock, and gave her his signet, bracelets and staff until payment was made (Genesis 38:17,18). The only use of "kid" prior to this is in Genesis 27 where, in another act of deception, the skins of a kid were used to trick Isaac into believing Jacob was his firstborn, Esau. A kid is, of course, a young goat. Goats are often used a symbol for those who are rejected:

> "And he (Jesus) shall set the sheep on his right hand, but the goats on the left. Then shall the King say unto them on his right hand, Come, ye blessed of my Father, inherit the kingdom prepared for you from the foundation of the world ... Then shall he say also unto them on the left hand, Depart from me, ye cursed ..."   (Matthew 25:33,34,41)

A signet speaks of authority. In Ahab's day, Jezebel used his signet to seal a letter which required Naboth's death (1 Kings 21:8). The bracelet was some sort of band: elsewhere the same Hebrew word is translated "wire", and "thread"; under the law we read of the necessity of a "lace" or "ribband" (same Hebrew) of blue (Exodus 28:28; Numbers 15:38), indicating holiness. Yet here such an item of decoration or clothing spoke of sin. A staff is used for aid in walking. The same Hebrew word is translated "rod", and used to speak of Moses' staff, which became a serpent (Exodus 4:4). Surely here we have a symbol of a man who had ceased to walk aright before his God.

Judah had every intention of paying his debt, for he sent the kid by Hirah. Of course, Tamar was nowhere to be found, and the locals stated openly that there had been no harlot plying her trade in that area (Genesis 38:20,21). Judah's statement, "Let her take it to her, lest we be shamed" (verse 23) seems to imply that he had at least attempted to pay her.

In due course Tamar was found to be pregnant, and this time Judah was quick to act:

"And it came to pass about three months after, that it was told Judah, saying, Tamar thy daughter in law hath played the harlot; and also, behold, she is with child by whoredom. And Judah said, Bring her forth, and let her be burnt." (verse 24)

Why was she to be burnt? Why not stoned? Under the law a daughter of a priest who acted as a whore was burnt (Leviticus 21:9). This language is picked up in Revelation where the pagan church, which originated of course in the true ecclesia (1 John 2:19), and is termed a whore, is later burned (Revelation 17:1,16). Maybe Judah was seeking to portray himself as some sort of priest – although by doing so he would be defiling the true type of the one who would come, the true king-priest of Judah, Jesus Christ (Hebrews 7:14; Revelation 5:5).

Tamar's righteousness

Once more, let us note the unmistakeable Bible truth that sin is never acceptable. Nonetheless, Tamar's intention was right. She longed for a son, desiring that he might be part of the great seed promised to Abraham. When she was taken, she produced the three items listed above which belonged to Judah, identifying him as the father of her child. His response tells us all we need to know of her faithfulness – and, indeed, his repentance:

"And Judah acknowledged them, and said, She hath been more righteous than I; because that I gave her not to Shelah my son. And he knew her again no more." (Genesis 38:26)

Judah was a man who made mistakes, but was quick to acknowledge them. The next time he appears in scripture is in Genesis 43, when the brothers had journeys to Egypt to buy corn. So this incident may well have been the catalyst which prompted him to return to the fold. In due course he would play a greater part than any in bringing about the reunion which Joseph sought with his brothers (witness his remarkable, moving speech in Genesis 44:18-34, and his willingness to sacrifice self that Benjamin might go free). Certainly his twin sons, Pharez and Zarah, born of Tamar, were numbered amongst the children of Israel, and were included with those who travelled down to

Egypt to be sustained by Joseph in time of famine (46:12). Indeed Pharez was the one through whom the promises were to be fulfilled. The line of Jesus traces back to Abraham, Isaac, and Jacob through Judah and Pharez:

> "Judas begat Phares and Zara of Thamar ..." (Matthew 1:3)

Time does not permit a consideration of the unusual incident regarding the birth of the twins, where a scarlet thread was bound round the wrist of one, only for his brother to be born first (Genesis 38:27-30). Nor can we examine the other Tamar, a daughter of David and sister of Absalom, treated shamefully by her half-brother, Amnon (2 Samuel 13). We are, however, left with some wonderful lessons from the actions and words of this remarkable woman.

Having been sent back to her father's house, she could have remained in the world, seeking the short-term pleasures of this age. Rather she longed to be associated with the family of Israel, this small but growing community. She had heard of the promises, possibly from her father-in-law or other family members – maybe even from Jacob himself – and desired to be part of this amazing family of living ones. No wonder, then, that when Ruth, another faithful Gentile bride was taken, the people of Bethlehem speak to her husband, Boaz, of this very incident:

> "And let thy house be like the house of Pharez, whom Tamar bare unto Judah, of the seed which the LORD shall give thee of this young woman." (Ruth 4:12)

We do not face anything like the same challenges as Tamar. We do, however, have opportunities to manifest the truth to those in darkness. As spiritual Israel, when opportunity presents itself, may we be found ready to show the hope we have by the way we speak and act. By speaking a "word in season" (Isaiah 50:4), we may be able to play our part in enlightening those currently in darkness. We too can be a "light to the Gentiles":

> "But sanctify the Lord God in your hearts: and be ready always to give an answer to every man that asketh you a reason of the hope that is in you with meekness and fear."
> (1 Peter 3:15)

4 |

Pharaoh's dealings with Joseph and his family

THERE are, surely, few more amazing characters in the Bible than Joseph. There are certainly very few more powerful types of Christ. We need not consider the horrendous events in his life which commenced when he was seventeen (Genesis 37:2). We know how he was stripped of his coat by his brothers and placed in a pit. In Reuben's absence he was sold to Ishmaelites (verse 28), who then traded him on to Midianites (verse 36). Last of all he was sold to Potiphar (verse 36), where initially he enjoyed success as overseer of his house (39:1-5).

However, just when it seemed that he was beginning to prosper, the unrequited love (or more correctly, lust) of his master's wife, and her subsequent lies resulted in his being placed in jail. We can read the words of Genesis 39:20,21 and imagine him to have been, almost instantaneously, placed in a position of authority in the prison. We might describe such a man today as a "senior trustee". Yet, as has been noted many times, the Bible is its own best commentary. Prior to his elevation in that place, Joseph suffered terribly:

> "He sent a man before them, even Joseph, who was sold for a servant: whose feet they hurt with fetters: he was laid in iron: until the time that his word came: the word of the LORD tried him." (Psalm 105:17-19)

Joseph: a light to the Gentiles
In all of these cases, we find this faithful descendant of Abraham coming into contact with an immense number of Gentiles. With

the exception of the commencement of his time in Potiphar's household, such relationships were almost entirely negative. Even his dealings with the butler and baker, which had concluded with his interpreting their dreams (Genesis 40), appeared to have concluded in dismal failure. He had made one final appeal to the butler – remember me when you are restored:

"Yet did not the chief butler remember Joseph, but forgat him." (verse 23)

Truly Joseph could have concluded that all Gentiles were worthless, untrustworthy, pagans! All his efforts to do right had come to nought. For his faithfulness to God (see 39:9) he had been cast into jail. There seemed no likelihood of his ever leaving that place. He could have become bitter and angry. It might have seemed logical for that spirit to have been manifested towards those round about him. Yet, as we have seen, the word of God was "trying him". We are reminded of Abraham, whom the Father tempted or "tried" (22:1). In due course the time came for him to be raised from prison and play his part in transforming the nation of Egypt and saving the people of the Lord.

In this chapter we do not wish to consider in any detail the events of Joseph's life. Rather we shall seek to examine the relationship which existed between Joseph, Pharaoh and the Egyptians. As we shall see, Joseph is a classic example of one manifesting his faith by the way that he acted towards those round about him.

Egypt

No Gentile land is mentioned more in God's word than Egypt. It was, of course, a place which many of God's people visited. Abraham (12:10), Jacob (46:6) and the Master (Matthew 2:14) all sojourned in the land. The Egyptians are often portrayed as oppressors of the people of God, and their ways are typical of the ways of this world. No wonder, then, that in 1 Corinthians 10 the Apostle Paul speaks of Egypt as representing the world. The language of the exodus is used, with the departure of Israel from Egypt described as a type of our own conversion:

"Now these things were our examples ... all these things happened unto them for ensamples: and they are written for our admonition, upon whom the ends of the world are come."

(1 Corinthians 10:6,11)

So, the crossing of the Red Sea is a type of our baptism. The wilderness wanderings describe our time of probation now. The Promised Land represents the kingdom of God, which means that Egypt is a type of the world. How appropriate that when Israel left the land, we find Egypt in a time of darkness:

"They saw not one another, neither rose any from his place for three days: but all the children of Israel had light in their dwellings." (Exodus 10:23)

In the world we find only darkness. By God's grace we have been enlightened, for He has caused His "face to shine upon" us (Numbers 6:25). Like Israel under Moses, we have come out from a land of darkness and death, and are journeying, by grace, towards a time of life, glory and rest (Hebrews 4:9-11).

Life in Potiphar's house

Despite having been "stolen away" from his father (Genesis 40:15), Joseph clearly gave all he could in the service of his mortal master.

"And his master saw that the LORD was with him, and that the LORD made all that he did to prosper in his hand." (39:3)

Joseph manifested the truth to Potiphar and his household. Not only did people realise he had talent, they also knew why! Did Joseph use the covenant name of Yahweh in his dealings with Potiphar? Did he speak about the laws of God which had been handed down to him, possibly regarding food and animals? Such things would be repeated under the law; however a number of instructions recorded through Moses had clearly already been given prior to their revelation in the mount (circumcision, sacrifices, etc.).

Did Joseph reveal the wisdom of God to Potiphar and his household? There is a strong indication that this is the case. However such things had been of no benefit, naturally speaking, to him. For his faith and chastity he had been placed in jail. Yet he refused to permit these previous experiences to change the way he acted. We could say that he was "stedfast, unmoveable, always abounding in the work of the Lord", because he knew that his labour was "not in vain in the Lord" (1 Corinthians 15:58). He was not "weary in well doing" (Galatians 6:9).

Joseph's elevation from prison
The butler and baker had heard Joseph's wise words. One of them had survived and been restored to his former office, exactly as foretold. Yet for two long years Joseph remained in prison (Genesis 41:1). Finally, the time came for him to be raised. Pharaoh had dreams and there was none able to interpret them for him. At this point the butler remembered Joseph and, having shaved and changed his clothing, Joseph was summoned to stand before the king (verses 9-14).

There are so many lessons that can be drawn from the actions of Joseph here, and so many reminders of the Master, who was raised from the grave to enjoy a position of privilege and glory. We wish simply to note Joseph's response to Pharaoh's comment that he was a man able to interpret dreams:

"And Joseph answered Pharaoh, saying, It is not in me: God shall give Pharaoh an answer of peace." (verse 16)

Later he made the same comment: that God had revealed these things, and that it was through His power alone such things would be accomplished (verses 25,28,32). Here is surely a lesson we can all apply. Joseph was a man who 'nailed his flag to the mast'. Right from his very first conversation with Pharaoh he ensured that the king – then, arguably, the most powerful man in the world – knew the reason why he had this ability. It was solely because the God he served had blessed him.

Joseph's God-given wisdom: revealed to the Egyptians
Pharaoh was a man who worshipped many different gods. In Exodus 12:12 we are told that the plagues were the judgements of the Father being executed against *all* the gods of Egypt. Yet

Joseph made it clear right from the very beginning that he worshipped one God alone. Again, he was manifesting the spirit of a law which would be given to the generations following:

"Hear, O Israel: The LORD our God is one LORD."

(Deuteronomy 6:4)

Pharaoh could have rejected such a man out of hand. Yet he was willing to listen. Joseph enlightened him regarding the dreams, and his words were accepted by the king and his men:

"And the thing was good in the eyes of Pharaoh, and in the eyes of all his servants. And Pharaoh said unto his servants, Can we find such a one as this is, a man in whom the Spirit of God is?"

(Genesis 41:37,38)

Note that Pharaoh uses the phrase "the spirit of God". The Hebrew here is "Elohim" ('mighty ones'): this is the same word used by Joseph earlier. The words of Joseph had been very clear: 'God alone – the mighty one of my fathers, Abraham, Isaac and Jacob – has revealed this unto me. Only in His might can I accomplish anything. Only in His mercy can I reveal anything to you.' And Pharaoh agreed:

"And Pharaoh said unto Joseph, Forasmuch as God hath shewed thee all this, there is none so discreet and wise as thou art: thou shalt be over my house, and according unto thy word shall all my people be ruled: only in the throne will I be greater than thou. And Pharaoh said unto Joseph, See, I have set thee over all the land of Egypt." (verses 39-41)

The Master said we should not hide our light under a bushel (Matthew 5:15). Joseph provides a wonderful example of this, for he manifested the God he served, and others were guided in the ways of righteousness.

Joseph's guidance of Pharaoh and his men

The book of the Psalms provides insight into the work and words of Joseph at this time:

"He (Pharaoh) made him (Joseph) lord of his house, and ruler of all his substance: to bind his princes at his pleasure; and teach his senators wisdom." (Psalm 105:21,22)

So the senators, or elders of Egypt were taught wisdom by Joseph. Once more, we conclude that it was the wisdom of God which flowed forth from his lips. He knew, partly from being taught at the feet of his father, and probably also by divine revelation, the things of the Almighty. Indeed, in the faithful service of the Egyptians, in obedience to Joseph's words, we have a 'cameo' of the Gospel. We believe that great changes are coming on the earth, as revealed by the Father through His faithful servants, and so we prepare now, in faith, for that time. A man or woman who hears the Gospel message but chooses not to respond would be like an Egyptian, enlightened by Joseph, yet refusing to lay up food for the years of famine that were to come. Is this what is hinted at above – those princes who were bound at Joseph's pleasure?

There is a further indication of the respect with which Joseph was held amongst Pharaoh and his men in the name (or, more correctly, title) which the king gave him:

"And Pharaoh called Joseph's name Zaphnathpaaneah ..."

(Genesis 41:45)

Gesenius' Lexicon suggests that this many mean "saviour of the age". Once again, we are reminded of the Master, the true Saviour of those who come to God through him.

Joseph's relationship with Pharaoh

When Joseph revealed himself to his brothers, as well as telling them not to be angry with themselves over what they had done to him, he also spoke of the amazing relationship which existed between him and the king:

"So now it was not you that sent me hither, but God: and he hath made me a father to Pharaoh, and lord of all his house, and a ruler throughout all the land of Egypt." (45:8)

"A father to Pharaoh"! Naturally we might think that the other way round would be more logical, that Pharaoh was a father to Joseph – however this was not the case. Joseph was not simply the lord of all the royal house and ruler of the entire land, he was also a father-figure to Pharaoh. This may have been because the king was very young. Throughout history many monarchs

have begun to reign whilst still young (as Joash, aged 7, in 2 Kings 11:21, and Josiah, aged 8, in 22:1). It is suggested that Tutankhamen began to rule aged 9 or 10. Two things are true of a very young king:
- a. He is almost always fatherless.
- b. He needs wise counsellors.

In both of these cases Joseph was able to aid, protect, educate and enlighten Pharaoh. And scripture supports the fact that in this time of guidance and education, Joseph taught the king the things of the truth.

Joseph's wife and children

Unsurprisingly, Joseph was blessed with a wife and children in the land of Egypt:

> "... and he (Pharaoh) gave him (Joseph) to wife Asenath the daughter of Poti-pherah priest of On. And Joseph went out over all the land of Egypt." (Genesis 41:45)

Some have suggested that Potipherah and Potiphar were one and the same person but there is little to support this. Marrying a priest's daughter was clearly of some importance in Egypt. Although we are told nothing of his wife above that which is recorded here, we can be certain that Joseph shared the wonderful truths he knew and loved with her. Certainly we do know that his two sons, Ephraim and Manasseh, were incorporated into the family of Israel. When Joseph spoke to Jacob shortly before his death, he blessed them in a very special way:

> "And now thy two sons, Ephraim and Manasseh, which were born unto thee in the land of Egypt before I came unto thee into Egypt, are mine; as Reuben and Simeon, they shall be mine." (48:5)

This was the "double portion" normally reserved for the firstborn (see Deuteronomy 21:17). Such was his faith that this special blessing was reserved for Joseph, who, in age order, was the eleventh son of Jacob (Genesis 30:24). Joseph's two sons had only ever known life in Egypt. Their mother's family could not have been more Egyptian; they were, like Timothy, naturally speaking, sons of division (Acts 16:1). Yet like others throughout scripture, they find a place within the household of faith, embracing the promises, and benefitting from the Father's mercy and love.

Joseph's servants
Might Joseph have preached the truth to his household servants? There is a strong indication that they knew of Joseph's ancestry, and the promises. When Joseph's ten brothers came to Egypt the first time, they returned home with their money concealed in the sacks of corn, at Joseph's instruction. When they came down again, this time with Benjamin, they returned the money to the steward of Joseph's house:

> "And he said, Peace be to you, fear not: your God, and the God of your father, hath given you treasure in your sacks: I had your money. And he brought Simeon out unto them."
> (Genesis 43:23)

Once again, we are reminded of the Gospel message:

> "Ho, every one that thirsteth, come ye to the waters, and he that hath no money; come ye, buy, and eat; yea, come, buy wine and milk without money and without price."
> (Isaiah 55:1)

The words of this Gentile man are remarkable. The "God of their father" was one of whom only a relatively few knew anything. Yet this Egyptian was sufficiently well-versed in the things of the truth to attribute their blessings to Him.

What wonderful things are recorded in this portion of the word of God! The story of the life of Joseph is one that many learned in their earliest Sunday school class. Yet the intricate details of the record paint a picture of a man who not only sought the salvation of his natural family, but also manifested the truth to those Gentiles with whom he came into contact. Like Jesus, Joseph therefore stands as a marvellous example of one who was a herald of the great things that are to come. Truly he "let [his] light so shine before men", that others – even pagan-worshipping Egyptians – came to know and love the truth, "glorifying [the] Father which is in heaven" (Matthew 5:16).

5 |

Pharaoh's daughter

WITH the exception of the dark days under Herod (Matthew 2:16-18), these were surely times of unparalleled horror for parents in Israel. The people of God had grown from numbering just seventy plus Joseph's family (Exodus 1:5) to become a mighty nation. Their Egyptian hosts were worried. What if there was a war and they chose to side with their enemies? Initially taskmasters were set over them, the clear intention being that many would die of exhaustion or beating and there would be fewer children born. However, the very opposite took place (verse 12). Midwives were commanded to kill all male babies born to Israelites (verse 16). This plan also failed. Finally the instruction was given to every man or woman of Egypt: they had to play their part in saving the nation. All males born to Israel would be cast into the Nile (verse 22).

It was into this time of unspeakable sadness and danger that Amram and Jochebed's second son was born (2:1,2; 6:20). It seems likely that other parents would have tried to save their children, however only one account of this practice taking place is recorded for us. In an act which was prompted primarily by faith, rather than love (see 2:2; Hebrews 11:23), Moses was placed in an ark by the river's bank.

Whether there was any further plan at this stage, we cannot know. Did they intend him to be found? Did they hope the law would be repealed or simply forgotten? Whatever they may have intended, their child was to be saved that day by the intervention of a member of the royal house of Egypt, through the guiding hand of Israel's God.

Pharaoh's daughter

As the baby's sister stood watching, the daughter of Pharaoh came to the banks of the river to wash. Upon seeing the ark, she commanded one of her maids to take it, and looked inside:

> "And when she had opened it, she saw the child: and, behold, the babe wept. And she had compassion on him, and said, This is one of the Hebrews' children." (Exodus 2:6)

The daughter of Pharaoh clearly had a very different mindset from many of her nation, including her father! She saw the child and had "compassion" on him. This is the language of love and mercy – and these are key attributes of our Heavenly Father.

> "And the LORD God of their fathers sent to them by his messengers, rising up betimes, and sending; because he had compassion (same word in both the English and Hebrew) on his people, and on his dwelling place." (2 Chronicles 36:15)

In Romans 1:31 and in 2 Timothy 3:3 the Apostle Paul was inspired to describe those who would be "without natural affection". We are reminded of the contrast in the life of Ahab's family. Athaliah, the daughter of Ahab and Jezebel, in a desperate attempt to hold on to power, commanded that all children of the royal house should be killed (2 Kings 11:1). The actions of the daughter of Herodias, herself a royal princess, resulted in the death of John the Baptist (Matthew 14:6-10).

In all of these situations we see the very opposite of the spirit manifested by the daughter of Pharaoh. Her natural affection for a defenceless child outweighed her loyalty to family or desire for personal or national security. Being royalty she was clearly able to appeal to her father that the law he had passed should not be applied.

In the time of the Medes and Persians, the king desired to save Daniel but was hamstrung by a law which could not be altered (Daniel 6:14,15). Obedience to the laws of Egypt was clearly open to discretion where the royal house was concerned! Not only was the child saved, but, as proposed by his brave sister, a nurse was employed (Exodus 2:7-9). He was then sustained until he was old enough to live in the palace.

How did Pharaoh's daughter know that the child was a Hebrew? He was three months old (verse 2). All males in Israel were circumcised on the eighth day (Genesis 17:12). We assume, therefore, that this outward demonstration of a spiritual principle enabled the child to be identified as an Israelite.

It is ironic that, in the eyes of the king of Egypt, daughters of Israel were perceived as no threat and could therefore be permitted to live (Exodus 1:22). Yet it was a daughter of the king himself who oversaw the salvation of a male Israelite. She had greater power than almost anyone else within Egypt. How remarkable, then, that her actions would, in due course, result in precisely what her father had been trying to avoid! He was concerned that the Israelites would turn against the Egyptians. He was grieved that Egypt would suffer if this took place. Little did he or his daughter know it, but eighty years on (7:7), the child they permitted to live would play his part in bringing these very calamities upon their land.

We are reminded of Samuel, who also stayed with his natural mother until he was old enough to live with Eli (1 Samuel 1:19-28). In both cases the word describes sons who would go on to play great roles within Israel, leading God's people through difficult and trying times.

The child is named Moses
Of course, a child will normally be named by his or her parents. There is no mention of Pharaoh's daughter being married so the choice of the name was hers alone:
> "And the child grew, and she brought him unto Pharaoh's daughter, and he became her son. And she called his name Moses: and she said, Because I drew him out of the water."
> (Exodus 2:10)

Once more, there is irony in her words. She had "drawn him" from the water. Israel would indeed be drawn out from Egypt, with Moses as the divinely appointed head. David later wrote of being saved by God, and used exactly the same phrase (2 Samuel 22:17).

We know very little of the life of Moses in the years that followed. Prior to his seeking the welfare of the children of Israel, we know from the words of Stephen a little of his time as the son of Pharaoh's daughter:

> "And Moses was learned in all the wisdom of the Egyptians, and was mighty in words and in deeds." (Acts 7:22)

It was almost certainly the example of Joseph which prompted Moses to seek after his natural people. When the exodus finally took place, Moses was determined that the bones of Joseph should be carried out with them:

> "And Moses took the bones of Joseph with him: for he had straitly sworn the children of Israel, saying, God will surely visit you; and ye shall carry up my bones away hence with you." (Exodus 13:19)

No wonder he felt a fellow feeling with Joseph. Both men were Israelites; both lived within the palace of Pharaoh; both enjoyed immense authority and influence, and achieved great things for Egypt. However both men also sought, and were instrumental in bringing about, the salvation of Israel. Both were blessed by the Father for their faithful acts. When the nation finally left Egypt, it was Moses who carried the bones of Joseph with him (verse 19). In time they would be laid to rest in the land, as he had requested (Joshua 24:32).

We do not know whether Pharaoh's daughter lived to see her son forsake the land of Egypt, nor are we told whether he spoke of the hope of Israel to her. What we do know is that his actions, in part, reflect hers:

> "By faith he forsook Egypt, not fearing the wrath of the king: for he endured, as seeing him who is invisible." (Hebrews 11:27)

Both Moses and the daughter of Pharaoh had chosen to ignore the king's commandment, doing what they believed to be right. Both turned their backs on the laws of that land, seeking to save those whom they loved. And both provide powerful examples for us, as we seek to serve our Heavenly Father in challenging and often dangerous times, as the Apostle Peter declared:

"... We ought to obey God rather than men." (Acts 5:29)

6 |

A mixed multitude

FINALLY the children of Israel had left Egypt. After so many false dawns, so many broken promises, at last the land of bondage and suffering was behind them. In all 600,000 men (Exodus 12:37), plus women and children departed. Even the infirm and elderly were given sufficient strength for the journey (Psalm 105:37).

Prior to this time the judgements of the God of Israel had been poured out on the people, animals and land of Egypt in the form of ten phenomenal plagues. When we list these, we note that sometimes warning was given, sometimes not. The first two plagues, when the river turned to blood and frogs appeared, were foretold through Moses (see Exodus 7:17; 8:2). The third plague, that of lice, came without any warning from God (8:16). This pattern was then repeated throughout the remaining plagues. Similarly, the first three plagues affected the land of Goshen, where the children of Israel dwelt. Only for the other seven plagues were God's people unaffected:

"And I will sever in that day the land of Goshen, in which my people dwell, that no swarms of flies shall be there; to the end thou mayest know that I am the LORD in the midst of the earth. And I will put a division between my people and thy people."

(verses 22,23)

Surely there is a lesson for us in these things. Whilst it is true that the Lord will care for His people, never suffering them to be tempted more than they are able to bear (1 Corinthians 10:13), it is also true that we must enter the kingdom "through much tribulation" (Acts 14:22). Like the people of Israel in Egypt, some of the problems that affect those in the world will touch us also. A life of discipleship is not one of ease and comfort. We only need to consider the most faithful man of all time to see that this is true. No one was more obedient than Jesus Christ, yet he is termed "a man of sorrows, and acquainted with grief" (Isaiah 53:3).

Differing reactions from the Egyptians

When Moses appeared before Pharaoh on the first occasion, the response of the king and, we presume, his servants, was very clear:

> "And Pharaoh said, Who is the LORD, that I should obey his voice to let Israel go? I know not the LORD, neither will I let Israel go." (Exodus 5:2)

This was to change, however. Pharaoh, so typical of many of this world, wavered in his attitude to the commands of God. His men, on the other hand, realised that Moses possessed a power far greater than anything they had ever witnessed:

> "Then the magicians said unto Pharaoh, This is the finger of God: and Pharaoh's heart was hardened, and he hearkened not unto them; as the LORD had said." (8:19)

These words were spoken by men capable of turnings rods into serpents (7:11,12), water into blood (verse 22) and bringing frogs upon the land (8:7). What made the production of lice beyond them? The context provides the answer for us:

> "And the LORD said unto Moses, Say unto Aaron, Stretch out thy rod, and smite the dust of the land, that it may become lice throughout all the land of Egypt." (verse 16)

Bringing life from the ground was beyond the Egyptians. How true this is! Only our God can bring life from the dust. He is the great life-giver; He sustains and He determines when life should end. When Adam was caused to live, the Lord God breathed into his nostrils the breath of life. In Egypt the magicians in Pharaoh's court realised that in their presence stood a man with power far greater than they possessed.

Over time, it became obvious to any with "eyes to see" that the land of Egypt was becoming decimated. Only the king refused to accept this. Indeed, his servants, realising that there was no hope for them, appealed to him to hearken to the request of Moses:

> "And Pharaoh's servants said unto him, How long shall this man be a snare unto us? let the men go, that they may serve the LORD their God: knowest thou not yet that Egypt is destroyed?" (10:7)

As we saw, the name of the God of Israel was not known to Pharaoh at the outset of these things. However that situation had changed: everyone had come to the name of Yahweh. Moses, his servant, was "a god to Pharaoh" (7:1). So whilst many of the Egyptians would have prayed to their own pagan deities (those against whom the plagues were being executed, 12:12), there is strong evidence that others saw the hand of Israel's God at work. Some, it seems, became associated with the people of Israel because of what they heard and saw. When Moses warned Pharaoh of the plague of hail, he exhorted him and his men to gather cattle and servants out of their fields. There were two very distinct responses amongst the Egyptians:

> "He that feared the word of the LORD among the servants of Pharaoh made his servants and his cattle flee into the houses: and he that regarded not the word of the LORD left his servants and his cattle in the field." (9:20,21)

Some heard the word of God and responded to it, and others did not. We find this pattern throughout the Bible, from the days of Cain and Abel onwards. Whether this willingness to hearken to the words of the Father was then followed by a desire to become associated with Him and His people, we can only surmise. However, there is a very strong indication that a number of the Egyptians did just this.

Light for Israel, darkness for Egypt

As we have seen time and again, when one knows the wonderful truths of God he or she is in a state of enlightenment. How fitting, then, that the plague of darkness, three days in duration, did not affect Israel:

> "They saw not one another, neither rose any from his place for three days: but all the children of Israel had light in their dwellings." (10:23)

Israel had been enlightened. The Father was calling for His people to manifest this: to "walk as children of light" (Ephesians 5:8).

This pattern was then repeated after the exodus had taken place. When the people saw the hosts of Pharaoh pursuing them, they cried out to Moses (Exodus 14:10). Moses reassured them and, at God's command, they began to walk towards the Red Sea, which was then parted by an east wind (verses 21,22). At this point the angel, manifesting God's power in the pillar of cloud and fire, moved from going before them:

> "And the angel of God, which went before the camp of Israel, removed and went behind them; and the pillar of the cloud went from before their face, and stood behind them: and it came between the camp of the Egyptians and the camp of Israel; and it was a cloud and darkness to them (Egypt), but it gave light by night to these (Israel): so that the one came not near the other all the night." (verses 19,20)

As God's people left the land of sin and death, they were in light whilst their enemies were in darkness. Truly this is a fitting picture of all that Egypt had been for the children of Israel.

A mixed multitude

In excess of two million people left Egypt on Passover night. However it seems very likely that others chose to join them:

> "And a mixed multitude went up also with them; and flocks, and herds, even very much cattle." (12:38)

What does this mean? Are we simply being told that there were different types of Israelites? Surely such a comment would be superfluous – two million people would *have* to include male and female, young and old, rich and poor, manual labourers and skilled artisans. Surely we are being told that others, in addition to those of Israel, left the land of Egypt and commenced

that great journey to the Promised Land. The use of the same expression in Nehemiah 13:3 supports this, for Israel took Gentile wives from whom they were later exhorted to separate. Who were these people in the time of the exodus? There are two logical suggestions:
- a. There were other slaves in Egypt who leaped at the opportunity to flee from a land of bondage and hardship alongside the Israelites.
- b. Some Egyptians realised that the God of Israel was the only true God, and desired to become His servants.

Maybe both of these are true. What we do know is that a great mixture of people left Egypt, and whilst the majority of these were Abraham's seed, others (such as Caleb, for example, see chapter 9) were Gentiles.

A symbol of the ecclesia

We know from 1 Corinthians 10 that these things point forward to the ecclesia. Whilst there are many types of Christ in scripture, there are very few types of us. One of these is the Apostle Paul:

"Howbeit for this cause I obtained mercy, that in me first Jesus Christ might shew forth all longsuffering, for a pattern to them which should hereafter believe on him to life everlasting." (see 1 Timothy 1:15,16)

So Paul is presented as a "pattern" of those who believe. Perhaps the reason for this is that very few have ever brought more hardship on the people of God than Saul of Tarsus. What Paul was teaching, therefore, was that if he could be forgiven and accepted, anyone can!

One other type of us is the nation of Israel at the time of the exodus (1 Corinthians 10:6,11). The people are "our examples", and those who came out, as we have seen, were a "mixed multitude".

Within an ecclesia, it would be illogical – even slightly worrying – to find a large group of people who agree on every minor issue. Certainly when discussing the first principles, there can be no difference of opinion (Galatians 1:8,9). However we are a family unit. We have different talents (as depicted in the parable of the Master, Matthew 25) and, in respect of trivialities, different opinions. Any ecclesia is a mixed multitude!

We must, like Israel, journey together, trying not to look back to that which we have left behind. For the most part those who left Egypt failed dismally in this respect. They were the "many" with whom God was not well pleased (1 Corinthians 10:5), "whose carcases fell in the wilderness" (Hebrews 3:17). Indeed when the phrase "mixed multitude" is used elsewhere in the days of the wilderness wanderings, we are faced with a stark warning:

> "And the mixt multitude that was among them fell a lusting: and the children of Israel also wept again, and said, Who shall give us flesh to eat?" (Numbers 11:4)

After they had crossed the Red Sea, Moses had promised that the people would never see the Egyptians again (Exodus 14:13). Oh that this could have been the end of it! Most were constantly focused upon the things of Egypt throughout the forty years. They murmured (15:24) and longed for the food of Egypt (Numbers 11:4-6). They even made and worshipped idols (Exodus 32:4-6), similar to those they had bowed to in the land of their captivity (Ezekiel 20:8). Truly the majority of the people were "mixed" in their hearts. They were "double minded" (James 1:8; 4:8), and were trying to "serve two masters" (Matthew 6:24).

How important, then, that we seek to apply these vital lessons today. These things were "written for our learning" (Romans 15:4), so that we might be patient, comforted by the scriptures, hoping for something better. Our Heavenly Father desires that we look forward, with the eye of faith, to the promised land of God's kingdom – a place of glory, beauty, righteousness and light:

> "And the city had no need of the sun, neither of the moon, to shine in it: for the glory of God did lighten it, and the Lamb is the light thereof." (Revelation 21:23)

7

Zipporah and her family

IN this life some are born into privilege, others into poverty. A few, such as Moses, taste life at both extremes. He was born the son of slaves, but was elevated to the house of the king. He performed great and mighty acts (Acts 7:22) and was, doubtless, held in immense respect by many. Then aged forty he sought the welfare of his own people and, having killed an Egyptian overlord, had to flee the land (Exodus 2:11-15). At that stage he must have wondered what the future held for him. He had rejected a position of immense responsibility and riches in an effort to save the Israelites, believing he was their appointed deliverer:

"For he supposed his brethren would have understood how that God by his hand would deliver them: but they understood not." (Acts 7:25)

It seems highly likely that Moses knew the promises made to Abraham. He would know that Israel would live in a land that was not theirs for 400 years, being afflicted by their masters (Genesis 15:13). Surely he would know also how these promises concluded:

"And also that nation, whom they shall serve, will I judge: and afterward shall they come out with great substance."

(verse 14)

Yet his efforts to bring about the Israelites' departure had come to nought. Having lost everything, naturally speaking, he sat down by a well in the land of Midian. Little did he know it, but this was to be the commencement of the second of three very distinct periods in his life, each of them numbering forty years (Acts 7:23; Exodus 7:7; Deuteronomy 34:7).

The Midianites

Midian was a son of Abraham by his wife Keturah (Genesis 25:1,2). Unlike the other five sons she bore him, of whom we know very little (verse 2), the descendants of Midian were a mighty people. Appropriately, the name means 'brawling, contentious' (Strong), for there were numerous wars between Israel and Midian.

In Genesis 37:28 a group of Midianite merchants bought Joseph, later selling him to Potiphar in Egypt (verses 28,36). The land of Midian appears to have been to the south of Israel; Smith's *Bible Dictionary* suggests it was "probably the peninsula of Sinai". During the wilderness wanderings the children of Israel encountered the Midianites on numerous occasions. This supports the above suggestion for the location of their land. When the Israelites appeared in their land, the elders of Midian and Moab hired Balaam to curse them (Numbers 22:7). Although this plan failed, the instruction of Balaam that the females of the nations should entrap the men of Israel (Revelation 2:14) had a great deal of success (Numbers 25:1,6). This explains the instruction of the Lord to Moses later in this chapter:

"Vex the Midianites, and smite them: for they vex you with their wiles, wherewith they have beguiled you in the matter of Peor ..." (verses 17,18)

The final instruction of God to Moses was to wage war with the Midianites (31:1,2). This resulted in all the males of Midian being killed (verse 7). Presumably this refers to only one area of the land, as in Judges 6 the Israelites were delivered into the hand of the Midianites for seven years. In due course Gideon would lead Israel to conquer the Midianite army (Judges 7 and 8).

We see, then, that for much of the Old Testament the Midianites were hostile towards God's people. Yet Moses was to encounter a Midianite, and receive nothing but good at his hand.

Zipporah and her father

As Moses sat at the well, seven sisters arrived to give their flocks drink (Exodus 2:16). In a repetition of the events in the life of Jacob, there appeared to be a delay in this process (Genesis 29:10). In Jacob's time there was a system whereby a number of men removed a stone from the well's mouth, presumably after a levy had been paid by those wishing to use it (verse 8). Moses saved the women who were being refused access to the well by other shepherds (Exodus 2:17). In an act foreshadowing the work of Jesus (John 4:10; 10:11), and also his own future role as leader of the nation (Isaiah 63:11), he then provided water for all their flocks. When the women returned home earlier than usual, their father inquired why (Exodus 2:18), and then welcomed his daughters' deliverer into his home.

The man in question was called Reuel (2:18), a name elsewhere translated Raguel (Numbers 10:29). He was also called Jethro (Exodus 3:1) and Hobab (Judges 4:11). We have no need to question this. Many in scripture were known by more than one name. After his dealings with the angel (Genesis 32:28), Jacob was called by both his original name (33:1) and also by the name of Israel (35:21). Simon Peter was called both Simon (Luke 22:31) and Peter (Matthew 16:18) by Jesus after he had been given his new name (John 1:42). Solomon was given the name Jedidiah (2 Samuel 12:25). Thomas was also called Didymus (John 11:16).

What we do see in this man is an example of fairness, kindness and practicality. Unlike Jacob's dealings with his father-in-law Laban, in the house of Jethro Moses found not only a warm welcome but also a man of the utmost integrity.

Reuel means 'friend of God'. Jethro means 'his excellence'. Possibly "Jethro" was a title rather than a name. We do know that he was a priest of Midian (Exodus 2:16), an indication that he was a man of some standing in the community. This reminds us of Moses' predecessor, Joseph, whose wife was also the daughter of a priest (Genesis 41:45). In due course Moses benefitted in two ways, naturally speaking, from his association with this man. He was permitted to lodge with him, and he married one of his seven daughters:

> "And Moses was content to dwell with the man: and he gave Moses Zipporah his daughter." (Exodus 2:21)

It was in this state of 'contentment' that Moses and Zipporah were blessed with a son, called Gershom (verse 22). His name reflects Moses' feelings at this time, and perhaps also in Egypt:

> "... for he (Moses) said, I have been a stranger in a strange land."

Later a second son was born, called Eliezer (18:4). His name means 'God of help'. It seems that despite his separation from the people of Israel, the things of the truth were never far from Moses' mind. He went on to work for his father-in-law as a shepherd. This arrangement would only be interrupted when the God of his fathers spoke to him at the burning bush (Exodus 3).

Having received the call from God, and despite his many reservations, Moses declared to Jethro his intention to return to Egypt:

> "And Moses went and returned to Jethro his father in law, and said unto him, Let me go, I pray thee, and return unto my brethren which are in Egypt, and see whether they be yet alive. And Jethro said to Moses, Go in peace." (4:18)

How very different from the experiences of Jacob! Laban did everything in his power to further his own ends at the expense of Jacob, including deceiving him into marrying Leah instead of Rachel (Genesis 29:23), and changing his wages ten times (31:7). Even when Jacob declared his intention to depart, Laban did all he could to keep him, for he knew how he had benefitted from his presence (30:27). Jethro, however, could not possibly have been more different. Despite the fact that he stood to lose a faithful shepherd and much loved son-in-law, he refused to stand in the way of what he believed to be the plan and purpose of Almighty God.

"Go in peace": it is a phrase used only a few times in the Old Testament. Eli used the same expression when talking with Hannah (1 Samuel 1:17). Jonathan said the same thing to David (20:42). Elisha used these words to Naaman regarding the entering of the house of Rimmon (2 Kings 5:19). On each occasion a new beginning was anticipated. How apt, then, that this Midianite, who may well have learned of the things of the truth from Moses, should use this phrase.

Moses' departure from Jethro's house

There then follows what appears to be one of the strangest incidents in scripture. In obedience to the commandment of God, Moses, accompanied by Zipporah and their sons, began the journey to Egypt.

> "And it came to pass by the way in the inn, that the LORD met him, and sought to kill him. Then Zipporah took a sharp stone, and cut off the foreskin of her son, and cast it at his feet, and said, Surely a bloody husband art thou to me. So he let him go: then she said, A bloody husband thou art, because of the circumcision." (Exodus 4:24-26)

What do we make of this highly unusual series of events? Why would God command a man to return, then attempt to kill him as he obeyed? These are not easy things to explain, and many students of the word have come to different conclusions as they have pondered this.

We can be sure that if Moses was obeying the command of God in returning, it would be utterly illogical, indeed contrary to all that we know of the Lord, for such a man to be killed in an act of divine judgement. Our Father takes no pleasure in the death of the wicked (Ezekiel 33:11); why then should He seek to kill a man who was serving him faithfully?

The context helps us here. The message that Moses was to present to Pharaoh was simple and powerful:

> "And thou shalt say unto Pharaoh, Thus saith the LORD, Israel is my son, even my firstborn: and I say unto thee, Let my son go, that he may serve me: and if thou refuse to let him go, behold, I will slay thy son, even thy firstborn." (Exodus 4:22,23)

So the firstborn sons of Egypt were to be killed. One of the key things which marked the people of God out as different was circumcision. It was a token of the establishment of the Abrahamic covenant (Genesis 17:11). This section of scripture, where circumcision is mentioned for the first time, concludes with the following statement:
"And the uncircumcised man child whose flesh of his foreskin is not circumcised, that soul shall be cut off from his people; he hath broken my covenant." (verse 14)

The uncircumcised firstborn sons of the Egyptians were to die. Could the one that the Lord, through his angel, was seeking to slay, have been Gershom, Moses and Zipporah's firstborn? He stands as a symbol of those outside the covenant. Such people would not be saved when the children of Israel were delivered from Egypt. Indeed, when those of the second generation were about to enter the Promised Land, it was essential for all the males to be circumcised (Joshua 5:2-5). Unsurprisingly, based on what we learn of them in the books of Exodus and Numbers, the first generation had not obeyed the command regarding circumcision during the wilderness wanderings. Their uncircumcised children were barred from entering the land until this was rectified – this is how the Father regarded this vital "token of the covenant" between Him and His people.

After the son was circumcised, Moses departed from family and met with Aaron. It would be some time before he would meet Zipporah again.

Moses' reunion with Jethro and Zipporah
Having been instrumental in bringing one of the most powerful and advanced nations to its knees, Moses led the Israelites to Sinai (Exodus 16:1). Unsurprisingly, such a movement of people provoked a response amongst the nations of the land. Jethro was a wise man. He knew what had taken place and unlike other Midianites (see above), went out to meet Moses in love:
"Then Jethro, Moses' father in law, took Zipporah, Moses' wife ... and her two sons ... and ... came ... unto Moses. And

Moses went out to meet his father in law, and did obeisance, and kissed him; and they asked each other of their welfare; and they came into the tent." (18:2,3,5,7)

There is a beautiful picture of mutual respect and love here. Each man asked of the welfare of the other. The Hebrew word for welfare is *shalom*; indeed this is the same word used by Jethro earlier when Moses sought to depart ("go in peace"). "Kissing" was a special act of love amongst the people of God, often associated with the establishment of a covenant. David and Jonathan kissed each other, having promised that there should be a special relationship between them and their respective seeds forever (1 Samuel 20:41,42).

Entering a tent might be describing nothing more than being in a place of comfort and refuge. However "dwelling in tents" appears to have been a practice associated with the faithful in Israel (Genesis 25:27; Jeremiah 35:10; Hebrews 11:9). Was Jethro aware of the promises? Was Moses sharing fellowship with his father-in-law?

Jethro's reaction to the exodus

In the verses following, we are left in no doubt as to the state of mind of Jethro. Others saw the events of the exodus and sought to fight with the Israelites. Some (including certain Midianites) desired that Israel should be cursed. Jethro could not have been more different:

"And Jethro rejoiced for all the goodness which the LORD had done to Israel, whom he had delivered out of the hand of the Egyptians. And Jethro said, Blessed be the LORD, who hath delivered you out of the hand of the Egyptians, and out of the hand of Pharaoh, who hath delivered the people from under the hand of the Egyptians." (Exodus 18:9,10)

Jethro did not simply marvel that Israel had been brought out. He did not simply rejoice that a group of slaves had been set free. He saw Yahweh's hand at work. The following verses are similarly remarkable:

"Now I know that the LORD is greater than all gods: for in the thing wherein they dealt proudly he was above them."

(verse 11)

Who were the other "gods" (Elohim, mighty ones) of whom Jethro spoke? Those of Egypt? Those of Midian? This was an amazing statement from a man who had seen none of the plagues or the crossing of the Red Sea. What he had seen, however, was the outworking of the promises of the God of Israel. He had heard of the prophecies that had been made, and had witnessed the end result of these things. He was a man with "... an heart to perceive, and eyes to see, and ears to hear ..." (Deuteronomy 29:4).

"And Jethro, Moses' father in law, took a burnt offering and sacrifices for God: and Aaron came, and all the elders of Israel, to eat bread with Moses' father in law before God."

(Exodus 18:12)

Here is a further demonstration of the mindset of Jethro. This Gentile man brought a burnt offering and sacrifices for the God of Israel. He clearly knew something of the law – which animals were permitted, what state such creatures had to be in, and why. Surely he was able to see beyond the process of simply bringing animals to be sacrificed, to that which such things represented. In the case of the burnt offering atonement was made (Leviticus 1:4). Other offerings were also presented and, we assume, accepted.

In addition to this, Moses, Aaron and the elders of Israel sat and ate bread with Jethro. This may be nothing more than a simple meal. However if this was the case, why were all the leaders of the nation summoned? The phrase "before God" surely implies that it was something of far greater significance. On six occasions in Deuteronomy (12:7; 12:18; 14:23; 14:26; 15:20; 27:7), the Father spoke to the second generation of coming before him and "eating". Elsewhere the practice is connected with fellowship:

"But now I have written unto you not to keep company, if any man that is called a brother be a fornicator, or covetous, or an idolater, or a railer, or a drunkard, or an extortioner; with such an one no not to eat." (1 Corinthians 5:11)

Jethro was being accepted by the elders of the nation, and permitted to take part in things normally reserved only for Israel. Truly this Gentile man had an immense respect for the truth, having been enlightened by the God of Israel.

Jethro's advice for Moses

In the verses that follow, we have the record of Jethro beholding Moses' judging of the nation. This took "from the morning unto the evening" (Exodus 18:13). Upon seeing this, he expressed his immense concern for the well-being of his son-in-law:

"Thou wilt surely wear away, both thou, and this people that is with thee: for this thing is too heavy for thee; thou art not able to perform it thyself alone." (verse 18)

He then made a simple suggestion to Moses. Why not permit issues of lesser importance to be judged by other capable men? Matters of great significance could still be brought to Moses. On the surface this seems practical; however would such a suggestion be accepted by God? Once more, Jethro was thinking like a man of Israel:

"If thou shalt do this thing, and God command thee so, then thou shalt be able to endure, and all this people shall also go to their place in peace." (verse 23)

Note the concern of this man. 'Make these changes – but only subject to the approval of the Almighty.' What a thoughtful, kind and wise man Jethro was! Having seen all this, it might seem strange that the chapter then concludes with his departure:

"And Moses let his father in law depart; and he went his way into his own land." (verse 27)

Did he remain there? Did he come back to the camp of Israel? Based on all that we have seen, it would seem highly appropriate if he did, although scripture is silent on this matter. Did Zipporah stay with Moses? We know from 1 Chronicles 23:14-17 that their sons were numbered amongst the tribe of

Levi, so we can assume that they stayed with Moses when Jethro departed.

Jethro's son

The final reference to the family of Jethro and Zipporah is in Numbers 10. There is no mention of sons born to Jethro in the book of Exodus. However one of his sons, a man by the name of Hobab, met with Moses later in the record, and received a very personal invitation from him:

> "And Moses said unto Hobab, the son of Raguel the Midianite, Moses' father in law, We are journeying unto the place of which the LORD said, I will give it you: come thou with us, and we will do thee good: for the LORD hath spoken good concerning Israel." (Numbers 10:29)

This man was Zipporah's brother (or half-brother). The offer of Moses was initially rejected. Hobab determined to return to his own land, and his own kindred. His name means 'cherished'. Moses' appeal, however, was not based solely on family loyalty. There was a reason why he cherished the company of Hobab:

> "And he said, Leave us not, I pray thee; forasmuch as thou knowest how we are to encamp in the wilderness, and thou mayest be to us instead of eyes. And it shall be, if thou go with us, yea, it shall be, that what goodness the LORD shall do unto us, the same will we do unto thee." (verses 31,32)

Moses knew that, even though the nation was guided by the Father through the pillars of cloud and fire (Exodus 40:38), a man who knew the lie of the land could be of great benefit to the nation. By associating himself with the nation of Israel, Hobab and his family could enjoy Israel's hope. If hardship was endured, a reward would be enjoyed. Jesus said the same thing to his disciples in Matthew 19:28. Surely the same promise is made to us: if we "endure hardness" (2 Timothy 2:3) there awaits a "crown of righteousness" for us, by grace (4:8).

Whether Hobab, Jethro and Zipporah chose to accept this call we are not told at this stage. However there is a strong

indication elsewhere that some did hearken to Moses' words, and were incorporated into the nation of Israel:
> "And the children of the Kenite, Moses' father in law, went up out of the city of palm trees with the children of Judah into the wilderness of Judah, which lieth in the south of Arad; and they went and dwelt among the people." (Judges 1:16)

The fact that Moses' father-in-law is called a Kenite, rather than a Midianite, should create no great problems for us. If a man is known by the area in which he lives, a pilgrim will be called by more than one title. Maybe the lands of the Midianites and the Kenites were very close geographically. Perhaps, like Ammon and Moab, the two nations acted together. Possibly the one was part of the other, as we might say a man from France is also a European.

What we do know is that unless Judges 1:16 describes another son of Jethro, this must be speaking of Hobab. If this is the case, then we see that Moses' offer had been accepted. Indeed, there is yet another indication of this in Judges 4, where we read of Heber, another descendant of Jethro and Hobab. He and his wife had severed themselves from the Kenites and were now living alone (see chapter 12: Jael and Heber).

Clearly Jethro and Hobab knew the things of the truth, and were offered the hope of life in the land of promise as part of the nation of Israel. We see, then, a further type of faithful Gentiles today. Many in the ecclesia will not be able to trace their ancestry back to Abraham; however they have come to know of the hope of Israel (Jeremiah 14:8; 17:13; Acts 28:20). By baptism into the saving name of Jesus Christ (Galatians 3:27-29), they have been able to embrace the things of the covenant made with the fathers of old, just like the family of Zipporah –

> "... that the blessing of Abraham might come on the Gentiles through Jesus Christ; that we might receive the promise of the Spirit through faith." (Galatians 3:14)

8

The kindness of the Kenites

SAUL'S days as king of Israel were numbered. He knew what was right and, like Adam in the garden (1 Timothy 2:14), had chosen not to do it. Prior to a key battle with the Philistines, instead of waiting for Samuel to come and offer the sacrifices, he had slain the offerings himself (1 Samuel 13:8,9). The type of the true king-priest had been defiled (Hebrews 6:20-7:3). The judgements of God, presented through Samuel were unmistakeable:

"And Samuel said to Saul, Thou hast done foolishly: thou hast not kept the commandment of the LORD thy God, which he commanded thee: for now would the LORD have established thy kingdom upon Israel for ever. But now thy kingdom shall not continue: the LORD hath sought him a man after his own heart, and the LORD hath commanded him to be captain over his people, because thou hast not kept that which the LORD commanded thee." (1 Samuel 13:13,14)

From that moment on the king became increasingly suspicious of any potential rivals, and more and more erratic in his behaviour.

The Amalekites

One day, he was given a final commission through Samuel: all Amalekites were to be wiped out:

"Now go and smite Amalek, and utterly destroy all that they have, and spare them not; but slay both man and woman, infant and suckling, ox and sheep, camel and ass." (15:3)

Why was it that the judgements of the Lord on Amalek were so severe? Under the law, strict instructions were given regarding other nations which were *not* to be afflicted: Egyptians, because Israel had dwelled in their land, and Edomites, because they were brothers (Deuteronomy 23:7). So why were Amalekites so utterly abhorrent in the sight of God? The reason is revealed in Samuel's words to Saul earlier in the chapter:

> "Thus saith the LORD of hosts, I remember that which Amalek did to Israel, how he laid wait for him in the way, when he came up from Egypt." (1 Samuel 15:2)

So the Amalekites had "laid wait" for Israel. This is amplified in Deuteronomy:

> "How he met thee by the way, and smote the hindmost of thee, even all that were feeble behind thee, when thou wast faint and weary; and he feared not God."
> (Deuteronomy 25:18)

The Amalekites smote those who were weakest. Unlike other Gentiles who came out to do battle with Israel, they were cowardly, picking off those unable to fight back.

Are there echoes of the life of a disciple in these things? Does Amalek represent the flesh? Our sinful, human nature moves us do wrong (Romans 7:21). Often when we are weakest we find the promptings of the flesh to be particularly strong, as David's dealings with Bathsheba and Uriah prove. Was Saul, then, being challenged to put to death the flesh, in symbol? This is, surely, the call for every one of us (8:13; Colossians 3:5).

Saul spares the Kenites

Saul then assembled the men of Israel, 210,000 in total, and approached the enemy. However there were, living in the general area inhabited by the Amalekites, a number of Kenites. In the days of the wilderness wanderings, they had shown kindness towards the children of Israel:

> "And Saul said unto the Kenites, Go, depart, get you down from among the Amalekites, lest I destroy you with them: for ye shewed kindness to all the children of Israel, when they

came up out of Egypt. So the Kenites departed from among the Amalekites." (1 Samuel 15:6)

Although the Kenites are listed amongst those who would be disinherited when Abraham's seed took the land (Genesis 15:19), for the most part their contact with Israel was positive. As we saw in chapter 7, Moses' father-in-law, although called a Midianite in Numbers 10:29, is also called a Kenite in Judges 1:16. The Kenites were a nomadic race, and would therefore be known not only by their ancestry, but also by the place where they happened to be living at the time.

Who, then, were these Kenites of whom Saul spoke? It seems likely that this refers to Moses brother-in-law, Hobab, who we considered in chapter 7:

> "And Moses said unto Hobab, the son of Raguel the Midianite, Moses' father in law, We are journeying unto the place of which the LORD said, I will give it you: come thou with us, and we will do thee good: for the LORD hath spoken good concerning Israel." (Numbers 10:29)

As we noted previously, although there is no direct evidence of Moses' offer being accepted, there is a strong indication that this did happen (see Judges 4). This would almost certainly be the act of kindness of which Saul was speaking. Where the Kenites went after they were given opportunity to flee by Saul we are not told. Possibly they became incorporated into the nation of Israel (see also chapter 26, the Rechabites).

The goodness and severity of God

Was Saul right to act as he did towards the Kenites? As we are given no indication to the contrary, we must assume that this was acceptable in the sight of God. An act of kindness on the part of these Gentiles was not forgotten by the people of Israel or their God, and they received a blessing as a result. In this context the Father had said that He "remembered" the sins of Amalek (1 Samuel 15:2). Perhaps we are being directed back to the promises made to the father of the nation, Abraham:

"And I will bless them that bless thee, and curse him that curseth thee: and in thee shall all families of the earth be blessed." (Genesis 12:3)

What we see very clearly from these things is that the Mighty One of Abraham, Isaac and Jacob will bless some and not others. The Apostle Paul spoke of the "goodness and severity of God", and we see it demonstrated perfectly in this chapter. Two groups of Gentiles were regarded totally differently by the Father, based on their treatment of His people. It is a pattern that we see repeated elsewhere in God's word. Leaders who set themselves against the nation of Israel invariably come to nought. Haman the Agagite, or Amalekite (see below) is a classic example of this (Esther 6:13). In recent times Saddam Hussein and Muammar Gaddafi have opposed Israel and been removed from power. Just as this is true for natural Israel, it is true for spiritual Israel also. We are, by grace, the "jewels" of whom Malachi was inspired to write (Malachi 3:17).

Saul's failings regarding the Amalekites

We cannot consider the rest of 1 Samuel 15 in any detail. However, we know that Saul failed to execute the judgements of God against Amalek. Tragically, instead of destroying all the people and animals, he not only spared the best of the flocks and herds, but also permitted Agag, the king of the Amalekites to live (verse 9). How ironic it is that the king had done right in permitting the Kenites to live, yet had then applied this same command in relation to a man "appointed to death". Surely this confirms the teaching that not all people in the world are regarded in the same light by the Lord. Pharaoh was "raised up" with one specific intention: that the power of the Almighty one of Israel might be shown (Exodus 9:16; Romans 9:17).

Clearly there are lessons for us in these things. We are not commanded to wage war against those of this world, for the servant of the Lord must not strive (2 Timothy 2:24). However we must "walk in wisdom towards them that are without ..."

(Colossians 4:5), being "wise as serpents and harmless as doves" (Matthew 10:16).

Are all people in the world evil, hateful, to be shunned at all cost? Surely experience teaches us that this is not the case. Even now, in what we hope and believe to be the "last days", there are still some who may be searching for the truth. Many brethren and sisters have embraced the hope we are privileged to share as a result of coming into contact with a member of the ecclesia. If we refuse to have any contact whatsoever with those in the world round about us, how can anyone ever see our light which should be shining before men (5:16)?

However there are others who desire only our destruction. The sole desire of some in the world is to do wrong. Many seem determined to make us conform to their standards (Romans 12:2), and when we refuse, they "speak evil" of us (1 Peter 4:4). There are men like Agag – people who will never change – and any unnecessary association with them can only have a negative effect upon a disciple of Jesus Christ. As we "see the day approaching", in a world becoming increasingly more Godless, may we be found watching the signs, aware of the dangers, and determined to fellowship only those who know, believe and apply the truth:

"Wherefore come out from among them, and be ye separate, saith the Lord, and touch not the unclean thing; and I will receive you, and will be a Father unto you, and ye shall be my sons and daughters, saith the Lord Almighty."

(2 Corinthians 6:17,18)

9 |

Caleb the Kenezite

THERE were, surely, few more important times in the history of the nation of Israel. God's people had seen the plagues which had decimated Egypt. They had kept the Passover, and departed from their land of bondage. They had passed through the Red Sea and seen the Egyptians dead on the sea shore. Finally, they had arrived at the border of the Promised Land. This had been foretold to the ancestors of the nation, Abraham, Isaac and Jacob.

We accept that inheritance of the land by the true seed can only take place in the kingdom age, for that "seed ... is Christ" (Galatians 3:16). However, there was to be a foreshadowing of this when the natural descendants of Abraham left the land of slavery, sin and death after 400 years (Genesis 15:13,14), to take possession of the land where the patriarchs had once dwelt as strangers and pilgrims (Hebrews 11:8-16).

The twelve spies
So it was, that two full years after that amazing exodus (Numbers 9:1), the land was within their sight. Before they went in, the Father instructed Moses to send spies, that the land might be viewed by these chosen representatives before the rest of the people entered. These men were not randomly picked. They were leaders of their tribes:

"And the LORD spake unto Moses, saying, Send thou men, that they may search the land of Canaan, which I give unto the children of Israel: of every tribe of their fathers shall ye send a man, every one a *ruler* among them. And Moses by the commandment of the LORD sent them from the wilderness of Paran: all those men were *heads* of the children of Israel."

(13:1-3)

These men were "rulers" (Strong: "an exalted one, i.e., a king or sheikh"), and "heads". The Hebrew for "heads" is the word *rosh*, as used in Ezekiel 38 and 39. The names of these men, and the tribes they represented, appear in Numbers 13:4-15. The leader of the tribe of Ephraim was Oshea, renamed Joshua by Moses (verses 8,16); the leader of Judah was Caleb (verse 6).

We know what followed: the twelve spies travelled through the land for forty days and returned with two very different reports. Ten said the land was good, but the walls of the cities were high and the men of the land were giants. Two men, Joshua and Caleb, said that although the men of the land were tall, they would be no match for the God who had destroyed the Egyptians, and preserved his people since their exodus:

"If the LORD delight in us, then he will bring us into this land, and give it us; a land which floweth with milk and honey."

(14:8)

On the surface, this may not appear particularly strange to us. Two groups of men – even men who know the truth – may regard the same thing, but come to very different conclusions. Cain and Abel heard the words of the Elohim, but reacted very differently. Esau and Jacob both knew of the promises, but only one believed them. The fact that Joshua and Caleb were faithful, and the other ten were not is hardly amazing – except when we consider the ancestry of Caleb, for he was, in fact, a Gentile.

The Gentile ancestry of Caleb

When the Father declared to Israel that the first generation would not enter the Promised Land, he said that only two men, along with the faithful Levites, would go in:

"... Caleb the son of Jephunneh the Kenezite, and Joshua the son of Nun: for they have wholly followed the LORD." (32:12)

This is the first of three occasions where Caleb is termed a "Kenezite", the other two being in Joshua 14. He is, in fact, the only Kenezite named in the Bible.

We know nothing of Caleb's history. How he (or his ancestors) came to be part of the nation we are not told. It seems likely that his forbears were taken captive by the Egyptians, and placed amongst their other slaves, the majority of whom were, of course, Israelites. Caleb's ancestors were therefore incorporated into the tribe of Judah, and later embraced the ways and religious practices of Israel.

The Kenezites

The only other occasion where these people are mentioned in the Bible is when Abraham was promised the land. Having told him that he would inherit the land from the river of Egypt to the river Euphrates (Genesis 15:18), the Lord then identifies the nations which would be dispossessed in order for this to take place:

"The Kenites, and the Kenizzites, and the Kadmonites ..."

(verse 19)

So the Kenizzites (the name is spelled differently but is identical in the original record) would *not* possess the land. Yet Caleb, who traced his roots back to these people, would. The reason for this great irony will become obvious as we consider this man in more detail.

There is some debate amongst scholars as to the precise meaning of Caleb's name. It is possibly from the same Hebrew as *keleb*, which means 'dog'. The Jews regarded Gentiles as dogs (see chapter 34, the Syrophenician woman), so maybe this is an ironic reminder of the ancestry of this great man.

Searching the land ... for forty days

The rulers of the tribes passed through the land for forty days. Few of us are ever likely to face such a task, as espionage is hardly a suitable occupation for a brother or sister in Christ! Yet these twelve men went through the land, noting the structure of the

cities and the kinds of people that dwelled there, with two key instructions from Moses:
"And be ye of good courage, and bring of the fruit of the land." (Numbers 13:20)
As we know, this vital exhortation was heeded by only two men: Joshua and Caleb. Only they manifested the courage that Moses demanded. And when the fruit of the land was brought, what are we told?
"And they came unto the brook of Eshcol, and cut down from thence a branch with one cluster of grapes, and they bare it between two upon a staff; and they brought of the pomegranates, and of the figs." (verse 23)
Although the bearers of this immense cluster of grapes are not named, who else could they have been but Caleb and Joshua? The ten would return saying that the land could *not* be taken, so why would they bother bringing evidence of its fruitfulness?

The name Eshcol, appropriately, means 'cluster' (see Strong). One great bunch of grapes, one immense cluster, was brought. It is as though Caleb was saying to the nation: 'This is what we can be like: one great group of faithful believers.' This is the same name that appears in Genesis 14:13,24 (see chapter 2, Abraham). In Abraham's life a Gentile by the name of Eshcol had embraced the promises and been incorporated into the group of believers. How tragic that this situation was not replicated here, because it was this very location which prompted the ten spies to doubt their ability to take the land. When speaking to the two and a half tribes who would take possession on the other side of Jordan, Moses refers to this very incident:
"For when they (the ten) went up unto the valley of Eshcol, and saw the land, they discouraged the heart of the children of Israel, that they should not go into the land which the LORD had given them." (Numbers 32:9)
Surely we are being told that when people of the truth and people of the world behold the same thing, they must draw different conclusions. People around us behold the world and see a place of opportunity, challenge and excitement. We see a place

which can only divert us from the way that leads to life. Many in the world look at the land of Israel and see a place which will never be at rest. We see God's land, where one day the Prince of Peace will reign (Isaiah 9:6), sitting on David's throne (Luke 1:32). The ten spies beheld the giants and felt insignificant and small:

"And there we saw the giants, the sons of Anak, which come of the giants: and we were in our own sight as grasshoppers, and so we were in their sight." (Numbers 13:33).

When people of the truth and people of world behold the same thing and arrive at the same conclusions, there is something very wrong!

The faith of Caleb

The ten spies, tragically, had become just like the world around them, looking not with the eye of faith, but simply beholding the height of the walls and size of the men, who, apparently, were *all* giants (verse 32). What did Caleb say?

"Let us go up at once, and possess it; for we are well able to overcome it." (verse 30)

Here is a Gentile arguing to Jews that they could defeat Gentiles! What a remarkable irony! Was this powerful exhortation heeded? Numbers 14:4 tells us: the people said they would be better off appointing a leader and returning to Egypt. Once again, Caleb and Joshua appealed to the people: if God delights in us, then we will be able to take the land. Then they used a particularly powerful phrase to describe these giants, of whom the ten were afraid:

"... for they are bread for us: their defence is departed from them ..." (verse 9)

What did they mean? The KJV margin tells us that the Hebrew for defence is "shadow". What happened to Israel's bread when there was no shadow? What happened to manna when the sun was immediately overhead?

"... and when the sun waxed hot, it melted." (Exodus 16:21)

This is precisely what Caleb was saying: the inhabitants of the land will melt before us! Indeed, when another two spies entered the house of Rahab the harlot thirty-eight years later, this is what she said was happening in Jericho:

"And as soon as we had heard these things, our hearts did melt ..." (Joshua 2:11)

Joshua and Caleb could not have been more certain: the land was there for the taking, if only Israel would go forward in faith. Tragically, their words almost cost them their lives:

"But all the congregation bade stone them with stones ..." (Numbers 14:10)

The Lord Jesus Christ faced the same response from the leaders of his day, simply because he told them the truth (John 10:31). Note the words of the Father regarding Caleb later in this same chapter. The people would *not* enter the land, but:

"... my servant Caleb, because he had another spirit with him, and hath followed me fully, him will I bring into the land whereinto he went; and his seed shall possess it." (Numbers 14:24)

Caleb had "another spirit". This was surely a declaration that the natural man possesses a spirit of disobedience, faithlessness and wickedness, for the heart is deceitful above all things (Jeremiah 17:9). This was the spirit that the majority of the nation manifested; it was also the spirit Caleb possessed naturally, but it was a spirit that he conquered. He was a normal, fleshly, sinful man, yet he nourished "another spirit" within his heart, and the "new man" (Ephesians 4:24) grew and developed.

Note the conclusion of Numbers 14:24: how can we read this and not think of Abraham? He walked through a land, and was promised that one day it would be his. Caleb did the same thing. Truly, he is a wonderful example of Abraham's (spiritual) seed, for he manifested the faith of Abraham, though he was unable to trace his lineage back to that great patriarch. Indeed, the words of the Father about Caleb in Deuteronomy 1:36 are reminiscent of the promises to Abraham, for he and his children were promised all the land "he hath trodden upon".

At the end of the forty years

As we read on through the Old Testament, we see how the first generation died in the wilderness. Only Joshua, Caleb, and the Levites were preserved. So when the forty years were concluded, the time came for Caleb's immense faith to be manifested. His words to Joshua at this time are particularly powerful:

> "Now therefore give me this mountain, whereof the LORD spake in that day; for thou heardest in that day how the Anakims were there, and that the cities were great and fenced: if so be the LORD will be with me, then I shall be able to drive them out, as the LORD said." (Joshua 14:12)

Forty years of wilderness wanderings, suffering as a result of the lack of faith of others, had not quenched his unshakeable faith. Which part of the land, then, was he to possess?

"And Joshua blessed him, and gave unto Caleb the son of Jephunneh Hebron for an inheritance." (verse 13)

The city of Hebron

Hebron, of all places! It was the very location where Abraham had built an altar after receiving the promise of the seed (Genesis 13:18). It was also the site of the cave of Machpelah, where Abraham, Sarah, Isaac, Rebekah, Jacob and Leah were all buried (23:19; 25:9; 50:13; 49:31). Hebron was to become a city of refuge (Joshua 20:7), and the place from which David, guided by God, reigned over Judah (2 Samuel 2:1).

There were surely few more important places in the whole of the land of Israel – and a Gentile possessed it. Indeed, as we consider the words and actions of Caleb, we see that he was, in truth, more like the fathers of the nation than almost any other man. He was "an Israelite indeed" (John 1:47) and "a Jew ... inwardly" (Romans 2:29).

So was Hebron finally taken? Were the giants dispossessed? Judges chapter 1 tells us. It is, for the most part, a catalogue of dismal failure. Gentiles were *not* destroyed but permitted to survive amongst the nation (see Judges 1:27-33). Indeed, the

Danites were chased off into the mountains by the Amorites (verse 34).

Yet amidst all this weakness, this dismal incapacity and unwillingness to fulfill the commands of God and take the land, there was one wonderful example of success:

> "And they gave Hebron unto Caleb, as Moses said: and he expelled thence the three sons of Anak." (verse 20)

Here is the faith of Caleb in action. He had claimed that if God delighted in His people, then the giants would be no match for Israel. Were they simply dispossessed? Did Caleb merely chase them away? Knowing the character of Caleb, we would be surprised if this was the case! The comparison record in Joshua 15:14 names these giants: Sheshai, and Ahiman, and Talmai. They met their end:

> "And Judah went against the Canaanites that dwelt in Hebron: (now the name of Hebron before was Kirjath-arba:) and they slew Sheshai, and Ahiman, and Talmai." (Judges 1:10)

So these sons of the giant were slain by Caleb, and their city taken. These were the very men of whom the ten were afraid:

> "... and moreover we saw the children of Anak there." (Numbers 13:28)

Caleb was a man who "practised what he preached". Despite a gap of forty-five years, his bold declarations of faith, made in the face of fierce and potentially violent opposition, were shown to be more than just idle words. The time had come for this eighty-five-year-old man, divinely strengthened and preserved for this very day (Joshua 14:10,11; see also Psalm 91:16), to manifest his belief in the God he served. He faced the giants, fought with them and overcame them. So he was blessed with the city which spoke, as much as almost any other place, of the patriarchs and the promises made unto them.

Lessons from the life of Caleb for the ecclesia today

What then are the lessons for us from the life of this great man? Though we may be called upon to fight when the Master returns (Psalm 149:7-9), in this age we "must not strive" (2 Timothy 2:24).

Nonetheless life in the truth is one of trial, hardship and warfare. We are commanded to "fight the good fight of faith" (1 Timothy 6:12), and to "war a good warfare" (1:18), bearing "the sword of the spirit, which is the word of God" (Ephesians 6:17).

In the life of Caleb, therefore, we see a representation of our own lives. Perhaps more especially, we see a man who foreshadowed the work of the Lord Jesus Christ. Our Master conquered the mightiest giant of all: the sin that dwelled within him (Romans 7:17; 8:3). And in doing so he provided the way for faithful believers of all ages – those with a faith like that of Caleb – to enjoy immortality at his side, when he comes again to reign:

> "And having spoiled principalities and powers, he made a shew of them openly, triumphing over them in it."
>
> (Colossians 2:15)

10

Rahab the harlot

THE forty years was at an end. The men of war had been "wasted out from among the host" (Deuteronomy 2:14), and Israel could enter the land through which Abraham had walked over 400 years previously. Now, at last, this part of the promises would be fulfilled. The precise details of how the land would be taken were yet to be revealed. How would the river Jordan be crossed? How long would the manna last? How would the land be divided up? How long would it take for the inhabitants to be subjugated? Such questions would be answered soon enough. Israel were about to enter the Promised Land. This was to be a time of immense rejoicing for God's people.

The nations of the land
Of course, one person's joy may be another's grief. As one inherits, another may well be disinherited. As Israel neared the borders of the land, having travelled north from Sinai, the nations who dwelled there would have watched proceedings with growing uncertainty. Some may have scoffed at the idea of a race of pilgrims entering their land and taking it. Others knew differently. Here was a mighty army and, despite their own defences, many in Canaan would know that Israel's impending arrival would spell potential disaster for every one of them. Such a one was Rahab of Jericho.

At the start of the forty years, twelve spies had been sent to search the land, only two of whom bought back a faithful assessment. This time only two were sent:

"And Joshua the son of Nun sent out of Shittim two men to spy secretly, saying, Go view the land, even Jericho. And they went, and came into an harlot's house, named Rahab, and lodged there." (Joshua 2:1)

The location here is of particular interest. Shittim is only mentioned once prior to this:

"And Israel abode in Shittim, and the people began to commit whoredom with the daughters of Moab." (Numbers 25:1)

So Shittim was a place which had previously identified with sin. It was a place where the men of Israel had fallen, having been enticed by Gentile women and their ways, at the instruction of Balaam (Micah 6:5; Revelation 2:14). We see that they committed "whoredom". How ironic, then, that one generation later two men arrived at the house of a "harlot", for this is exactly the same word in the original Hebrew as "whoredom" in Numbers 25:1. However, far from being beguiled by her, she was the one who would be influenced by their words and faith, and subsequently would be welcomed into their nation.

Rahab the harlot

Rahab's name means 'proud' (Strong). Yet any pride she may have had in Jericho would be dispelled over the coming days, as she turned, in faith and humility, to Israel's God, embracing Israel's hope and being saved as a result.

Many commentators seek to avoid describing Rahab as a "harlot", preferring to speak of her as a "landlady". Here was one who refused to take part in the sin, we are told, for she merely owned the building where these acts took place. This is not supported by the word of God. The Hebrew term used to describe her occupation means exactly what we would expect: one who commits adultery. The word is translated in a whole host of ways, all to do with sins of the flesh (as in Numbers 25).

Rahab was a pagan harlot, living in a pagan city. Yet in the love of the Lord God of Israel, she was offered a way out, and she took it with both hands. What a person is *before* he or she comes to the truth does not matter in the slightest, as the lives of people like Saul of Tarsus prove. It is such a person's life *after* he or she responds to the call of salvation that matters. Rahab, who had previously been "dead in trespasses and sins" (Ephesians 2:1), was to be transformed by her knowledge of the truth, and her life would reflect this.

Rahab and the two spies
The spies, under angelic guidance, arrived at Rahab's house. Although this would have been a typical occurrence, there was clearly something about these two men that caused them to stand out (a lesson for us when we are in the world). News of their arrival reached the king, who sent men to take the spies. Yet Rahab lied to protect the two Israelites, and the men of her city believed her words. Nowhere in the word of God does He commend sin. Nowhere are we called to do that which is wrong, that right may prevail. Yet Rahab had not, as yet, embraced the truth, and so she did what she believed to be right. In the providence of God, this resulted in the spies being preserved.

> "But she had brought them up to the roof of the house, and hid them with the stalks of flax, which she had laid in order upon the roof."   (Joshua 2:6)

The men were covered over and concealed by flax. Flax is a crop which is dried to form linen, which is then used to be made into clothing. The same Hebrew word is often translated "linen" (as under the law: four times in Leviticus 13). This covering brought about their salvation. We are reminded of the immortal bride of the Lamb:

> "Let us be glad and rejoice, and give honour to him: for the marriage of the Lamb is come, and his wife hath made herself ready. And to her was granted that she should be arrayed in fine linen, clean and white: for the fine linen is the righteousness of saints."   (Revelation 19:7,8)

So fine linen represents righteousness; in its fullest sense it speaks of immortality. An immortal multitude of redeemed ones will be united with their Lord in the age to come, having refused to be associated with the people of this world. Just as the spies were covered by the flax (which was to become linen), we are clothed with the righteousness of the Son of God, by putting him on in baptism (Galatians 3:27). This is in anticipation of that greater change, when, by grace –

"… this corruptible must put on incorruption, and this mortal must put on immortality." (1 Corinthians 15:53)

We are reminded also of the act of love of Boaz, who spread his skirt over Ruth (Ruth 3:9), and of the fine linen brought by Joseph of Arimathaea to cover the body of the Master (Mark 15:46).

Rahab's faith and her appeal for salvation

The men of her city having departed, Rahab approached the spies. In her words to them, we see a marked difference between what she believed and what was accepted by the people of her city. To demonstrate this difference, the parts of her speech which relate only to her are italicised below:

"And she said unto the men, *I know that the* LORD *hath given you the land*, and that your terror is fallen upon us, and that all the inhabitants of the land faint because of you. For we have heard how the LORD dried up the water of the Red sea for you, when ye came out of Egypt … And as soon as we had heard these things, our hearts did melt, neither did there remain any more courage in any man, because of you: *for the* LORD *your God, he is God in heaven above, and in earth beneath*."

(Joshua 2:9-11)

The key to understanding the mindset of this amazing woman is to see how the pronouns change in the words recorded above, from "I" to "us", "we", "our". Everyone knew the children of Israel were coming, but only she knew why. Everyone knew the city would be taken, but only she believed that this was because of the power of their God, and the promises He had made. All of Jericho knew they were as good as dead, but only Rahab did anything about it. This is made all the more remarkable when we consider that these words were spoken by a Gentile woman who had, almost certainly, little or no association with anyone from Israel prior to this. Her use of the Yahweh name in her conversations with the spies is similarly amazing. We can only surmise at the source of this knowledge, and who she may have met to have revealed such things to her. What we do know is that she was a woman of the utmost faith. Faith is "the evidence of things not seen" (Hebrews 11:1) and Rahab possessed it in abundance!

Having spared the men, she then requested that they save her and her family when the city was taken:

"Now therefore, I pray you, swear unto me by the LORD, since I have shewed you kindness, that ye will also shew kindness unto my father's house, and give me a true token: and that ye will save alive my father, and my mother, and my brethren, and my sisters, and all that they have, and deliver our lives from death." (Joshua 2:12,13)

She required a "true token". The Hebrew word means a 'signal', and is translated in a number of different ways, often speaking of a sign of a covenant having been made. Bearing in mind the request of Rahab, it is appropriate that this same word is used to describe the covenant made with Abraham:

"And ye shall circumcise the flesh of your foreskin; and it shall be a token (same word in both the English and Hebrew) of the covenant betwixt me and you." (Genesis 17:11)

The context in Genesis speaks of all the land of Canaan – all of Rahab's land – being given to Abraham and his seed. Yet Rahab was to be incorporated into the nation, and so these promises, in the grace of God, would apply to her also.

The scarlet line

Having received this promise from the spies, she then let them down from a window of her house. Note how the men of her city, in searching for the spies, had gone to the fords (Joshua 2:7). She instructed the spies to head for the mountain (verse 16). The two Israelites were men who sought "those things which are above" (Colossians 3:1). Indeed in the actions of these two groups, we see a demonstration of the truth of the Master's words in

Matthew 7:13,14: for there are two very different ways, one of which leads to life and one to death.

Before the spies left, they had words of instruction for Rahab. She was to remain silent as to the agreement they had made, and any who were with her in her house when the city was taken would be saved along with her. She was also told that her house needed to be identified when they returned:

"Behold, when we come into the land, thou shalt bind this line of scarlet thread in the window ..."   (Joshua 2:18)

Scarlet represents sin:

"Come now, and let us reason together, saith the LORD: though your sins be as scarlet, they shall be as white as snow ..."   (Isaiah 1:18)

It was as though Rahab was being called to placard her sinfulness, that she might be forgiven by the God of Israel, and welcomed into the nation by Him.

What, then, of the "line"? We may have seen children's books where an immense red rope is shown hanging from Rahab's window, all the way down to the ground. The word translated "line" means 'cord'; however it is used in symbol to speak of "expectancy" (Strong). Indeed, every other use of this word outside Joshua 2 refers to "hope" or "expectation":

- In the valley of dry bones, Israel say: "our *hope* is lost" (Ezekiel 37:11).
- Naomi said to Ruth: "If I should say, I have *hope*, if I should have an husband also to night ..." (Ruth 1:12).

So this was more than a simple method of identification of a property. This was a manifestation of the hope of a Gentile woman. Rahab's faith in sparing the men, and her belief that she could be saved (see James 2:25) was being shown for all outside the city to see. When Jericho was taken she would be rewarded by Israel's God.

"I have waited for thy salvation, O LORD"

These are words of Israel himself, in the promises made to his twelve sons, as his death approached (Genesis 49:18). However they also describe very well the actions of Rahab after the spies had left. Day by day she would have looked out, knowing that one day her saviours would come, led by Joshua, the warrior appointed by the Father. Surely her position then is the same as ours today.

We dwell amongst people of the world, and wait in faith for the promised Saviour, the 'greater Joshua' to come. We believe that, by grace, when he comes, we shall be saved from wrath and united with him.

There is a further allusion to the sacrifice of the Master, which is foreshadowed by the Passover (1 Corinthians 5:7). There are strong connections between the faith of Rahab and what the children of Israel had to do when the Passover lamb was slain:

Rahab	Joshua	Passover	Exodus
Scarlet hope / line / cord	2:18	Blood of lamb (scarlet in colour) on doorpost	12:7
Family in the house	2:18	Family / neighbours in house	12:22
Death all round	6:21	Death all round	12:29
Spies sent to save	6:22	Angel passed over, Israel saved	12:23
Out of Jericho	6:23	Out of Egypt	12:41
"Token"	2:12	"Token" (same word)	12:13

Doubtless after she was incorporated into the nation, she would have been educated as to the relevance of the Passover meal, and would have seen in her own salvation a representation of these things.

Rahab and Achan

So Rahab was to be saved. She had looked out, and had seen with the eye of faith that the children of Israel would come one day.

She longed, and probably prayed, that she might be with them. In due course her faith was to be rewarded. However there was another who looked in, for Achan, of the tribe of Judah, beheld her city and lusted after the treasures there. As we know, his sin was brought to light, and he and his family (who had, presumably, been complicit in this) were all stoned (Joshua 7:24,25). When we compare these two contrasting responses, we see a serious warning from the word of God for us today.

When Achan took items that should have been devoted to the Lord (6:19; 7:1), he was bringing the world into the camp of Israel. His sin was highlighted by the initial defeat suffered at the hands of the people of Ai (verses 4,5). Note the outcome of this tragic event:

"... wherefore the hearts of the people melted, and became as water." (verse 5)

This had happened before, to the men of Jericho, as Rahab had said:

"And as soon as we had heard these things, our hearts did melt ..." (2:11)

So Achan brought the things of the world into Israel, and the result was that God's people felt just like the people of the land, for their hearts melted. Indeed, the very place where he was stoned is mentioned later in the Old Testament, and once again we read that same word translated "line" – this time referring to the place where Achan had died (7:24):

"And I will give her her vineyards from thence, and the valley of Achor for a door of *hope*" (same word as "line").

(Hosea 2:15)

Scripture often presents two different types of people to us, one of whom was faithful and the other who was not. We think of Cain and Abel, Isaac and Ishmael, Jacob and Esau, or perhaps the two different builders spoken of by the Master (Matthew 7:24-27). To this list we could add Rahab and Achan. Both looked, and longed for what they saw. Both acted, and both received the reward of the actions. Who, then, are we most like?

Rahab's salvation and the line of David

The walls of the city fell down, "by faith" (Hebrews 11:30), and the spies rescued Rahab and her family. Initially, as required by the Law of Moses, she would have remained without the camp (Deuteronomy 21:10-13; Joshua 6:23) and then brought inside. The New Testament commentary on her actions is particularly powerful:

> "By faith the harlot Rahab perished not with them that believed not, when she had received the spies with peace."
> (Hebrews 11:31)

Others, such as the men of her city and Achan, "believed not" (the Greek is *apeitheo*, from which we get our English word 'apathy'). Yet her amazing faith – and she is one of only two faithful women named in Hebrews 11 – is recorded as a lesson and challenge for us all. Note also that her former life is mentioned: she was a "harlot"; the Greek word is *porne*, from which we get the English word 'pornography'. Surely we are being told that none is beyond the reach of the love, mercy, and salvation of Israel's God, if only that person will respond in faith, like Rahab, the harlot of Jericho.

However, this is not the last time we read of Rahab in the Bible:

> "And Salmon begat Booz of Rachab; and Booz begat Obed of Ruth; and Obed begat Jesse." (Matthew 1:5)

This is a slightly different version of the name that appears in Hebrews 11 and James 2. However, it seems very likely that it is the same person we read of in the book of Joshua. The RV, RSV and NKJV, for example, all render the name "Rachab" as "Rahab".

So having been welcomed into the nation, she married Salmon and they were blessed with a son, Boaz. And Boaz, as we know, was the great-grandfather of David. What, then, is the lesson of the life of Boaz? Is it not the salvation and redemption of a Gentile bride (Ruth), through faith and love? No wonder, then, that he was so kind and generous towards this "stranger" (Ruth 2:8-10,14-16), for his ancestor had been the recipient of this kind of love when she first encountered the people of Israel.

Being an ancestor of David, Rahab was therefore also an ancestor of Jesus Christ, for the Son of God was born of David's line (Luke 1:27). Indeed, the salvation of Rahab prefigures the wondrous work of redemption and deliverance wrought for us by our gracious Heavenly Father, through the death and resurrection of His only begotten Son:

"But God commendeth his love toward us, in that, while we were yet sinners, Christ died for us. Much more then, being now justified by his blood, we shall be saved from wrath through him." (Romans 5:8,9)

11

The Gibeonites

FEAR can provoke a whole host of different responses. Some panic and flee; others freeze. Some 'fight fire with fire', striking out at what makes them afraid. A few consider the danger and act in wisdom, desiring to nullify whatever threatens them by reason and logic. Some of these do so in faith. In the words and deeds of one Gentile tribe in the days of Joshua we see precisely this course of action. The children of Israel were in their land; a mighty and powerful nation had come to dispossess them. What could possibly be done? The men of the city of Gibeon did the one thing they could: they acted wisely in order to secure their own salvation.

The entry of Israel into Canaan
Some, like Rahab (see chapter 10), knew that this day would come (Joshua 2:9-11). They had heard of the exodus and knew that Egypt had been decimated. Then the news they feared had been received: Israel had crossed the Jordan. Very soon they would be amongst them and, based on what had happened to others, the enemy would destroy them and take their homes. Sihon and Og, two great and mighty leaders, had been killed (Numbers 21:24,35). All their military might had been useless. What hope was there?

The Gibeonites
This was the dilemma facing the Gibeonites. The city of Gibeon was in the area eventually allotted to the tribe of Benjamin

(Joshua 18:25), and would be one of the cities given to the priests (21:17). In the days after the death of Saul, a battle between those loyal to him and those who followed David commenced with a minor skirmish at Gibeon (2 Samuel 2:16). The city would have an immensely important part to play later on under the rule of David and Solomon, as we shall see in due course.

Gibeon means 'hilly'; it is derived from the same word elsewhere translated "Gibeah". The land had been described by Moses as a place of "hills and valleys" (Deuteronomy 11:11). There were many who lived in cities built on hills. Yet those of Gibeon were different. They wanted to embrace the hope of Israel. There were four key cities of the Gibeonites (Joshua 9:17). Gibeon itself appears to have been the most powerful, for it is termed "a great city", a "royal" city, and its men "mighty" (10:2).

The Gibeonites are called "Hivites" in Joshua 9:7 and 11:19. The Hivites were descended from Ham through his youngest son, Canaan (Genesis 10:6,17). Time and again the children of Israel were promised that the Canaanites would be driven out and that they would possess their land. When the inhabitants of the land are listed, invariably the Hivites are named (Exodus 3:8). They appear to have been a nomadic people, living in many parts of the land of Canaan, including in the shadow of Hermon (Joshua 11:3) and as far north as the mountains of Lebanon (Judges 3:3). Only the Hivites dwelling in Gibeon appear to have been faithful, and their faith would be rewarded.

In 2 Samuel 21:2 the Gibeonites are described as being "of the remnant of the Amorites". The Amorites were another ancient people, listed amongst those who would be disinherited when Abraham's seed took the land (Genesis 15:21). Jacob describes having taken an area of land from the Amorites in battle (48:22). In Numbers 13:29 we are told they lived in the mountainous areas of the land. Sihon (see above) was the king of the Amorites. The children of Israel requested that they be permitted to pass through the land during their wilderness wanderings. This request was refused and Sihon came out ready for battle. Israel enjoyed an immense victory and took the Amorites' cities (21:21-31).

When we look more closely at the use of this name in the Old Testament, we see that it appears to be a general title, used to describe a large area of the land. In Joshua 7:7, when Israel had suffered at the hand of the men of Ai, Joshua describes them as having been delivered "into the hand of the Amorites". In Joshua 10 five kings (one of whom was king of Jerusalem) came against the men of Gibeon, and are described as being Amorites (10:5). In Amos 2:10 the Father speaks of the ancestors of the nation surviving the forty years in the wilderness and possessing "the land of the Amorite".

The key phrase is in 2 Samuel 21:2: the Gibeonites were "*of the remnant* of the Amorites". As we shall see shortly, the Amorites sought their destruction when they realised Gibeon had become associated with Israel. So although the main body of the people called "Amorites" still existed, the Gibeonites, having separated themselves, are described as being a remnant.

The actions of the Gibeonites

As Joshua and the people of Israel came closer, we can imagine a meeting being called. The leaders of Gibeon would have voiced their concerns. Possible solutions would have been discussed. Fighting back was useless. Fleeing to another part of the land would not work, for Israel had been promised an immense area, stretching from the river of Egypt to the Euphrates (Genesis 15:18). This will only ever be inherited in the kingdom age, but how were the men of Gibeon to know this? Could they travel yet further? The dangers would be too great.

Eventually they would have arrived at the conclusion that there was only one hope of saving their lives and those of their children. They must send representatives to Joshua who would claim to be from a far-off land. They would then make a peace treaty with Israel. An agreement would be arrived at whereby they would promise not to attack each other. Then when the Israelites came to take their part of the land, the treaty would be in place, and they would be permitted to live. This plan was then put into action:

> "They did work wilily, and went and made as if they had been ambassadors, and took old sacks upon their asses, and wine bottles, old, and rent, and bound up; and old shoes and clouted upon their feet, and old garments upon them; and all the bread of their provision was dry and mouldy. And they went to Joshua unto the camp at Gilgal, and said unto him, and to the men of Israel, We be come from a far country: now therefore make ye a league with us." (Joshua 9:3-6)

What do we make of the actions of these men? The God we worship is a God of holiness, abundant in goodness and truth (Exodus 34:6). Lying lips are an abomination to Him (Proverbs 12:22). Time and again the Son of God condemned the leaders of his day for being "hypocrites" or 'play actors' (Matthew 6:2,5,16). The members of the ecclesia at Laodicea were condemned for being "neither cold not hot" (Revelation 3:15,16). Pretending to be one thing whilst being something else may be regarded as acceptable by some in the world, but it is never right in the sight of the Father. We should never do wrong, that right may prevail. The end never justifies the means, if this necessitates our sinning.

Were the Gibeonites at fault? In reality, we have to answer 'Yes'. A lie is a lie regardless of the reason for its being told. However, at this stage they had not been incorporated into the nation of Israel and were not yet under the law. Our sins committed prior to our association with our gracious Heavenly Father and His Son are forgiven on the occasion of our baptism (Acts 22:16). We should, therefore, never judge anyone too harshly based on his or her actions prior to an acceptance of the truth. Rahab lied to spare the lives of the spies (Joshua 2:4,5); once again, these things took place prior to her being accepted into the nation.

The Gibeonites did the only thing they could think of to ensure their survival. Ironically, this course of action was a compliment to Israel. They knew that the Israelites were people of their word. If an agreement was made, then it would be applied.

The KJV speaks of their acting "wilily" (Joshua 9:4). This is an old-fashioned expression which implies 'with deceit' (in Ephesians 6:11 we read of "the wiles of the devil"). The NKJV translates this as "craftily"; the RSV says "with cunning". The Hebrew word here means 'trickery' or 'discretion' (Strong). Interestingly, the same word occurs twice in Proverbs 8 and is rendered "wisdom" (verse 5) and "prudence" (verse 12). Regardless of the rights and wrongs of the actions of these men, they acted wisely; they "walked in wisdom toward them that [were] without" (Colossians 4:5). Others could have desired peace with Israel, yet only the men of Gibeon did so (Joshua 11:19).

The Gibeonites meet with the children of Israel

When the ambassadors from Gibeon arrived in the camp of Israel, an interrogation took place. The visitors stated their wish to make a "league" with Israel (9:6). This is the same word we have seen many times, elsewhere translated "covenant" (especially in relation to the seed of Abraham inheriting the land: Genesis 15:18). How did the men of Israel know they were from a far-off land (Joshua 9:7)? What if they lived among them?

The men of Gibeon then told their tale, claiming that they had travelled many miles, having commenced their trip with fresh bread and new skins for their water. These things were now old. Such was the length of the journey even their shoes were worn out (verses 12,13). This was something the children of Israel had not seen throughout their wilderness wanderings (Deuteronomy 29:5). Much as we cannot condone the actions of these men, there are two statements in their speech which demand our attention.

Firstly, they state that they had come not solely because of all that Israel had done to the enemy, but also –

"... because of the name of the LORD thy God: for we have heard the fame of him, and all that he did in Egypt."

(Joshua 9:9)

This is a remarkable statement from the lips of these Gentiles. They knew the name of the God whom Israel worshipped, and had heard of His fame. They knew that salvation from Egypt was accomplished by the hand of Yahweh alone. Regardless of the untruths which issued from their lips, this statement demonstrates a considerable insight into the actions of the Father with His people. The name of the God that Israel worshipped had prompted these men to travel to meet with His people. We are reminded of the words of the Apostle James at the Jerusalem Conference:

> "Simeon hath declared how God at the first did visit the Gentiles, to take out of them a people for his name."
> (Acts 15:14)

The second statement is later in their speech, and is in the form of a request:

> "We are your servants: therefore now make ye a league with us." (Joshua 9:11)

Their wish was to serve Israel. This was not some desperate plea made after they had been discovered. Rather, this had been their desire right from the outset. Did they know of the curse placed on their ancestor, Ham, by Noah?

> "... Cursed be Canaan; a servant of servants shall he be unto his brethren." (Genesis 9:25)

A willing servant is always acceptable in the sight of God. Time and again throughout the law the importance of faithful and reverential service was stressed. Time and again, especially in the days of prophets such as Jeremiah, a lack of service was bemoaned. The Lord Jesus is introduced to us, especially in the prophecy of Isaiah and Mark's Gospel record, as the ultimate servant of God (Isaiah 42:1; 53:11; Matthew 12:18). This intention of the Gibeonites was good. By serving Israel they would be serving Israel's God.

The response of Joshua and the leaders of Israel

Following these discussions, the leaders of the nation had a decision to make:

"And the men took of their victuals, and asked not counsel at the mouth of the LORD. And Joshua made peace with them, and made a league with them, to let them live: and the princes of the congregation sware unto them." (Joshua 9:14,15)

It is so easy to be wise after the event. Should they have asked counsel of the Lord? Surely the answer is 'Yes'. Should they have (as the KJV margin suggests) "received the men by reason of their victuals"? Surely we would answer 'No'. When speaking of the Lord Jesus, the prophet Isaiah wrote that he would:

"… not judge after the sight of his eyes, neither reprove after the hearing of his ears." (Isaiah 11:3)

In making a judgement based upon what they could see, Joshua and the leaders were ignoring the fact that what a man can behold may not always be a representation of the truth. God looks on the heart (1 Samuel 16:7). In failing to seek His guidance in this matter the men of Israel were deceived and there would be consequences of their actions, for them and for the Gibeonites, in due course.

The deceit of the Gibeonites is revealed

Only three days later the truth came to light (Joshua 9:16). There then followed an uncomfortable meeting between the two peoples. The children of Israel promised to spare the Gibeonites; however the people murmured against the leaders of Israel because of their actions (verse 18). This is a worrying reminder of what had taken place throughout the wilderness wanderings, when "murmuring" in the camp of Israel was a common sound (Exodus 15:24). Despite these complaints, however, the leaders were true to their word. The Gibeonites were spared. Joshua chided with them, asking why they had chosen to act in such a way (Joshua 9:22). Their response underlines the insight of these faithful Gentiles:

"And they answered Joshua, and said, Because it was certainly told thy servants, how that the LORD thy God commanded his servant Moses to give you all the land, and to destroy all the inhabitants of the land from before you, therefore we were sore afraid of our lives because of you, and have done this thing." (verse 24)

Not only did they know that the land would belong to Israel one day, they also knew that the Lord had revealed this to Moses, and that all inhabitants of the land would be wiped out when this took place. We marvel at the knowledge of these men. Others in the land may have scoffed at a nation of pilgrims entering and taking their cities. Indeed the first generation, prompted by the ten spies, had refused to accept that the land could be conquered (Numbers 13). These Gentiles from Gibeon knew differently. Regardless of the rights and wrongs of their actions, they manifested their belief in an effort to be saved and become incorporated into the nation.

Hewers of wood and drawers of water

The request of the Gibeonites that they should be servants of Israel was therefore granted:

"And Joshua made them that day hewers of wood and drawers of water for the congregation, and for the altar of the LORD, even unto this day, in the place which he should choose." (Joshua 9:27)

So these Gentiles would be permitted to perform acts of service for God's people. However they were not to do this merely "unto all the congregation" (see verse 21), but more especially "for the altar of the LORD". They would serve the priests and Levities by performing menial duties around the tabernacle. This is of particular importance when we consider where the tabernacle was established later, prior to its removal to Jerusalem.

The Gibeonites are saved by Israel

News travels fast. It didn't take long for the nations round about to learn what the men of Gibeon had done. A number of kings of the land, led by Adonizedek of Jerusalem, came together to attack the Gibeonites (10:3-5). The men of Gibeon sent a message to Joshua, appealing for assistance (verse 6). This time guidance was given from the Father:

"And the LORD said unto Joshua, Fear them not: for I have delivered them into thine hand; there shall not a man of them stand before thee." (verse 8)

What followed was a crushing victory for God's people, commencing at Gibeon itself (verse 10). In addition to the might of Israel, the enemy had to endure an immense hailstorm, which was so severe that the hailstones killed more than had died in the battle (verse 11). There is an echo of these things in the seventh plague (Exodus 9:18), and a pointer forward to the time when the northern host will be destroyed at the commencement of the Millennium (Ezekiel 38:22).

There then followed an incident which is unique in God's word:

"Then spake Joshua to the LORD in the day when the LORD delivered up the Amorites before the children of Israel, and he said in the sight of Israel, Sun, stand thou still upon Gibeon; and thou, Moon, in the valley of Ajalon. And the sun stood still, and the moon stayed, until the people had avenged themselves upon their enemies ... There was no day like that before it or after it, that the LORD hearkened unto the voice of a man: for the LORD fought for Israel." (Joshua 10:12-14)

Although there are events that bear a resemblance to this, such as the shadow on the sundial of Ahaz returning ten degrees in Hezekiah's day (Isaiah 38:8), in truth there has never been a day such as this. The Lord hearkened to the voice of a man and the sun stood still. How astounding that this unique event should have commenced with the nation of Israel coming to the rescue of a tribe of Gentiles.

The city of Gibeon in David's day

Moving on to the time of King David we read of the city of Gibeon again:

"So he left there before the ark of the covenant of the LORD Asaph and his brethren ... Zadok the priest ... before the tabernacle of the LORD in the high place that was at Gibeon." (1 Chronicles 16:37,39)

This city had been the home of Gentiles, who looked at the children of Israel and longed to be incorporated into the nation. How fitting, then, that their home should in time become the temporary resting place of the tabernacle of the Lord. The ark was there at Gibeon. Nothing spoke of the things of the truth more than the ark of the covenant. The God of Israel is portrayed as dwelling "between the cherubim" (1 Samuel 4:4). It was placed, at least for a time, in a city inhabited by men of Gentile ancestry. Maybe it was the service of the Gibeonites which made this such a logical step. Or perhaps their spirituality and desire to be associated with the things of the truth resulted in the tabernacle being placed there.

Later in David's reign we read of these men once more. A terrible famine, lasting three years, had decimated the land. David desired to know the reason for this. He was told it was as a result of the sin of Saul. In his misplaced zeal for Israel, Saul had put to death the majority of the Gibeonites. David approached the survivors and asked what they wanted. They stated openly that they desired neither silver nor gold, but wanted seven of Saul's sons to be handed over to them that they might be executed (2 Samuel 21:1-9). We can only assume that those who were selected had acted alongside their father, as the record concludes with the phrase:

"… And after that God was intreated for the land." (verse 14)

Gibeon in the reign of Solomon

Under Solomon, the tabernacle remained in this city (2 Chronicles 1:13). Gibeon was a key location, known for the offering of sacrifices. It was a "great high place" where Solomon offered one thousand burnt offerings upon an altar (1 Kings 3:4). What follows is particularly appropriate:

"In Gibeon the LORD appeared to Solomon in a dream by night: and God said, Ask what I shall give thee." (verse 5).

We know what transpired. Solomon asked for, and was granted, the gift of wisdom, that Israel might be judged faithfully.

How apt that in a location where men had acted wisely (see above, Joshua 9:4), this blessing of wisdom should be requested.

The Gibeonites after the captivity

Scripture is silent regarding the Gibeonites for the next few hundred years. In the days of Jeremiah a false prophet called Hananiah came from Gibeon (Jeremiah 28:1). Later, when most of the nation had been carried away to Babylon, there was a conflict between some of those left behind at Gibeon (41:12,16). However, it is in the days of the Medo-Persian empire that we read of the Gibeonites again.

The call had gone forth from Artaxerxes the king. All who wished to return to Jerusalem with Nehemiah could do so. Nehemiah chapter 3 describes the different parts of the wall and gates of Jerusalem which were rebuilt, and by whom. All sorts of people did all kinds of jobs. Skilled artisans worked side by side with manual labourers. Males and females all played their part. How marvellous it is to read that amongst those of Israel who had chosen to return and repair God's city, a number of Gibeonites are listed:

"And next unto them repaired Melatiah the Gibeonite, and Jadon the Meronothite, the men of Gibeon, and of Mizpah, unto the throne of the governor on this side the river."

(Nehemiah 3:7)

Ninety-five men of Gibeon had chosen to return (7:25). Of itself, this is not particularly amazing. Compared with other groups in this chapter, it is not an especially large number. Yet when we consider that these were Gentiles by their ancestry, this is surely worthy of note. The forefathers of these men had come out of the Gentile world to become incorporated into the nation of Israel. Later their children had been carried away captive, back into the lands of the Gentiles. Yet when opportunity came for their descendants to return, they refused to stay in the area of Medo-Persia, choosing rather to face the dangerous journey back to the Promised Land. Truly they were Abraham's seed in spirit, for in returning to the land they would have retraced the steps of the great ancestor of the nation.

One day, we hope and pray very soon, the city walls of Jerusalem will be built again. Yet unlike former times, when invading armies came and destroyed this "city of the great King", it will stand forever. Zion will become "the joy of the whole earth" (Psalm 48:2). The faithful will walk round her, admiring her towers (verse 12).

"Do good in thy good pleasure unto Zion: build thou the walls of Jerusalem." (51:18)

And in that great day, who will be united with the Son of God? Those with a desire to serve the God of Israel – those like the faithful Gibeonites of old. May we be privileged to play our part in establishing that city which has foundations, whose builder and maker is God (Hebrews 11:10).

12 |

Jael and Heber

AS has been noted many times, the Bible contains just about everything. In sixty-six amazing books we have law, history, prophecy, letters and poetry. There is a great variety of incidents, from acts of love and devotion to deeds of hatred and selfishness. In the actions of one faithful woman called Jael we see the kind of things which would probably form the basis of a particularly gruesome horror movie today. Yet she was commended for her actions by the inspired prophetess Deborah. Her act of faith was killing the captain of the enemy of Israel. Yet as we shall see, she was a Gentile, having come from the land of the Hittites with her husband.

The acts of Deborah and Barak
In a pattern so typical of the book of Judges, Israel had sinned. Great judgements were poured out by the Father through Gentile nations. Finally His people had cried unto Him and Barak was instructed to lead them in battle with the enemy. His initial uncertainty has been portrayed as cowardice by some. Yet his actions later when leading the army and pursuing the enemy on foot hardly support this (Judges 4:14-16; 5:15). It seems likely that he was unarmed (5:8). He is also listed as one of the faithful in Hebrews 11:32. A man acting in faith is never a coward. Nonetheless, when the prophetess Deborah agreed to accompany him, she made it clear that when the victory was secured, the leader of the invasion, Sisera, would be killed by a woman. That woman was Jael, the wife of Heber the Kenite.

Heber and Jael
We are first introduced to Heber around the time that Deborah and Barak led ten thousand men of Israel to do battle with Sisera's army:

> "Now Heber the Kenite, which was of the children of Hobab the father in law of Moses, had severed himself from the Kenites, and pitched his tent unto the plain of Zaanaim, which is by Kedesh." (Judges 4:11)

The Kenites are considered elsewhere in this book (see chapters 8, 9 and 26). They are listed amongst those who would be disinherited when the seed of Abraham possessed the land (Genesis 15:19). Despite this, there were a number of men and women of faith who were of Kenite ancestry. Heber was a descendant of Moses' father-in-law, Hobab (also called Jethro, Raguel and Reuel, see chapter 7). How Heber had come to separate from the rest of his family, we are not told at this stage. All we do know is that this man had departed from his immediate family and was living in the land of Israel in a tent.

Straightaway we are reminded of the father of the faithful, Abraham. He also severed himself from his people and lived in the Promised Land in tents. Although we know very little of Heber, his wife Jael certainly shared Abraham's vision of the things of the truth.

Heber's name means 'community' (Strong). It may seem strange that a man whose name spoke of a collection of individuals, working together for the common good, lived apart from his people. Maybe we are being told that he was seeking a different kind of community, one made up of like-minded people. Amongst the Kenites he was unable to find this. Yet within Israel such things existed, and could be enjoyed by Gentiles who desired union with people of the truth.

The home of Heber and Jael: Kedesh in Galilee
Kedesh, the nearest city to the place where Heber had pitched his tent, was in Galilee, in the area inherited by the tribe of Naphtali (1 Chronicles 6:76). It was a city of refuge (Joshua 20:7). This

will become relevant as we consider the events recorded later in Judges 4. Galilee as an area was later despised by those in the south of the land. In New Testament times one man was synonymous with Galilee: the Lord Jesus Christ. He had grown up in the area and was known to all as "Jesus of Nazareth". Some of his closest followers were recognised by their Galilean accents (Matthew 26:73; Acts 2:7). The leaders in Christ's day had concluded that he couldn't possibly be the Messiah, as he was (apparently) from Galilee, and "out of Galilee ariseth no prophet" (John 7:52). However, in the work which Jael was to perform we shall see one of the most powerful types of the Master in the whole of the Old Testament.

Earlier in the chapter this same place, Kedesh, is mentioned again:

"And she sent and called Barak the son of Abinoam out of *Kedesh-naphtali* (this is the same name in the Hebrew) and said unto him, Hath not the LORD God of Israel commanded, saying, Go and draw toward mount Tabor, and take with thee ten thousand men of the children of Naphtali and of the children of Zebulun? ... and Deborah arose, and went with Barak to *Kedesh*. And Barak called Zebulun and Naphtali to *Kedesh* ..."   (Judges 4:6,9,10)

So Heber and his wife lived in the very area from which Barak had been called, and from where Israel would be summoned to do battle with the enemy. This is highly relevant as a woman who dwelled there would play an immense part in the victory that would be enjoyed by Israel.

Victory for Israel

Despite being so vastly outnumbered, and Barak's initial uncertainty, Israel achieved a crushing victory over their enemies that day:

"And the LORD discomfited Sisera, and all his chariots, and all his host, with the edge of the sword before Barak; so that Sisera lighted down off his chariot, and fled away on his feet. But Barak pursued after the chariots, and after the host, unto Harosheth of the Gentiles: and all the host of Sisera fell upon the edge of the sword; and there was not a man left."

(verses 15,16)

The reason for this is made clear in the following chapter: "They fought from heaven; the stars in their courses fought against Sisera. The river of Kishon swept them away ..."

(5:20,21)

Quite what verse 20 means, we can only surmise. Perhaps it is a poetic way of saying that the weather acted against Sisera – hence the rain cloud that caused the chariots to become stuck. Elsewhere Israel were blessed with light, with their foes remaining in darkness (Exodus 14:20; Esther 8:16). Was there some sort of unusual solar activity which caused these Gentile warriors to be blinded? One thing we do know: all but Sisera were killed. The commander of the army fled on foot as his chariot sank in the mud. It is here that we meet the heroine of this incident, Heber's wife, Jael:

"Howbeit Sisera fled away on his feet to the tent of Jael the wife of Heber the Kenite: for there was peace between Jabin the king of Hazor and the house of Heber the Kenite.

(Judges 4:17)

Jabin was the king of Canaan; Sisera was the captain of his army. These men were the enemies into whose hand the Lord had "sold" His people (verse 2). How could there have been peace between these men, and a man like Heber? How could there have been any union between Jabin and a woman like Jael? The answer to this question surely lies in a careful consideration of the above verse. There was peace between the *house* of Heber and the king, but not necessarily between the *man* Heber and the king. Could this have been the reason for Heber's departure from his family? They were willing to foster friendly relationships with this man. They were quite content to agree a peace treaty with one who afflicted Israel. Heber and Jael sought the well-being of the people of God. They therefore refused to have anything to do with Jabin and had chosen to live alone.

If this is the case, we are surely being reminded of a simple Bible truth that we do well to note. Association with the people of God will, at times, bring hardship and trial. None can declare an allegiance to the God of Israel without making some sort of sacrifice. When the Apostle Paul spoke of entering the kingdom of God he said we must do so "through much tribulation" (Acts 14:22). Fitting words from a man who had just been stoned and left for dead (verse 19), and was due to return to the same place of danger shortly afterwards (verses 8,21). As we seek to maintain our separation in an increasingly dangerous and ungodly world, may we be encouraged by these examples of faith and courage.

The perilous days of Heber and Jael

We are given an insight into life for the faithful in Israel in the following chapter:

> "In the days of Shamgar the son of Anath, in the days of Jael, the highways were unoccupied, and the travellers walked through byways. The inhabitants of the villages ceased ..."
>
> (Judges 5:6,7)

Assuming this Jael is the same one mentioned in chapter 4 and later in chapter 5 (and logic suggests that this is the case), what a worrying picture of everyday life this is. "Travellers walked through the byways": on the surface it seems simply to be saying that men and women travelled through the land using familiar footpaths. This cannot be all that Deborah was saying, for such a statement would be an unnecessary description of everyday life in the land in Bible times.

The commencement of verse 7 implies a time of trial and danger, with people in unwalled villages "ceasing". Perhaps they had been slain, or had chosen to move to much larger cities, seeking protection behind city walls. When we look closer at verse 6, we are left in no doubt as to the seriousness of this situation. The Hebrew word translated "byways" means something 'winding' (Strong): the RV margin has "crooked ways". The only other use of this Hebrew word is of interest:

"As for such as turn aside unto their crooked ways (same word), the LORD shall lead them forth with the workers of iniquity: but peace shall be upon Israel." (Psalm 125:5)

So the people of Israel were walking in "crooked ways" in the days leading up to the victory over Sisera and his men. This could be a literal statement, or it could be a summary of the failure of God's people. They were no longer "upright", walking the "straight" way (see 5:8). Certainly when anticipating the coming of the Messiah the call was to make a "straight highway" for him (Isaiah 40:3,4; 42:16; 45:2).

Probably this is both a literal and symbolic depiction of the nation at this time. They would walk winding and dangerous paths in an effort to escape from the enemy. Yet they were also "crooked" in their ways. They had perverted what was right and true, refusing to rectify their lives in accordance with God's word. Then everything changed, when two women rose up and offered the service which God was demanding. Deborah moved Barak to lead the army against the enemy, and the Gentile Jael executed the captain of the host.

Jael's treatment of Sisera
As Sisera approached the tent of Heber, Jael came out to meet him.

"And Jael went out to meet Sisera, and said unto him, Turn in, my lord, turn in to me; fear not. And when he had turned in unto her into the tent, she covered him with a mantle. And he said unto her, Give me, I pray thee, a little water to drink; for I am thirsty. And she opened a bottle of milk, and gave him drink, and covered him." (Judges 4:18,19)

Jael's name means 'goat', or 'mountain goat'. The same Hebrew word is used elsewhere in the Old Testament, for example:

"The high hills are a refuge for the *wild goats*; and the rocks for the conies." (Psalm 104:18)

Goats' hair was used in the tabernacle (Exodus 25:4). They could be offered in sacrifice under the law (Leviticus 1:10). The scapegoat is probably the best known example of this (see

16:27). Although different Hebrew words are used regarding the animals which could be offered, we never read of a wild goat being brought. Such a sacrifice would not have been acceptable under the Mosaic system.

In the parable of the sheep and goats, the goats represent those who are rejected, placed at the left hand of the Master (Matthew 25:31-46). So a goat stands as a representative of those who were without. How fitting that Jael, like her husband, was almost certainly a Gentile. She was outside the camp of Israel. Her actions, however, would benefit the nation and show her faith in Israel's God.

Despite the apparent kindness shown to Sisera, there was only one thing on Jael's mind, as the following verses prove. She knew precisely who this man was, and what he had done to God's chosen people. Her sole intention was that this oppressor of Israel should be killed. However, how would this have looked had someone from Israel been watching her? Her actions would have appeared those of one siding with the enemy. She would have been condemned as a collaborator and, doubtless, killed alongside him. We see in these things, therefore, an example not simply of faith but also of immense courage. Indeed her actions after this are surely some of the most courageous on the part of any woman in the whole of scripture:

"Then Jael Heber's wife took a nail of the tent, and took an hammer in her hand, and went softly unto him, and smote the nail into his temples, and fastened it into the ground: for he was fast asleep and weary. So he died."   (Judges 4:21)

To describe such things as gruesome is an understatement. A man on a battlefield will be accustomed to death. Soldiers of Israel in Bible times were quite used to killing. Yet this is something very different from the kind of things that even battle-hardened warriors would have seen. For a man to be killed by a woman in Bible times was a degrading thing (see 9:54). This was an insult to Sisera's family and his nation. More than that, this was a symbolic blow to the sinfulness which had filled the land for so long.

On the surface Jael's actions were, to put it mildly, somewhat deceptive. She pretended to be Sisera's friend, whilst all the time plotting his downfall. If we knew no better, we might be tempted to describe this as cowardice. However as we read the divine commentary of this incident, and see the types and shadows contained here, we are left in no doubt as to what kind of a person Jael was. Did she see beyond the incident in question to the fulfilment of the promises made regarding the true seed, and all that would be done when sin would finally be crushed?

A symbol of the work of the Master

From the beginning of time, one promised seed had been anticipated. Abraham was told how the seed would inherit the land. David was promised he would rule as a king. In Genesis 3, the emphasis is upon his conquering of sin:

> "And I will put enmity between thee and the woman, and between thy seed and her seed; it shall bruise thy head, and thou shalt bruise his heel." (Genesis 3:15)

These things speak powerfully of the work of the Master. He would slay the seed of the serpent, or sin (Matthew 3:7; 23:33; Revelation 20:2). In doing so he would be bruised and would suffer (Isaiah 53:5). A blow on the heel is never fatal. So Jesus would suffer and die, yet he would rise from the dead. Yet the "bruising" that he would inflict upon the enemy would cause death. A severe blow to the head can, and does, kill. In doing so he would overcome sin and deal it the 'death blow':

> "Forasmuch then as the children are partakers of flesh and blood, he also himself likewise took part of the same; that through death he might destroy him that had the power of death, that is, the devil." (Hebrews 2:14)

Did Jael understand this? Did she look for that one chosen seed who would destroy sin? Other women, from Eve onwards, anticipated that time when the promised Son would come:

> "And Adam knew his wife again; and she bare a son, and called his name Seth: For God, said she, hath appointed me another seed instead of Abel, whom Cain slew." (Genesis 4:25)

Jael's comprehension of the promises and the need for a deliverer to conquer sin was the same. This is made clear by the words of Deborah, as Israel sang of the victory that had been accomplished that day:

> "Blessed above women shall Jael the wife of Heber the Kenite be, blessed shall she be above women in the tent."
>
> (Judges 5:24)

There then follows a record of how she killed Sisera. Deborah even spoke of her having "smote off his head" (verse 26). It is unlikely to mean that she did the same as David to Goliath (1 Samuel 17:51,54). This is, however, the only use of the Hebrew word, which means 'to crush' (Strong). Rotherham's literal translation speaks of her having "shattered" his head.

In case we are in any doubt as to the magnitude of the work of Jael, and the symbolism in her actions, the phrase "blessed above women" is used again prior to the birth of Jesus. Twice in Luke 1 Mary was blessed, firstly by Gabriel (verse 28) then by Elisabeth (verse 42). On both occasions the same phrase is used: "blessed art thou among women". They saw in these things the fulfilment of the promises made to the Fathers, and of the work of Jael in slaying the enemy by bruising him in the head. Like the faithful in Israel, this remarkable Gentile woman looked to the ultimate fulfilment of these things, when the Son of God would come and make that once-for-all offering for sin. Her example speaks of all that the Master would do, and all that we must try to do, while we wait for that great day when he will be in the earth once again:

> "For if ye live after the flesh, ye shall die: but if ye through the Spirit do mortify the deeds of the body, ye shall live."
>
> (Romans 8:13)

13

Ruth the Moabitess

THIS is, surely, one of the most moving stories in the whole of the Bible. Few books remind us more forcibly of the relationship which exists between the Master and his ecclesial bride (Ephesians 5:23-27). When we read that the male hero in the story, Boaz, was the great-grandfather of David (Ruth 4:21,22), the types and shadows become even more powerful.

In this chapter we cannot, of course, consider in any great detail the story of Ruth. Detailed study guides have been written, and many Bible Class studies presented on this subject. Time does not permit us more than a cursory glance at the record. All we wish to do is to establish the fact that, despite her Gentile ancestry, Ruth was, in her heart, a "daughter of Abraham". She returned from her homeland with her mother-in-law, partly out of love for Naomi and a desire to care for her. There was a far greater motivating factor at work, however. Her love for the things of Israel and a desire to become part of the nation burned like a fire in her heart. Having learned the truth from Naomi she determined to embrace it, and manifested that remarkable faith in all of her ways.

Moab
Like the Ammonites (see chapter 16), the people of Moab traced their family tree back to Lot and one of his daughters (Genesis 19:37,38). By the time of the exodus the Moabites were established as a powerful race. In the song of deliverance, Moses spoke of the "mighty men of Moab" trembling at the

news of Israel's arrival in their borders (Exodus 15:15). Prior to Israel's conquest of the land, Moab had suffered at the hands of the Amorites. Land had been lost and captives taken (Numbers 21:26,29).

The Moabites appear to have occupied a number of different areas in and around the Promised Land. In Numbers 22:1 the plains of Moab are recorded as being on the west of the Jordan river near Jericho. However it seems that during their battles with the Amorites, the Moabites had been forced out of this area, resulting in their living on the east of the Dead Sea. The river Arnon, which gave its name to the Moabite city Ar (21:28) flows into the Dead Sea from the east. This is recorded as the border of the land of Moab (verse 13).

Balak was the king of Moab in the days of the wilderness wanderings. He was the prime mover in the hiring of Balaam, his intention being that Israel should be cursed (22:1-6). Later there were numerous conflicts between Israel and Moab. In the days of the Judges, Eglon, king of the Moabites, ruled over Israel for eighteen years (Judges 3:12,14). During David's fugitive years he arranged for his parents to live in Moab (1 Samuel 22:3,4). Later there were conflicts between the two nations in the days of David, Jehoshaphat and Ahab. In Isaiah chapters 15 and 16 we read a detailed prophecy regarding the judgements which would be meted out on the Moabites. They would be left "very small and feeble" (16:14). Similar times of suffering were foretold in Jeremiah 48, Amos 2, and Zephaniah 2.

The Moabites worshipped the pagan deity Chemosh, which is called "the abomination of Moab" in 1 Kings 11:7. Tragically this was one of the gods that Solomon worshipped in later life.

Restrictions upon Israel's treatment of the Moabites

Unlike some Gentiles, the Moabites were not to be "distressed" by Israel. The Father stated how He had given them their land and His people were not to contend with them in battle (Deuteronomy 2:9). However, events were to take place which would cause this command to be modified. When Israel came to the borders of Moab and Ammon, they were treated with great hostility. Not only did their enemies refuse them food or water, they hired Balaam against them (see above). This caused the Lord to state that Ammonites and Moabites were to be refused entry into His congregation "to their tenth generation" (23:3).

Despite the best efforts of Balak, Balaam was unable to curse Israel. He did, however, teach Moab how to trap the men of Israel (Revelation 2:14).

"And Israel abode in Shittim, and the people began to commit whoredom with the daughters of Moab." (Numbers 25:1)

We need not dwell on the unsavoury incidents which took place at that time, or on the plague which struck the nation. What we do know is that those from Moab and Midian – the women of those nations especially – would be treated with deep suspicion by many in Israel. Yet later a "daughter of Moab" was to come to Israel and become incorporated into the nation in a very special way.

In the days that the Judges ruled

The days of the Judges were times of unspeakable hardship for many in Israel. A famine in the land caused some to leave and seek opportunities elsewhere. Elimelech and Naomi were of Bethlehem. The decision was made to leave the 'house of bread' with their two sons for the land of Moab. In due course Elimelech died. The two sons married Moabite women. Later both the sons died (Ruth 1:1-5). At this stage Naomi determined to return home to Bethlehem-Judah. One daughter-in-law, Orpah, having originally said that she would return with her, changed her mind (verse 14). The other one, Ruth, refused to be parted from her.

What was it that prompted such loyalty on the part of this Gentile woman? Would her family have refused to accept her had she returned to them? Was this simply a commendable act of charity towards an older woman who had lost everything? Scripture leaves us in no doubt that, although there was a great closeness between these two women, it was the hope of Israel which prompted Ruth to desire to leave Moab:

"Entreat me not to leave thee, or to return from following after thee: for whither thou goest, I will go; and where thou lodgest, I will lodge: thy people shall be my people, and thy God my God: where thou diest, will I die, and there will I be buried: the LORD do so to me, and more also, if ought but death part thee and me." (verses 16,17)
"Thy God [will be] my God." Orpah, like Lot's wife, the grandmother of the man Moab, had turned back. She hearkened to Naomi's words and returned "unto her gods" (verse 15).

Ruth, however, desired to worship the one true God of Israel. As with so many faithful Gentiles, her use of the covenant name of Yahweh teaches us a great deal. Her intention to be buried in the land is surely reminiscent of Jacob (Genesis 47:30) and Joseph (50:25; Hebrews 11:22).

Note especially the final words recorded above: "if ought but death part me and thee". "Ought" is in italics in the KJV. The RSV has "if even death parts me and you". Rotherham's Literal Translation says: "if death itself part me and thee". So Ruth was not thinking of this life when she returned with Naomi. She believed in life after death. She was thinking about eternity.

The journey home

The return to Bethlehem must have been an emotional time for Naomi. The journey may have been dangerous. The river of Jordan would have been crossed. We can imagine Naomi explaining to her daughter-in-law how the nation entered the land under Joshua. Were the stones which had been set up as pillars by Joshua still visible? (Joshua 4; see also chapter 32). Was the meaning of this expounded? Did they pass the city of Jericho?

As we noted in chapter 10, the salvation of Rahab the harlot proves that the hope of Israel is open to any, regardless of nationality. Even if such things were not spoken of on the journey home, we can be certain they were discussed later, for Boaz was the descendant of Rahab (Matthew 1:5).

Ruth gleans in the field of Boaz
Once they had settled in Bethlehem, Ruth requested permission from Naomi to glean in one of the fields nearby. This shows that she had a knowledge of the Law of Moses, which made provision for the poor. However this would normally take place *after* a crop was gathered in:

> "And when ye reap the harvest of your land, thou shalt not wholly reap the corners of thy field, neither shalt thou gather the gleanings of thy harvest. And thou shalt not glean thy vineyard, neither shalt thou gather every grape of thy vineyard; thou shalt leave them for the poor and stranger: I am the LORD your God." (Leviticus 19:9,10)

Her willingness to work, and the kindness of Boaz and his men in permitting her to do so, manifests the characteristics the Father is seeking from His people. Later the Lord would say through Malachi that Israel were complaining that serving Him was a "weariness" (Malachi 1:13). Oh that more in Israel had shared the determination of Ruth.

What of the ecclesia today? Could it be said that, even in the little things, we give of our best? Are we like the woman who anointed Jesus, of whom he said: "she hath done what she could" (Mark 14:8)?

Ruth's first meeting with Boaz
In this world, many books have been written about the subject of romance. Television programmes, films and songs abound where love is the central theme. Glossy magazines and novels are produced in immense numbers packed full of romantic stories. If only those seeking such entertainment were to read the book of Ruth (chapters 2 and 3 especially), they would find a love story of the greatest beauty, significance and purity. When Boaz first met Ruth as she gleaned in his field, he behaved in the most kind, generous, chivalrous, Christlike way. Unsurprisingly, she was greatly moved at this:

> "Then she fell on her face, and bowed herself to the ground, and said unto him, Why have I found grace in thine eyes, that

thou shouldest take knowledge of me, seeing I am a stranger? ... Let me find favour in thy sight, my lord; for that thou hast comforted me, and for that thou hast spoken friendly unto thine handmaid, though I be not like unto one of thine handmaidens." (Ruth 2:10,13)

She openly acknowledged that she was unlike his other female servants, and was "a stranger". This word is often used to speak of Gentiles. Two other uses of this same Hebrew word indicate the mindset of Ruth at this time:

"But king Solomon loved many strange (same word) women, together with the daughter of Pharaoh, women of the Moabites ..." (1 Kings 11:1)

Gentile women in Solomon's life – some of whom were from Moab – caused his heart to be turned away. Yet his great-great grandmother was a Moabitess, and her influence upon others in Israel was only ever good.

"I am become a stranger unto my brethren, and an alien (same word) unto my mother's children." (Psalm 69:8)

The following verse in the Psalm, describing the zeal of God's house "eating up" the one of whom David was writing, is quoted regarding the Master in John 2:17. So Jesus felt, at times, just like Ruth had when she arrived in the land.

Salvation and redemption for a faithful Gentile

After their initial meeting, Boaz instructed his men to allow "some of the handfuls of purpose" to fall for her (see also chapter 34, the Syrophenician woman). Truly he was one who did not permit his left hand know what his right hand was doing (Matthew 6:3). How fitting that he went far beyond the requirements of the law. Gleaning was permitted. The strangers, fatherless and widows were to be provided for (Deuteronomy 24:19). As a Gentile widow, Ruth fell into two of these groups. But permitting some of the very best to fall went beyond the law, and is surely a pointer to the new covenant.

The words of Boaz tell us all we need to know about Ruth's decision to leave Moab. She had come to care for Naomi, having left her parents and her homeland (Ruth 2:11). The major motivation, though, was the fact that in Israel she would worship the only true and living God:

> "The LORD recompense thy work, and a full reward be given thee of the LORD God of Israel, under whose wings thou art come to trust." (Ruth 2:12)

What wonderful, beautiful words. She had come "under the wings" of Israel's God. This is the language of the cherubim, whose wings were outstretched, covering the mercy-seat (Exodus 25:18-20). The Master used the same symbol when speaking of his desire to gather the children of Jerusalem together (Matthew 23:37). The same word translated "wings" is used later in the book, and this time it is Ruth speaking:

> "And he said, Who art thou? And she answered, I am Ruth thine handmaid: spread therefore thy skirt (same word) over thine handmaid; for thou art a near kinsman." (Ruth 3:9)

So Ruth understood the language used by Boaz perfectly. She appreciated the position she was in. She needed redemption. She required a kinsman to raise up seed to the name of the dead. Regardless of the probable age difference between them (verse 10), she knew that Boaz was the redeemer. His words reflect this:

> "And he said, Blessed be thou of the LORD, my daughter: for thou hast shewed more kindness in the latter end than at the beginning ..." (verse 10)

The word translated "kindness" is the Hebrew term usually rendered "mercy". When the covenant name was revealed and expounded to Moses, we read this characteristic of the Father:

> "Keeping mercy (same word as "kindness") for thousands, forgiving iniquity and transgression and sin ..." (Exodus 34:7)

Ruth was emulating and manifesting the God of Israel in her dealings with those around her. No wonder she was such a suitable bride for a spiritual giant like Boaz. His description of her at this time speaks volumes of her spirituality:

> "... all the city of my people doth know that thou art a virtuous woman." (Ruth 3:11)

Everyone knew what she was like. Initially some may have turned away from a Moabitess. She may have been shunned when she arrived in Israel. Naomi advised her to remain in the field of Boaz, "that they meet thee not in any other field" (2:22). The KJV margin suggests "fall upon thee" as an alternative. The RSV records Naomi warning of her being "molested". In time, those in Bethlehem who may have harboured feelings of hostility and uncertainty towards this foreigner came to change. Like Abraham before the people of the land (Genesis 23:6), everyone knew that this stranger was someone who could be trusted. In describing Ruth as "a virtuous woman" Boaz was using the language which would later be recorded in the book of Proverbs:

"Who can find a virtuous woman? for her price is far above rubies." (Proverbs 31:10)

The marriage of Boaz and Ruth

The near kinsman weighed up his options. He knew what the law required of him very well. He knew what his obligations were, but decided to refuse to play the part of the redeemer (Ruth 4:6). The people of the city were witnesses to this, and to the marriage which took place shortly afterwards between Boaz and Ruth, declaring:

"... The LORD make the woman that is come into thine house like Rachel and like Leah, which two did build the house of Israel: and do thou worthily in Ephratah, and be famous in Bethlehem: and let thy house be like the house of Pharez, whom Tamar bare unto Judah, of the seed which the LORD shall give thee of this young woman." (verses 11,12)

How wonderful that Rachel and Leah – the matriarchs of the nation – should be mentioned. Ruth, naturally speaking, had no association with them. She was a Gentile, a despised Moabitess. But because of her obedience, in the mercy of God, she was brought into the household of faith and became part of the line of promise. And how appropriate that Tamar should be named (see chapter 3). She had also most probably been outside the family of Israel, yet had been brought in, and was one of the ancestors of Boaz, and therefore, the Lord Jesus (Matthew 1:3).

The final comment recorded of Ruth in scripture was made by the women of Bethlehem. They may have had their doubts when she arrived from the land of Moab. In due course these were dispelled as they came to realise what she was truly like. When a son was born to Boaz and Ruth the women blessed the Lord and declared:

"... thy daughter in law, which loveth thee, which is better to thee than seven sons, hath born him." (Ruth 4:15)

The famine was over and a daughter-in-law was better than seven sons. Was this in the mind of Hannah? Her words certainly seem to reflect this:

"... they that were hungry ceased: so that the barren hath born seven ..." (1 Samuel 2:5)

What great lessons there are for us in this astonishing book. A faithful Gentile woman was redeemed and saved, and united in marriage with a great man in Israel. Joy abounded. New life sprang forth from the earth; a son was born. Surely in these things we see a foreshadowing of the time which is yet to come, when Eden will be restored upon earth and the ecclesial bride – made up of faithful Jews and Gentiles – will be gathered unto her Lord in love:

"Let us be glad and rejoice, and give honour to him: for the marriage of the Lamb is come, and his wife hath made herself ready." (Revelation 19:7)

14

David's army

ANY king, any ruler, any government requires military might. An army is essential, firstly to ensure that law and order is enforced within the country itself, and secondly in dealings with other nations. If attacked, a country needs to be able to defend itself. If a leader deems it necessary to invade another nation, then a well-trained, well-equipped, well-led army, large enough to overcome that of the country being attacked (Luke 14:31) is absolutely vital.

In our day and age, of course, one weapon can do the work which, years ago, thousands of men would have done. Hence in Bible times armies were, of necessity, larger than today (see, for example, 2 Chronicles 14:9; 17:14-19). David had a vast army (1 Chronicles 21:5): no wonder then, that with the blessing of the Lord (11:9) he was such a successful king.

David's mighty men
David's army would have been made up of a number of different groups. Some of these soldiers may have been more adept with different weapons (swords, spears, bows). Amongst these men, none were more courageous, faithful, or loyal than his "mighty men". There are two records of this group of warriors: 2 Samuel 23 and 1 Chronicles 11, though they are mentioned on other key occasions (2 Samuel 10:7; 16:6; 20:7; 1 Kings 1:8). There were, we are told, thirty-seven in all (2 Samuel 23:39), and within this group there were other subgroups. There appears to have been two key groups of three warriors who had a position of

authority over the other men, hence we read of Abishai, Joab's brother:

> "Was he not most honourable of three (by implication the second three)? therefore he was their captain: howbeit he attained not unto the first three." (verse 19)

Faithful Gentiles amongst David's army

There is an immense amount of information revealed concerning some of these men, which would require a separate book to do the subject justice. Nonetheless, as we read through the list of names recorded we notice that some of these men were Gentiles. 1 Chronicles 11:26-47 provides one of the records of the men who made up this special fighting unit, and amongst them we find:

- Zelek the Ammonite (verse 39);
- Uriah the Hittite (verse 41);
- Ithmah the Moabite (verse 46).

Uriah the Hittite is considered in chapter 15. We know nothing of the others listed above, except that they were clearly men of the utmost bravery and devotion to David.

The king had many warriors ready to do his bidding, but none were closer to him than his mighty men. And at least three of these men, naturally speaking, had no right to be there whatsoever, for they were Gentiles.

Ammon and Moab

The nations of Moab and Ammon are considered in chapters 13 and 16. Both were descended from Lot and his daughters (Genesis 19:37,38). They were, at times, incredibly hostile towards Israel, both in the days leading up to, and during, David's reign. They would continue this state of opposition after David's time.

Moab, along with Midian, had hired Balaam to curse God's people, and later sent their women into the camp to entice the men of Israel (Numbers 22:4,5; 25:1-8; Revelation 2:14). In David's reign he defeated the Moabites and caused two thirds of them to be put to death (2 Samuel 8:2). Enemies from Moab were clearly a very real threat to God's people, such as the two "lionlike men", killed by Benaiah, another of David's mightiest servants (23:20).

The Ammonites had, inadvertently, been the catalyst for Saul's finest hour. They had encamped around Jabesh-gilead, determining to take the city after a set period of time. They stated their intent to thrust out all the right eyes of the men of the city, in an open display of reproach for Israel (1 Samuel 11:1,2). Saul rallied the entire nation and led them to a great victory (verse 11).

In David's day, he sought to show kindness to Hanun, the king of Ammon, after the death of his father Nahash (2 Samuel 10:1,2). We shall consider the family of this man in chapter 16. This act was misconstrued by the Ammonites, who mistreated David's men (verses 1-4), and another great victory followed for Israel (verses 13-19). Later we read of Joab and the army of Israel doing battle with Ammon, although David remained behind in Jerusalem (11:1).

We see, then, that Moabites and Ammonites were naturally enemies of God's people. They often worked together in an effort to defeat Israel (as in the days of Jehoshaphat: 2 Chronicles 20:1; and Jehoiakim: 2 Kings 24:2). Later, when Jerusalem was rebuilt under Nehemiah, association with them caused further difficulties for the faithful within the nation (Nehemiah 13:23). Under the law anyone from Moab or Ammon was restricted from entering Israel:

"An Ammonite or Moabite shall not enter into the congregation of the LORD; even to their tenth generation shall they not enter into the congregation of the LORD for ever." (Deuteronomy 23:3)

Despite this, we find men who had originated amongst these despised Gentile nations being incorporated into Israel. More than that, they were amongst the closest followers of the king of Israel, doubtless fighting at times against the Gentiles round about.

Ittai the Gittite

Other Gentiles were immensely loyal to David. Ittai was a Gittite, having come to David from Gath (2 Samuel 15:18,19). When Absalom's rebellion took place and David and his men were forced to flee, Ittai, having arrived relatively recently ("but yesterday", verse 20), was offered the opportunity to return home. Naturally speaking, this might have been an attractive proposition, but Ittai refused to be parted from David:

> "And Ittai answered the king, and said, As the LORD liveth, and as my lord the king liveth, surely in what place my lord the king shall be, whether in death or life, even there also will thy servant be." (verse 21)

How can we read these words and not think of Ruth's moving speech to her mother-in-law, Naomi (Ruth 1:16,17)? Once more, we find a despised Gentile manifesting the kind of faith and devotion required by the God of Israel.

Later Ittai was placed over one third of David's army (2 Samuel 18:2). What makes this most amazing is that this man was, as noted above, originally from Gath. This was one of the five Philistine cities (1 Samuel 6:17,18), and had been made famous by one key man and his family: Goliath (17:4). How would the people of Gath have regarded David? Naturally speaking they would have hated him with a passion! David had destroyed the one who had made their city great. They would have shared in the shame of Goliath's ignominious defeat at the hands of a shepherd boy, armed solely with a staff, sling and some stones (verses 43,49). Yet Ittai followed David from Gath, and refused to be parted from him when times were hard. Remarkably, a total of 600 men from Gath did the same (2 Samuel 15:18).

The Cherethites and Pelethites

There were other Gentile groups faithful to David, also of Philistine origin. Some of David's closest followers are termed "the Cherethites and the Pelethites". These two groups were specially chosen by David to pursue Sheba the son of Bichri, who had attempted to seize the nation when Absalom's rebellion had failed (20:6,7). Later, history appeared to be repeating itself. Absalom's younger brother, Adonijah, tried to take the throne (1 Kings 1:5). These men, along with Zadok the priest, Nathan the prophet, and Benaiah the son of Jehoiada, ensured that Solomon was installed as king (verse 38). One of these groups, the Cherethites, was of Philistine origin:

> "Therefore thus saith the Lord GOD; Behold, I will stretch out mine hand upon the Philistines, and I will cut off the Cherethims (same word as Cherethites), and destroy the remnant of the sea coast." (Ezekiel 25:16)
>
> "Woe unto the inhabitants of the sea coast, the nation of the Cherethites! the word of the LORD is against you; O Canaan, the land of the Philistines, I will even destroy thee, that there shall be no inhabitant." (Zephaniah 2:5)

Once more, we are surely struck by how unlikely this is. The Philistines had been a constant 'thorn in the flesh' for Saul and the nation of Israel. Goliath's challenge was that a man should come and fight him (a clear message to Saul, for none was nearer his height: 1 Samuel 9:2; 17:4). In Saul's final battle, many of Israel died at the hand of the Philistines, including three of Saul's sons (31:2,3). The king also perished at this time, falling on his sword along with his armour-bearer (verses 4,5).

We might describe this last war as a cameo of Saul's reign. He entered the battle in a state of faithlessness, uncertainty and terror. He and many of Israel were to die as a result of this conflict with 'the old enemy'. Saul's reign, for the most part, was one of fear and failure. No enemy nation was more hostile towards God's people during his days than the Philistines. Yet a great number of men from this very nation chose to be allied with Israel, following David, and serving with immense courage and devotion.

The Cherethites and Pelethites: a symbol for the saints

Who were these people? What, specifically, was their work? Our only source of information is found in the names (or titles) of these groups recorded in the word of God.

Strong's Concordance tells us that the Cherethites were executioners or life-guardsmen, and the Pelethites were couriers or official messengers. In the age to come, the saints will be charged with two principal tasks as the earth is transformed:
   a. Fighting those who would dare rise up against our Lord and Master (Psalm 149:6-9).
   b. Preaching the "everlasting gospel" (Revelation 14:6).

In the actions of these two groups of men therefore, we see the work of the immortalised bride of Christ prefigured. The saints will make war, and deliver the message of salvation to the Gentile nations, overseeing the transformation of the earth which will result. May we be amongst those who are the recipients of this immense honour when the Master comes!

David: a light to the Gentiles

Time and again we have noted that certain Gentiles, who would naturally have been hostile towards Israel, were anything but hostile! Not only did these men choose to be associated with God's people but they were amongst David's own personal fighting force, closer to the king than almost any other men. Why then did this happen? Surely the actions of these men emulate others who had acted in the same way. Rahab and Ruth both chose to leave their own people, and were incorporated into the nation. They embraced Israel's hope, and served the only true God with steadfastness and faith. A family tree of David (shown overleaf) shows that these Gentile women were amongst his ancestors.

Maybe it was his Gentile ancestry which had moved David to accept these men. However, more likely it was his recognition that, in accordance with the promises made to Abraham (Genesis 12:3; 22:18), any who wish to come to Israel, desiring to worship the Lord in truth and submit to His ways, are accepted by Him.

David doubtless looked in faith to the time of which he was inspired to write, when all nations would come and worship the only true God (Psalm 72:11,17). Surely by receiving faithful

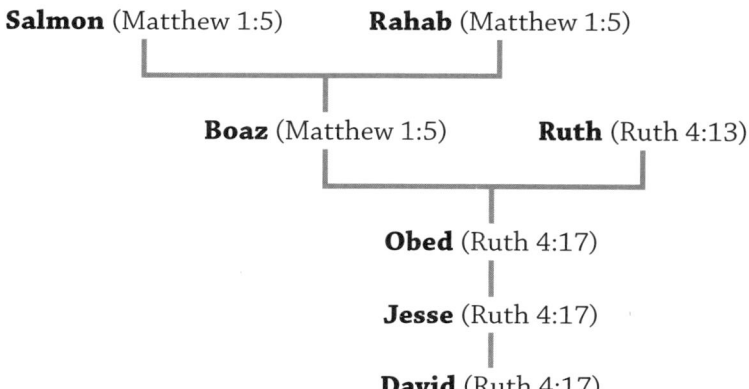

Gentile men into his army, he was demonstrating his acceptance of the words which would be spoken by Peter many years later:

"... God is no respecter of persons: but in every nation he that feareth him, and worketh righteousness, is accepted with him." (Acts 10:34,35)

15

Uriah the Hittite

DAVID'S mighty men were, we might say, 'a mixed bunch'. Of some we know a great deal. The works of Benaiah the son of Jehoiada are recorded in some detail (2 Samuel 8:18; 23:20-23). He also attained a position of great responsibility under Solomon (1 Kings 1:38; 2:35). Of others we know nothing but their names and their places of origin. Most were of Israel; a few, as we saw in chapter 14, were Gentiles.

Some were great warriors, but in need of guidance regarding the "weightier matter of the law". Abishai, the brother of Joab, killed 300 men with a spear (2 Samuel 23:18) but was, it seems, unable to comprehend the concept of mercy. When Saul slept and David had the opportunity to kill him, Abishai stated his willingness to perform this task (1 Samuel 26:8). Later, when Shimei, a relation of Saul, cursed David during Absalom's rebellion, he spoke of putting him to death; he made similar comments when David returned after the uprising was quelled (2 Samuel 16:9,10; 19:21,22). On both occasions David said that, despite his bravery and unflinching loyalty, Abishai had a great deal to learn regarding forgiveness.

Some, therefore, were known merely for their ability as warriors. Not so Uriah the Hittite, the final name to appear in the list of mighty men (23:39). He was a mighty warrior who knew and understood the vital principles of the truth perfectly. He regarded service in the army as an honour and a privilege, and was immensely loyal to David. He knew the Law of Moses, loved it, and sought to obey it. Truly, he was one of the mightiest men of all.

The Hittites

The Hittites were one of the most powerful nations in Old Testament times. They are listed amongst the people who would be disinherited for Abraham's seed to possess the land (Genesis 15:20). Ephron, who owned the field in which stood the cave of Machpelah (see chapter 2) was a Hittite (23:10). In the days of Moses, the Hittites still inhabited parts of Canaan (Exodus 3:8). In Numbers 13:29 we are told that they lived in the mountainous region of the land, although they clearly possessed a much larger area, stretching out towards the Euphrates (Joshua 1:4). In Solomon's day, some of the Gentile brides who turned his heart away were Hittites (1 Kings 11:1).

Speaking symbolically, to underline the sin of the people of Judah and how they had become like the nations round about them, the prophet Ezekiel was inspired to pen:

"... thy father was an Amorite, and thy mother an Hittite."

(Ezekiel 16:3)

Uriah the Hittite

However, not all Hittites were hostile to the truth. Uriah the Hittite was one of the greatest men in David's day. Uriah's name means "flame of Yah" – yet he was a Hittite.

This may appear to be somewhat strange: why would Hittite parents name their son after the God of the Israelites? There is, surely, only one logical answer. This Hittite man came to Israel, embraced Israel's hope, and chose (or was given by others) a Hebrew name. We read of this practice later in the Old Testament:

"One shall say, I am the LORD's; and another shall call himself by the name of Jacob; and another shall subscribe with his hand unto the LORD, and surname himself by the name of Israel." (Isaiah 44:5)

How Uriah came to Israel, we can only surmise. We know that he was the son-in-law of another of David's mighty men, Eliam (2 Samuel 11:3). Eliam was the son of Ahithophel (23:34), David's special advisor and familiar friend (Psalm 41:9), whose counsel was "as if a man had enquired at the oracle of God" (2 Samuel 16:23). When Absalom rebelled against David, Ahithophel was at his side (15:31). This may well have been because of David's treatment of his granddaughter, Bathsheba, and her husband. Did Ahithophel teach Uriah the truth? It would certainly explain the reason for his decision to turn against David. Indeed, such was the mind of Ahithophel that any man who learned from him would, surely, have been given a wonderful insight into the things of God.

One other faithful Hittite is named prior to this time. David had fled from Saul and had discovered the location of the king's encampment. He spoke with two of his closest men about venturing into the camp as Saul and his men slept. One of these was a man of Hittite ancestry called Ahimelech (1 Samuel 26:6). Although we cannot be certain, it is possible that this was another name for Uriah.

David's sin with Bathsheba

We are introduced to Uriah in 2 Samuel 11. It is, unquestionably, one of the saddest chapters in the whole of the Bible. Ever since Adam ate of the fruit, sin has been an intrinsic and inescapable part of human existence. To a degree, it is unavoidable (Romans 7:21), although we are all capable of doing better, "striving against sin" (Hebrews 12:4), as we seek to "resist the devil" (James 4:7). However faithful a man or woman might be, a record of such a person doing wrong is surely no great surprise:

"For all have sinned, and come short of the glory of God."

(Romans 3:23)

Nonetheless, the events recorded in this chapter, where we read of David's sin with Bathsheba, and his efforts to cover up his actions, reveal one of the greatest tragedies of all time. David was a man after God's own heart (1 Samuel 13:14; Acts 13:22). He was "the man who was raised up on high, the anointed of the

God of Jacob, and the sweet psalmist of Israel" (2 Samuel 23:1). Yet even he was tempted, and fell.

This is not the place to apportion blame, or to consider in detail the actions of David and Bathsheba. Nor can we examine the parable spoken by Nathan, or David's response to it. We wish simply to note the contrast between David, the mighty king of Israel, so often their saviour and spiritual guide, and this faithful, humble, godly, obedient Gentile man, Uriah.

"… at the time when kings go forth to battle …"
This is how 2 Samuel 11 begins. It was the very time when David should have been fighting alongside his men, and yet he "tarried still at Jerusalem" (verse 1). We do not know the reason for this. However, it is surely significant that 'living the truth' is portrayed elsewhere as fighting:

"Fight the good fight of faith, lay hold on eternal life …"
(1 Timothy 6:12)

This, David had ceased to do. He was in the wrong place. He was also in the wrong company: his own! One left to his or her own devices, without the influence of others (and more especially without the influence of the word of God) will always fail. This is one of the reasons why ecclesial life is so important, why we are not to forsake the assembling of ourselves together (Hebrews 10:25). If a brother is starting to stray from the path that leads to life, one kind word from another may be sufficient to stop him in his tracks (Galatians 6:1).

Without the guidance that others would doubtless have given, David was left to follow his own heart. And the heart of David, like yours and mine, was desperately wicked (Jeremiah 17:9).

We know what took place that day. Like Eve in the Garden of Eden (Genesis 3:6), like Ahab beholding Naboth's vineyard (1 Kings 21:1,2) and like Gehazi longing for Naaman's wealth (2 Kings 5:15,20), David saw, desired, and took what was not his. This is, perhaps, what James was alluding to when he was inspired to write of a man being "drawn away" and "enticed"; of lust "conceiving" and "bringing forth sin", which then "brings forth death" (James 1:13-15). The actions of this mighty man in this chapter could not have been more sinful, selfish, arrogant – or Gentile. Yet in his army at that very moment, doing battle for him, was a Gentile warrior who was able to show David what he had lost. Uriah, who David had wronged, was as different from Israel's king as it was possible for a man to be.

The contrast between David and Uriah
Desperate to conceal his sin and the consequences of it, David tried to arrange for Uriah to return home. The intention was that he would spend time with his wife, and the child born later would be regarded as his own (2 Samuel 11:6-8). But David reckoned without the steadfastness of his servant in this regard:

> "And Uriah said unto David, The ark, and Israel, and Judah, abide in tents; and my lord Joab, and the servants of my lord, are encamped in the open fields; shall I then go into mine house, to eat and to drink, and to lie with my wife? as thou livest, and as thy soul liveth, I will not do this thing."
>
> (verse 11)

These words are truly astonishing. Others may have chosen to enjoy the comforts of this life, but not Uriah the Hittite. He was effectively saying that David was in the wrong place. It was not a time for taking one's ease, but a time when great and mighty warriors should have been on the battlefield. Uriah was right – and David knew it.

We often speak of "God manifestation" – showing what our Heavenly Father is like in the way we act and speak. Jesus is, of course, the perfect example (1 Timothy 3:16). Uriah is a further, wonderful, faithful demonstration of this principle. He wanted to be like the ark; nothing spoke of Israel more than that. The tabernacle was the Father's dwelling place amongst men (Exodus 25:8), inaccessible by any but the priests and Levites (Numbers 1:50). The Most Holy, where the ark stood, was accessed once a year by the High Priest only (Hebrews 9:7). The ark was the place where the Father "met with" Israel (Exodus 25:22). Nothing could have been more separate; nothing could have been less Gentile. Yet Uriah, of Gentile origin, desired to be like the ark, thinking and acting like the God of Israel, manifesting him to a king who, temporarily, had lost sight of the truth altogether.

Although speaking of Moses, the words of Hebrews 11 remind us, surely, of the faith of Uriah:

"... choosing rather to suffer affliction with the people of God, than to enjoy the pleasures of sin for a season."

(Hebrews 11:25)

Three times in 2 Samuel 11:9,10 the record speaks of Uriah refusing to go "down" to his house. We might say, using the language of Colossians 3:1, he was a man who sought "those things which are above".

David tried harder, retaining Uriah for a second night, and then getting him drunk. Surely now he would go home and lie with his wife? Such was the steadfastness of Uriah that, even with his mind numbed by alcohol, he acted as before, sleeping at the door of the king's house with David's servants (2 Samuel 11:13). David was now truly desperate:

"And it came to pass in the morning, that David wrote a letter to Joab, and sent it by the hand of Uriah. And he wrote in the letter, saying, Set ye Uriah in the forefront of the hottest battle, and retire ye from him, that he may be smitten, and die." (verses 14,15)

Surely this is one of the most horrendous events in the whole of the Bible. Someone in the world with a long history of violence may arrange the death of another. This is sad, but hardly surprising. Another who is normally totally law abiding may even, in times of immense pressure, be moved to act in such a vile way. But for David – of all people – to do what he did to one of his closest followers, is hard for us to comprehend. We are not to judge. None of us knows how we may act in a time of weakness when a particular temptation strikes. We are all dependent upon the mercy of our God. David, having been shown the error of his ways through Nathan the prophet, acknowledged his sin and was forgiven immediately (12:13). Yet Uriah's death was a blot on his reign, and the consequences of this tragedy were always with him.

Uriah as a type of Jesus Christ

Surely in the life of Uriah we have portrayed one of the most powerful types of the Master in the whole of the Old Testament:

- He refused the comforts of this life which were available to him, for he was warring a good warfare (1 Timothy 1:18). He slept at the door of David's house. Jesus had "not where to lay his head" (Matthew 8:20).
- His wife was desired by another. We, by grace, will be the Lamb's wife (Revelation 19:7), and sin desires to rule over us now (Romans 6:12).
- He refused to conform to the standards of those round about him, and was content to be treated as a servant (2 Samuel 11:13; Philippians 2:7).
- He carried his own death warrant (2 Samuel 11:14). Did Jesus carry scrolls with him day by day, perhaps of Psalm 22, or Isaiah 53?
- He died all alone (2 Samuel 11:15). Of Jesus we read, "all forsook him and fled" (Mark 14:50).
- His death meant that his friend and his wife could live. If David's sin with Bathsheba had been discovered, then according to the law, both adulterer and adulteress should have been stoned (Leviticus 20:10). Hence we might say that Uriah was a man who "laid down his life for his friends" (John 15:13).

What a man Uriah the Hittite was. What an example he was for David – and indeed for every one of us. Have we wronged others? Have we acted in a way we know to be inappropriate? Have we been made aware of our actions? If so, how have we responded?

If the account of David's actions teaches us anything, it is that where there is confession and genuine repentance, our Father will always forgive His children.

"He that covereth his sins shall not prosper: but whoso confesseth and forsaketh them shall have mercy."

(Proverbs 28:13)

Our sins, just like those of David, are "put away" (2 Samuel 12:13), and removed as far as the east is from the west (Psalm 103:12). Did David hearken to the words of Nathan, and the example of Uriah? We only need to read the words of Psalm 51 (amongst others) to see that he did. Much as the consequences of his actions were forever with him, he knew that he had been washed from his iniquity and cleansed from his sin (51:2), and could therefore, like Uriah, teach others (verse 13).

Uriah the Hittite: the legacy of his life

Although Uriah's life ended in the most terrible way, "he being dead yet speaketh" (as Abel, Hebrews 11:4). His life of faithfulness and courage cry out to us that, regardless of a person's ancestry, his or her future is assured, if the promises made to the fathers are embraced in faith and love (Romans 6:22).

In the genealogy of the Master, Uriah's name appears for the last time in the word of God:

"And Jesse begat David the king; and David the king begat Solomon of her that had been the wife of Urias."

(Matthew 1:6)

Why was Matthew inspired to include Uriah's name here? Why is Bathsheba not named? Possibly this refers to the Law of Moses, where a man whose brother had died had to marry his widow and raise up children in the name of the dead (Genesis 38:8; Deuteronomy 25:5,6). Joseph, the husband of Mary, is therefore portrayed in symbol as a descendant of Uriah, whose name is not "blotted out"; rather he is recorded in the lineage of the family of our Lord and Master.

It is as though the relationship between David and Uriah is being shown as restored. David, in symbol, acted as a brother of the dead man. He raised up seed in the name of Uriah, ensuring that his name was not lost.

Times of trial and temptation come upon every man and woman. We can, and must, seek to avoid placing ourselves in a position where we are likely to be tempted. Even so, none of us knows what is round the corner, nor do we know how we will react when faced with a particular situation for the first time. The life of Uriah, his association with Israel, and David's dealings with him were not written so that we can feel superior, or judgemental. Rather, they have been preserved as part of the inspired record to underline three crucial things:

1. The remarkable faith of a Gentile man.
2. The genuine, heartfelt repentance of his friend.
3. The abundant love and mercy of our gracious Heavenly Father.

In our dealings with each other, and our consideration of our own shortcomings, we do well to take these lessons to heart.

16

Shobi the Ammonite

IT was a time of great sadness for the faithful in Israel. David, under whose hand God's people had enjoyed immense natural and spiritual prosperity, had fled from Jerusalem (2 Samuel 19:9). Had this been because of a challenge from a foreign king or even one of his own generals, this might not have been as painful for him. However it was Absalom, one of his own sons, who had sought to seize the throne (15:7-12). Most of the nation had followed this man, for he had stolen their hearts (verse 6). The rebellion was given authority and a sense of spirituality by Ahithophel, David's former counsellor (verse 12). Truly there was none like this man:

> "And the counsel of Ahithophel, which he counselled in those days, was as if a man had inquired at the oracle of God: so was all the counsel of Ahithophel both with David and with Absalom." (16:23)

David's flight from Jerusalem

David was totally outnumbered (15:13), with only his closest men choosing to flee Jerusalem with him. This would, for many, have been a case of history repeating itself. In Saul's day, David had been hunted as "a partridge in the mountains" (1 Samuel 26:20). During this time, he had been joined by a group of four hundred men, many of whom had been in distress, in debt or discontented (22:2). Later this number increased to six hundred (27:2). In chapter 14 we considered the number of faithful Gentiles amongst David's mighty men, and Ittai the Gittite. Ittai, who was originally from Gath, remained loyal to David and fled from Jerusalem with him (2 Samuel 15:19-21). How ironic, that whilst a man of Israel was seeking to take the throne from David, some of his most loyal and faithful followers were Gentiles.

The king and his men left the city, seeking sanctuary and a time to regroup prior to the inevitable attack. It seems very likely that the king was seriously unwell at this time. In Psalm 41:8 we read of the Psalmist suffering from "an evil disease". Later we read that he "lay" in a place of safety (2 Samuel 19:32). Perhaps the hope was that in time he would recover and be able to lead his men against the rebels (18:2). The group reached a place called Mahanaim (17:24,27). It was here that three men provided for David and those who were with him.

Mahanaim, appropriately considering the nation had split in two, means 'double camp'. It was here that Jacob had encountered angels, following his departure from Laban (Genesis 32:2). When the Promised Land was taken, Mahanaim fell into the area allotted to the tribe of Gad (Joshua 13:26), and was therefore on the east of the river Jordan (verse 32). Considering that David found a place of safety within the city, it is fitting that Mahanaim is listed amongst the cities of refuge (21:38). Following the death of Saul and Jonathan, Abner, former commander of Saul's army, had made another of his sons, Ishbosheth, king at Mahanaim (2 Samuel 2:8). Clearly the city was well fortified, giving ample protection for anyone seeking to maintain a position of power.

Provision for David and his men

Three men succoured David and those who followed him. They are listed in 2 Samuel 17:27:
1. Shobi the son of Nahash of Rabbah of the children of Ammon.
2. Machir the son of Ammiel of Lodebar.
3. Barzillai the Gileadite of Rogelim.

Machir owned a house where Mephibosheth, the lame son of Jonathan, had lived prior to his being permitted to sit at David's table (9:4,7). Whether this was simply an inn, or whether Machir was a man who cared for those unable to fend for themselves, we are not told. Based on the actions of this man when David fled from Jerusalem, it would be fitting if Machir was someone who fed the poor and needy. In doing so, he would be a powerful type of the Master (Psalm 72:13; 74:21; 82:4; Isaiah 41:17).

When the rebellion was crushed, Barzillai, who was eighty years old at the time, was offered the opportunity to live at Jerusalem with David. This faithful, elderly man declined the king's kind invitation, requesting rather that his servant Chimham be the beneficiary of David's generosity instead (2 Samuel 19:31-39).

Shobi the Ammonite

The first of the three men is an Ammonite called Shobi. Very rarely do we read anything good of these people. Yet this man of Ammon was instrumental in providing for David, and in due course the rebellion came to naught and the king returned to the city of the great King (Psalm 48:2; Matthew 5:35).

It is so easy for us to read over these verses, knowing the end as we do. However, at the time, there would have been no guarantee that David would win. How would Absalom have treated the friends of David, had he been successful?

Normally a man seeking to establish himself as king would put to death the family and friends of his rivals. We see this in the case of Abimelech (Judges 9:4,5), Baasha (1 Kings 15:29) and Athaliah (2 Kings 11:1); see also Nathan's words to Bathsheba when Adonijah tried to seize the kingdom (1 Kings 1:12). Those who had succoured David would probably have faced a similar fate, had Absalom won. Surely their willingness to be associated with a man "despised and rejected of men" (compare Isaiah 53:3), shows an immense degree of faith.

What they were stating by their actions was a belief that the rightful king, the one anointed by God, would return one day, and that they wished to be associated with him. Surely this is a challenge and an exhortation for every one of us, as we await the return of our King, the one who was rejected by those of his day but will come again to rule from Jerusalem in righteousness (Luke 1:32; Acts 17:31).

How amazing that one of those who provided for David was an Ammonite. His name means 'captor' (Strong), and he had given gifts to David and his men. Once more, we are reminded of the Master:

> "Wherefore he saith, When he ascended up on high, he led captivity captive, and gave gifts unto men."   (Ephesians 4:8)

The Ammonites

The people of Ammon were descendants of Lot and his younger daughter (Genesis 19:31-38). His brother, Moab, was the son of Lot and his older daughter. Unsurprisingly considering their origins, these two nations appear together on many occasions, often fighting against God's people (2 Kings 24:2; 2 Chronicles 20:1; Zephaniah 2:8,9). They acted jointly in hiring Balaam to curse Israel. Both nations refused Israel any sustenance when they reached the borders of their lands (Deuteronomy 23:3,4). This caused the initial command that they were not to be distressed or dispossessed to be revoked (see 2:19).

Unlike other Gentile nations, it is not easy to identify the precise area inhabited by the Ammonites. We know that the tribe of Gad possessed half of their land, and that this was on the east of the river Jordan (Joshua 13:8,25). This is supported by the teaching that the latter-day people of Edom, Moab and Ammon will escape when the King of the North sweeps down into Israel (Daniel 11:41). Amman is the capital city of the modern-day kingdom of Jordan.

In scripture the Ammonites are portrayed as people who were not simply hostile towards their enemies, but who appeared to take a perverted pleasure in causing unnecessary suffering. In 1 Samuel 11 we read of their desire to make a covenant with the men of Jabesh-gilead, as long as they could thrust out the right eyes of every man, as a reproach to all Israel (verse 2). In

Amos 1:13 the prophet spoke of the Ammonites having "ripped up the women (of Gilead) with child", that their borders might be enlarged. It will come as no surprise that the Ammonites worshipped idols. Time and again we read of the pagan deity Molech (also called Milcom or Malcham), and the horrendous practice of child-sacrifice (see Leviticus 18:21). In 1 Kings 11:7 Molech is termed "the abomination of the children of Ammon".

Everything we have seen describes the Ammonites as a pagan, bloodthirsty, rebellious race. They hated Israel. They took delight in the pain meted out on God's people. They would do anything to secure their own borders. Then in David's day Shobi the Ammonite appeared, and acted in the most faithful, generous way. Truly, in his heart he was "an Israelite indeed".

Shobi was the son of Nahash of Rabbah, an Ammonite. "Nahash" was almost certainly a royal name or title in Ammon. The Ammonite king who besieged Jabesh-gilead was known by this name (1 Samuel 11:1). Assuming he was amongst those encamped around the city when Saul and the rest of Israel came to save the men of Jabesh, it seems certain that he would have been slain (verse 11).

The family of Shobi the Ammonite

As we have seen, Shobi's father was called Nahash (2 Samuel 17:27). This name or title appears elsewhere in the record of David life. An Ammonite king of the same name is recorded as having died (10:1,2). David had been cared for by this man, and therefore determined to show kindness to his son, whose name was Hanun. This offer was misconstrued on the part of the Ammonites, resulting in the shameful treatment of David's men (verses 3,4). An immense battle followed, with Israel defeating the Ammonites and their hired mercenaries from Syria (verses 13-19).

Could Nahash the father of Shobi in 2 Samuel 17:27, have been the same man whose death is recorded in 2 Samuel 10? There is a strong indication that this may have been the case.

When Shobi is introduced as one of the men who succoured David, his home city is mentioned:
> "... when David was come to Mahanaim, that Shobi the son of Nahash of Rabbah of the children of Ammon ... brought beds ..." (17:27,28)

Rabbah was the place where the kings of Ammon dwelled:
> "And Joab fought against Rabbah of the children of Ammon, and took the royal city ... And David gathered all the people together, and went to Rabbah, and fought against it, and took it. And he took their king's crown from off his head ..." (12:26,29,30)

Shobi's father was Nahash of Rabbah, the city of the Ammonite kings. Unless there were two men with the same royal title in this city, this would make the man mentioned in 2 Samuel 10:2 his father.

A family tree of the royal house of Ammon shows the connection between the two sons of Nahash:

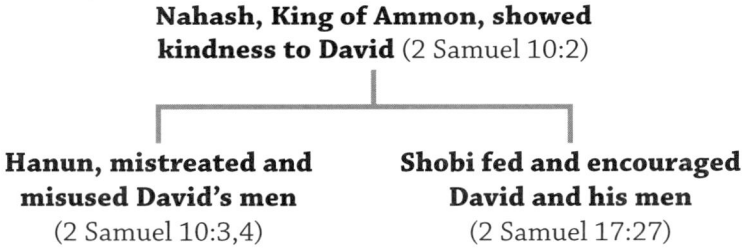

So these two sons of Nahash both came into contact with David. One mistrusted him, abused his men, and did battle with Israel. The other one loved him, fed him and his men, and was doubtless blessed by the king when Absalom was slain and he returned to Jerusalem.

The record speaks in detail of the generosity of Shobi and the other two men (17:28,29). Numerous items were brought including beds, basons and all sorts of food. When we think how many might have been with David – it seems likely there may have been as many as six hundred following him (1 Samuel 30:9; 2 Samuel 15:18) – this was no mean feat!

The account of this event concludes with the following phrase:

"... for they said, The people is hungry, and weary, and thirsty, in the wilderness." (17:29)

This is an insightful comment on the state of David and his men. In a place of death, the king was kept alive by the generosity of three men, who saw people in need and determined to do all they could to offer aid. The fact that one of these three was the son of an Ammonite king whose brother had insulted David and done battle with him, must surely strike us as highly unusual.

Whilst many of the nation of Israel had rejected David's leadership for the rule of a new, exciting, attractive, smooth-talking successor, Shobi of Ammon refused to 'follow the crowd'. And in doing so, he did what the Master said we should do, when we see one in need today:

"I was an hungred, and ye gave me meat: I was thirsty, and ye gave me drink: I was a stranger, and ye took me in: naked, and ye clothed me: I was sick, and ye visited me: I was in prison, and ye came unto me." (Matthew 25:35,36)

17

Araunah the Jebusite

FIRST impressions often last. In business an important meeting will be prepared for meticulously. An interview for a job will often be approached with similar attention to detail. In the world around us, a good initial impression is regarded as essential. It should come as no surprise therefore, that David determined that his very first act, having been made king over the whole nation, should be one of immense significance.

Saul's son, Ishbosheth, who had reigned for two years over the tribes of Israel, co-regent with David (2 Samuel 2:8-10), had been slain (4:5-8). The people had come before David: "So all the elders of Israel came to the king to Hebron; and king David made a league with them in Hebron before the LORD: and they anointed David king over Israel" (5:3). They looked to him at this crucial time. What would he do? What would be his first act as king over all of Israel?

"And the king and his men went to Jerusalem unto the Jebusites, the inhabitants of the land: which spake unto David, saying, Except thou take away the blind and the lame, thou shalt not come in hither: thinking, David cannot come in hither. Nevertheless David took the strong hold of Zion: the same is the city of David." (verses 6,7)

David's initial act, then, was to take the city of Jebus, later named Jerusalem, the castle of Zion and the city of David (1 Chronicles 11:5). This was, as we shall see, an act full of significance for those with 'eyes to see and ears to hear'.

17 – Araunah the Jebusite

The city of Jebus

Jebus (sometimes called Jebusi) or Salem was a location of great importance. It was right in the heart of the land and, being built upon a hill, virtually impregnable. Time does not allow us to look back to the days of Melchizedek, or forward to the life of Jesus, and all that he did in, and said of, this great city. Nor can we consider the age to come, when Jerusalem will be the centre of the kingdom of God upon the earth, with the Master sitting on David's throne.

Clearly these things were understood by David, so he determined that his first act as king over the whole land should be to purify this one key location. The Gentiles, who had taunted him with their blind watchmen and lame guards, were destroyed. Such was the strength of this "city … set on an hill" (see Matthew 5:14), that the Jebusites regarded themselves as untouchable. Their words suggest that either they had actually set those unable to see as lookouts and those unable to fight as soldiers, or were merely claiming that the blind and lame could defend the city – mocking David's intentions to take their fortress. Yet the city was taken and its inhabitants slain. At least for a time, Jerusalem became a place of peace and holiness, foreshadowing what it will be when the Master returns to the earth (see Isaiah 62).

The Jebusites

The Jebusites were an ancient race, descended originally from Ham (Genesis 10:6,16). As we have seen so often in our studies, they were amongst the people who dwelled in the land which was promised to Abraham (15:21).

Time and again throughout the wilderness wanderings, Israel was promised that the land of milk and honey, at that stage possessed by, amongst others, the Jebusites, would be theirs one day (Exodus 3:8; 13:5; 23:23; etc.). They are listed amongst the "seven nations greater and mightier" than Israel in Deuteronomy 7:1.

In a familiar refrain in the books of Joshua and Judges we read of Jebus and its inhabitants:

"As for the Jebusites the inhabitants of Jerusalem, the children of Judah could not drive them out: but the Jebusites dwell with the children of Judah at Jerusalem unto this day."
(Joshua 15:63)

"And the children of Benjamin did not drive out the Jebusites that inhabited Jerusalem; but the Jebusites dwell with the children of Benjamin in Jerusalem unto this day."
(Judges 1:21)

Yet following Joshua's victories over Jericho and Ai, the men of Jebus made an alliance with other cities in an effort to defeat Israel (Joshua 9:1,2), an indication of the effect their entry into the land was having upon the Canaanites.

Judges 19 describes one of the most distasteful of all scriptural events. A Levite of mount Ephraim, who had travelled to Bethlehem to retrieve his concubine who had returned to her family, was returning home late in the evening. Finding himself near to the city of Jebus, his servant suggested lodging there. The Levite was reluctant to do so, stating:

"... we will not turn aside hither into the city of a stranger, that is not of the children of Israel; we will pass over to Gibeah."
(Judges 19:12)

After so many years, with a great deal of the land now possessed by God's people, Jebus was still regarded as "the city of a stranger". In Solomon's day, there were still descendants of many of the Gentile tribes in the land, who were made to pay "a tribute of bondservice" (1 Kings 9:20,21). Amongst these people were Jebusites. Strong's Concordance tells us that Jebus means 'trodden, i.e., threshing place'. This is particularly appropriate, as we shall see in due course.

Araunah the Jebusite

The slaughter that followed Joab's act of great bravery in obtaining access to the city would have been immense (1 Chronicles 11:6-8). It seems unlikely that any Jebusites would have survived. Only by purging the city of the inhabitants of the land and the pagan idols which they would, doubtless, have worshipped, could

17 – Araunah the Jebusite

this place become a city of righteousness. Only then would it be a suitable dwelling place for the Lord's anointed. And yet, one Jebusite survived. Araunah (also called Ornan in the Chronicles record) was a Jebusite, and he was to meet with David at a time of heartache for the king and his people.

The children of Israel had sinned, and the judgements of the Father were to be poured out. David had numbered the people, and a time of pestilence followed:

> "So the LORD sent a pestilence upon Israel from the morning even to the time appointed: and there died of the people from Dan even to Beersheba seventy thousand men."
>
> (2 Samuel 24:15)

Seventy appears to be a number closely associated with Israel (see Exodus 1:5). The number slain, therefore, was representative of the nation as a whole. It is in this context that we are introduced to Araunah:

> "And when the angel stretched out his hand upon Jerusalem to destroy it, the LORD repented him of the evil, and said to the angel that destroyed the people, It is enough: stay now thine hand. And the angel of the LORD was by the threshingplace of Araunah the Jebusite." (2 Samuel 24:16)

There are allusions to the Passover in this chapter. In Egypt an angel passed over, and Israel was preserved (Exodus 12:13). In David's time an angel killed many of the nation but, upon reaching Jerusalem, his hand was stayed; he was caused to "pass over" the city. In Egypt, the blood of the lamb, on the doorposts and lintels of the houses resulted in the angel sparing the people of Israel (verse 23). In David's day, using the language of the Passover, the king referred to the people as "sheep", or lambs about to be slain (2 Samuel 24:17). The Master picked up this same teaching, describing himself as the good shepherd, the one willing to die for his flock (John 10:11,15).

A further connection is found in the words of the Lord to his angel: "stay now thine hand". Is not this an echo of His words to Abraham?

> "... Lay not thine hand upon the lad ..." (Genesis 22:12)

The location of these two incidents is precisely the same, for both took place at Moriah (verse 2; 2 Chronicles 3:1).

The threshingfloor of Araunah

As we have seen, the angel paused at the threshing place or floor of Araunah. Threshing implies separation. It is a time when that which is good (the grain) is kept and that which is worthless (the chaff) cast away. There were specific places in the land where this process, also known as 'winnowing', took place. The harvest would be cast up into the air, and as it fell to the ground the wind would blow the chaff away. The grain, being heavier, would fall to the ground and was kept. The practice is mentioned in Ruth 3:2, where barley was winnowed, and also Isaiah 30:24. Elsewhere the process is compared with judgement:

> "For thus saith the LORD of hosts, the God of Israel; The daughter of Babylon is like a threshingfloor, it is time to thresh her ..." (Jeremiah 51:33)
>
> "Thou didst march through the land in indignation, thou didst thresh the heathen in anger." (Habakkuk 3:12)

The children of Israel were being judged. 70,000 men were weighed in the balances of the Almighty and found to be wanting. And yet, at a time when many of God's people had angered Him and were destroyed as a result, one faithful Gentile came to the fore. At a plot of land owned by a Jebusite, the plague ended.

Why had Araunah not been put to death with the other inhabitants of his city? Possibly he or his forebears had severed themselves from the pagan practices rife amongst the people of the land, and had become incorporated into Israel.

Later, when David and his men cleansed the city, Araunah may have been amongst the warriors of Israel, and claimed the land which then became his threshing floor. Alternatively, he may have been granted what had belonged to his family in previous years, for his faithfulness to David. His name means 'strong'. He was indeed a man of spiritual might, as his actions before David prove. He had been threshing wheat when the plague struck. Upon seeing the mighty angel he and his four sons hid themselves (1 Chronicles 21:20). Although describing his time as a fugitive from Saul, we are surely reminded of the words of David:

> "Be merciful unto me, O God, be merciful unto me: for my soul trusteth in thee: yea, in the shadow of thy wings will I make my refuge, until these calamities be overpast."
> (Psalm 57:1)

The faith and service of Araunah

David was instructed by the prophet Gad to rear up an altar to the Lord in this threshing floor (2 Samuel 24:18). As he approached this key location, Araunah came out to meet him:

> "... and Araunah went out, and bowed himself before the king on his face upon the ground. And Araunah said, Wherefore is my lord the king come to his servant?" (verses 20,21)

David explained to this Gentile man that his land was required. In an action replicating that of Ephron the Hittite in Genesis 23, Araunah offered all that he had as a free-will offering to David (2 Samuel 24:22). Indeed the language describing not only his offering, but Araunah the man, is truly amazing:

> "All these things did Araunah, as a king, give unto the king. And Araunah said unto the king, The LORD thy God accept thee." (verse 23)

Rotherham's literal translation is particularly emphatic:

> "The whole did Araunah give, as a king, to a king".

Those well-versed in Hebrew tell us that this is a very accurate translation. Araunah was a king, and he gave, or was willing to give, to another king. We can only assume that his 'kingship' related to the area of Jerusalem which he possessed.

There are many types of Christ in the Bible. Some are actually identified as such by the word (e.g., Isaac: Hebrews 11:19; and Moses: Deuteronomy 18:15,18). There are many others who foreshadow the Master. Although scripture does not mention the similarity directly, by noting the Christlike attributes of the individual in question, we are able to identify such a person as one who manifested the mind of our Lord. Such a man, unquestionably, was Araunah. We have listed some of the other connections between him and Jesus in the following table:

Araunah	Jesus Christ
His name means 'strong'	He was "made strong" by God (Psalm 80:15,17)
He was a possessor of something of great value (2 Samuel 24:18)	"Though he was rich" (2 Corinthians 8:9)
He lived in Jerusalem	His "eternal dwelling place" will be Zion (Psalm 2:6)
He was humble (2 Samuel 24:20)	"He humbled himself" (Philippians 2:8)
He chose to reject the things of this world and embrace the things of truth	"Thou hast loved righteousness, and hated iniquity …" (Hebrews 1:9)
He had immense respect for the will of God	"thy will be done …" (Matthew 26:42)
He was willing give what he had as a freewill offering that others might benefit (2 Samuel 24:23)	"… yet for your sakes he became poor, that ye through his poverty might be rich." (2 Corinthians 8:9)

David's refusal of Araunah's gift

Like Abraham before him (Genesis 23:10-15), David refused this offer made by a faithful Gentile. His words to Araunah are an exhortation to us all:

"… Nay; but I will surely buy it of thee at a price: neither will I offer burnt offerings unto the LORD my God of that which doth cost me nothing …"   (2 Samuel 24:24)

Any sacrifice has to cost the one who is doing the giving, or it means nothing. There are numerous examples of this vital principle in scripture. When something or someone is given as a sacrifice, the one who does the giving has to feel it. Abraham and Hannah were both willing to offer their sons as sacrifices to the Lord (Genesis 22:12; 1 Samuel 1:11,24-28). Imagine the pain they felt. It 'cost' them; they were willing to 'pay the price' demanded by their God. Of course, the greatest example of this principle was seen when our gracious Heavenly Father permitted His Son to lay down his life for his friends.

What, then, of our own lives? What have we given up for the truth? Some have been offered positions of great responsibility, authority and wealth, and have refused them. Others have turned their backs on friends, or even family. What have we rejected in the service of the Lord? What are we still struggling to reject? The examples of Araunah and David, are before us.

The record of this incident, and the contact between these two great men, concludes in a particularly positive way:

"And David built there an altar unto the LORD, and offered burnt offerings and peace offerings. So the LORD was intreated for the land, and the plague was stayed from Israel."

(2 Samuel 24:25)

In the Chronicles record the Father instructs the destroying angel to cease, and we read that he put his sword into his sheath (1 Chronicles 21:27). There is an echo of these things in the events in Gethsemane. Peter, who had lashed out at the enemy, was corrected by Jesus, and told to put his sword into its sheath (John 18:10,11).

So the place was selected and the plague was stayed (a phrase used previously in Israel's history: see Numbers 16:48-50; 25:8). In due course, a great and glorious temple would be built. The reign of Solomon, for the most part one of peace, prosperity and righteousness (1 Kings 4:20,21), was typified by the temple which was constructed. In due course the ark would have a permanent home, and Israel would have a place, divinely selected, as a focal point. Time and again the Father had spoken of one key location where Israel would come and worship (note the repetition of the phrase "the place" in Deuteronomy chapters 12,14-18). The threshing floor of this faithful Gentile was the location selected for this wondrous structure (2 Chronicles 3:1).

One day, we hope and pray very soon, another temple will be built. However, unlike all places of worship and holiness which have gone before, this mighty, holy, glorious temple will stand the test of time. Solomon's temple was glorious, yet it was destroyed. Herod's temple took forty-six years to build (John 2:20), but was razed to the ground by the might of Rome in AD 70. Yet the temple which is to be built in the millennium will be age-abiding. And it will surely be built on that same site where once had stood the threshing floor of that faithful, obedient Gentile man, Araunah the Jebusite.

"And many nations shall come, and say, Come, and let us go up to the mountain of the Lord, and to the house of the God of Jacob; and he will teach us of his ways, and we will walk in his paths: for the law shall go forth of Zion, and the word of the Lord from Jerusalem." (Micah 4:2)

18

Obed-edom the Gittite

IT was a time that summed up the tragic days of Eli very well. The men of Israel, in an act of supreme folly, had concluded that the ark of the covenant could save them in their war with the Philistines. Eli's two sons, Hophni and Phinehas, who were probably the most evil men ever to defile the attire of the priest (1 Samuel 2:12-17), were with the ark as it was carried into the battle (4:3,4).

The Philistines, realising what was happening, were moved to fight with greater determination, and what followed was a disaster for all concerned. Israel lost the battle and thirty thousand soldiers were killed. The ark was captured by the enemy. Eli died when he heard this news, and his sons were amongst those slain in battle (verses 9-18). The Philistines then suffered terribly while the ark was in their land (1 Samuel 5). When it was returned to Israel, the men of Beth-shemesh looked into the ark, and 50,070 men were killed by God as a result of this (6:19). The days that Eli judged God's people were, for the largest part, times of sinfulness, suffering and death. Truly, "the glory [had] departed from Israel" (4:22).

Later, David desired to bring the ark up to "the city of David" (2 Samuel 6:1,2,10), even Jerusalem. In an act replicating that of the Philistines (1 Samuel 6:7-12), it was transported on the back of a cart pulled by oxen (2 Samuel 6:3). As they passed a threshing floor, the oxen stumbled and one of the men overseeing the operation, Uzzah, touched the ark to steady it and was killed by the Lord (verse 7). Surely we are being taught that if we act like those in the world, no good can come. Such was David's distress at this that he felt unworthy to permit the ark to come to the city which was known by his name:

> "And David was afraid of the LORD that day, and said, How shall the ark of the LORD come to me?" (verse 9)

However it was at this time that a man of great spirituality came to the fore. The ark was placed in his house and he and all his were blessed. Remarkably, it seems he was a Gentile;[1] and strangely, considering where the ark had been, he was a Philistine. Obed-edom, originally of Gath, was privileged to have the ark of the covenant under his roof. As we shall see, this was highly appropriate for he was a man with an immense love for the things of the truth and the God of Israel.

Obed-edom the Gittite

As we saw in chapter 14, a number of those who followed David were Gentiles. Moabites, Hittites and Ammonites are all named. Philistines, including the Cherethites and Ittai the Gittite, are also listed amongst David's closest men. A man who was a Gittite was originally from the city of Gath (2 Samuel 15:18). Goliath was of Gath (1 Samuel 17:4); he is termed "the Gittite" in 2 Samuel 21:19. It is almost as though he is being presented as a representative of the city. Being from Gath made a man one of Goliath's people. Yet not all Gittites were like him. Obed-edom could not possibly have been more different.

> "So David would not remove the ark of the LORD unto him into the city of David: but David carried it aside into the house of Obed-edom the Gittite." (6:10)

It might seem strange that, of all people, a man originally of Gath should be chosen for this great honour. However after the ark returned from the land of Philistia it rested for a while at Kirjath-jearim (1 Samuel 6:21-7:2). This was a city of the Gibeonites (Joshua 9:17), a tribe of Gentiles who had made

---

[1] An alternative view is given by J. J. Blunt in *Undesigned Scriptural Coincidences*, pages 140,141 (pub. *The Christadelphian Magazine and Publishing Association*, Nineteenth Edition, 1983).

peace with the Israelites when they first crossed the Jordan (see chapter 11). Were the children of Israel being told that they were still thinking and acting like the nations of the land? Were they being shown how to act by these men who were, by their ancestry, Gentiles? What we do know is that when the ark came to rest in the house of Obed-edom this was not blind chance. David himself made the decision to carry it there. David was a man "after God's own heart" (1 Samuel 13:14). For him to have made such a choice surely speaks volumes of the character of this faithful Philistine.

Obed-edom's name means 'servant of Edom' or, according to Strong, 'worker of Edom'. So as well as being a Philistine, his name speaks of Edom. The original Edomite was Esau. He despised the things of truth (Genesis 25:30-34), and is set forth as an example of those who are rejected because of their sin (Romans 9:13; Hebrews 12:16). Does Obed-edom's name indicate that he had been a slave in the land of the Edomites? Could he have been sold as a servant to a man of Gath, thus becoming known as a Gittite? Was he later sold to a man of Israel, and then granted his freedom, according to the Law of Moses? The law spoke of Hebrew slaves being freed (Exodus 21:2), although it is possible that a man of Israel could have applied this same command regarding a Gentile. Did his association with God's people come through David, who spent time in the city of Gath (1 Samuel 21:10)?

The ark of the covenant in the house of Obed-edom

For a period of three months the ark of God remained in the house of this faithful Gentile:

> "And the ark of the LORD continued in the house of Obed-edom the Gittite three months: and the LORD blessed Obed-edom, and all his household." (2 Samuel 6:11)

Both Obed-edom and his household received a blessing during this time. How was this blessing manifested? Possibly his flocks and herds conceived and brought forth great numbers of healthy offspring. Maybe his crops and trees were particularly fruitful. Perhaps his wife, daughters or daughters-in-law conceived? This would connect with the experiences of Abraham when in Gerar (Genesis 20:17), and is also supported by 1 Chronicles 26:4,5 (see below).

Elsewhere we read of "houses" (i.e., families) being blessed. Laban's house was blessed because of Jacob's presence (Genesis 30:30). The same is said of Potiphar in relation to Joseph (39:5). The promises to David speak of a blessing on him, his seed and his house (2 Samuel 7:12,29). In one of the Psalms of the sons of Korah, we read of blessings bestowed for those in a particular "house":

> "Blessed are they that dwell in thy house: they will be still praising thee." (Psalm 84:4)

Could this be said of Obed-edom? His house, for a while, was God's house. Within his house was that which spoke of the Almighty one of Abraham, Isaac and Jacob.

Surely in these things we see a demonstration of the promises to Abraham being fulfilled:

> "That in blessing I will bless thee, and in multiplying I will multiply thy seed as the stars of the heaven, and as the sand which is upon the sea shore; and thy seed shall possess the gate of his enemies; and in thy seed shall all the nations of the earth be blessed ..." (Genesis 22:17,18)

All nations can be blessed through Abraham's great seed. These things apply primarily to the Master and the privileges which arise through him (Galatians 3:16,29). However, we see a foreshadowing of these things in the life of men such as Obed-edom.

Can we imagine what it would have been like for Obed-edom to have had the ark of the covenant in his house? Did he pray before it? Was it shut away, lest any should try to touch it or look within? Others dwelt in the same area as the ark. Joash was preserved in the temple for six years (2 Kings 11:3). However, is there any other occasion where an item as holy as the ark was taken into a man's house? For Obed-edom to have been chosen for this immense honour tells us that he was a man of the utmost faith and uprightness. His house would have been a place of holiness, spirituality and love.

One of my abiding memories of my grandparents' house is a plaque which bore these words:

"Christ is the Head of this house, the unseen guest at every meal, the silent listener to every conversation."

These used to be quite common, even in the world. Very rarely are they seen today. However our houses should be places of holiness, where the Master would be welcomed if he was on the earth, and where the will of God and His law comes first. The house of Obed-edom was just such a place.

What we do know is that the God of Israel chose to bless this Gentile in such a way that those round about him took note:

"And it was told king David, saying, The LORD hath blessed the house of Obed-edom, and all that pertaineth unto him, because of the ark of God. So David went and brought up the ark of God from the house of Obed-edom into the city of David with gladness." (2 Samuel 6:12)

The blessings bestowed upon this faithful Gentile were sufficient to prompt David to reconsider his actions and bring the ark up without further delay. There is exhortation for us in these things. The Master taught that we should "let [our] light so shine before men" (Matthew 5:16) that others might see what we believe by the way we respond to the situations that come upon us. If we are blessed by God – and indeed we are – and we let others see that this is the case by the way we act and speak, then maybe they will be moved to ask of the hope that lies within us (1 Peter 3:15).

The ark is brought to Jerusalem

The time came for the ark to be brought to the city of God. Once more, the name Obed-edom appears. In 1 Chronicles 15:25 we have the comparison record of David's bringing the ark from his house. Three times in the previous verses we read of the name Obed-edom:

- Verse 18: Describing a man who was a porter.

- Verse 21: One who was a singer.
- Verse 24: One who was a doorkeeper for the ark (same Hebrew word as "porter" in verse 18).

Are these three different men? Are they one and the same? It seems strange for a man to be named in verse 25, and for the very same name to appear three times in the preceding seven verses yet describing another person altogether. If indeed this does describe the same man, then what a man he was! Not simply was he a worthy host for the ark but also a suitable doorkeeper for it and a member of a choir, praising God as His ark was brought to rest in His holy city, the "apple of his eye" (Zechariah 2:8).

Some may object to these connections. The men appointed to serve by David at this time were of the tribe of Levi (1 Chronicles 16:4). How could a Gentile – a man from Gath – enjoy such a privileged position? It seems that when a Gentile became associated with Israel, he was 'adopted' into one of the tribes. So Caleb (see chapter 9) is called a Kenezite, yet was a leader of the tribe of Judah (Numbers 13:6; 32:12). Could such men not have been incorporated into Levi, as well as into the other tribes? How fitting it would be for a man such as Obed-edom to be privileged to serve in this way:

> "But thou shalt appoint the Levites over the tabernacle of testimony, and over all the vessels thereof, and over all things that belong to it: they shall bear the tabernacle, and all the vessels thereof; and they shall minister unto it, and shall encamp round about the tabernacle. And when the tabernacle setteth forward, the Levites shall take it down: and when the tabernacle is to be pitched, the Levites shall set it up: and the stranger that cometh nigh shall be put to death." (1:50,51)

If indeed Obed-edom had become associated with the tribe of Levi, this would explain why he had been able to be so close to the ark, yet being a "stranger". What a worthy Levite he would have made!

The family of Obed-edom

Later in the first book of Chronicles the name appears again:

"Moreover the sons of Obed-edom were, Shemaiah the firstborn, Jehozabad the second, Joah the third, and Sacar the fourth, and Nethaneel the fifth, Ammiel the sixth, Issachar the seventh, Peulthai the eighth: for God blessed him … All these of the sons of Obed-edom: they and their sons and their brethren, able men for strength for the service, were threescore and two of Obed-edom." (1 Chronicles 26:4,5,8)

Note the phrase in verse 5, "for God blessed him". This is surely a reference back to the events of 1 Chronicles 13:14, where for three months he and his family were blessed as the ark abode amongst them. Assuming this speaks of the same man, once more his faith and willingness to serve is stressed.

He and his sons are termed "able men for strength of the service". So they had abilities, and they used them in the truth. As has been said regarding work in the ecclesia, sometimes we meet those who could if they would, and others who would if they could. Some possess immense talents and yet, for whatever reason, appear reluctant to use them in the service of God. Truly this accusation could never be levelled at Obed-edom or his family.

Later in the same chapter we read of him once more:

"To Obed-edom southward; and to his sons the house of Asuppim." (26:15)

What was this "house of Asuppim" which was allocated to this man and his children? The Authorised Version margin has "gatherings"; the Revised Version reads "store-house". Strong says this means a collection. Clearly when offerings were brought, especially in the case of non-perishable items such as wine or the meal offering, it would have been necessary for some of these items to have been stored. Other items, such as silver and gold, could have been gifted. These would also need to be held securely (see 2 Chronicles 25:24).

That Obed-edom should have been chosen for this task tells us a great deal about his character. Such a man would have to be totally trustworthy. None could bribe him. He did his work "as to the Lord, and not to men" (Ephesians 6:7). That a man with such attributes should have existed in Israel is of no great surprise. That a man like this should have been of Gentile origin is, surely, highly unusual. What a remarkable example he is of faithful service. What a challenge he is to every one of us.

If the ark of the covenant existed today, would we be chosen for it to be kept in our house? If there is work to do, are we able and willing to do it? Do we do so with all our might (Ecclesiastes 9:10)? If someone needs an item of value to be kept safely, would they ask us? In all of these things, this faithful Gittite demonstrated the spirit demanded by the God of Israel superbly. He is a classic example of those spoken of by the Apostle Paul in the letter to the ecclesia at Rome:

> "For he is not a Jew, which is one outwardly; neither is that circumcision, which is outward in the flesh: but he is a Jew, which is one inwardly; and circumcision is that of the heart, in the spirit, and not in the letter; whose praise is not of men, but of God." (Romans 2:28,29)

19

Hiram king of Tyre

DAVID'S desire had been a good one. He wanted to oversee the building of a house for God. Initially this appeared to be acceptable with Nathan (2 Samuel 7:1-3), however the prophet was told to return to David with a message from the Father:

"But the word of the LORD came to me, saying, Thou hast shed blood abundantly, and hast made great wars: thou shalt not build an house unto my name, because thou hast shed much blood upon the earth in my sight. Behold, a son shall be born to thee, who shall be a man of rest; and I will give him rest from all his enemies round about: for his name shall be Solomon, and I will give peace and quietness unto Israel in his days." (1 Chronicles 22:8,9)

Although he was unable to oversee the construction of the house, David was determined to make preparations for it. The details of this work are recorded in 1 Chronicles 22, which we need not examine in detail. Throughout the chapter there is an emphasis on quantity: we read phrases like "in abundance", "without weight", "no number" – such was the mass of items laid up for the work which Solomon would oversee. Of course only some of these materials were from the land of Israel. In addition to iron, brass (22:3), gold, silver, and stone (verse 14), timber was also provided:

"Also cedar trees in abundance: for the Zidonians and they of Tyre brought much cedar wood to David." (verse 4)

Although the king of Tyre with whom negotiations for this trade took place is not named here, his name appears earlier in David's reign, and afterwards during the time of Solomon. The king was called Hiram (2 Samuel 5:11; 1 Kings 5:1), sometimes rendered Huram in the Chronicles record (see 1 Chronicles 14:1).

Hiram king of Tyre

From the outset, Hiram appears in scripture as a man of great spiritual insight. When David requested timber for his own house, Hiram willingly provided it, together with carpenters and masons (2 Samuel 5:11). However it is at the commencement of the reign of Solomon that we begin to see the character of the man:

> "And Hiram king of Tyre sent his servants unto Solomon; for he had heard that they had anointed him king in the room of his father: for Hiram was ever a lover of David." (1 Kings 5:1)

What an amazing thing to read of a Gentile king. Whilst the love of others might have waned, the king of Tyre remained true in his respect and affection for David. Surely our love for David's greater Son should mirror that of this Gentile king.

Hiram's name means 'witness' (Strong). A witness is someone who gives evidence regarding an event, or has knowledge of a particular matter. Israel were called the witnesses of the Lord (Isaiah 43:10,12; 44:8); often this was done unwittingly. The Master, before Pilate "witnessed a good confession" (1 Timothy 6:13). Hiram, moved by David's faith and service, witnessed to these things in his attitude towards the people of God and their kings.

Tyre

The city of Tyre was on the Mediterranean coast, north-west of Galilee. It was the principal city of the Phoenicians. At times it appears that the nation was known by the name Tyre, and also after the other principal city in the region, Sidon or Zidon (the Sidonians / Zidonians are mentioned in many places in the Old Testament). The first mention of the city comes in Joshua 19:29, where the border of the tribe of Asher is said to have reached "the strong city of Tyre". The city was indeed strong, indicated by the meaning of the name, for Tyre means 'rock'. After the days of Solomon, the relationship between Israel and the Phoenicians changed. Judah is listed amongst a whole host of Gentile nations who sold a number their wares in the markets of Tyre (Ezekiel 27:17). Tragically, in Joel 3:4-6 and Amos 1:9 we read of Jewish slaves being sold by the Phoenicians.

Later in the Old Testament some of the most amazing and precise prophecies regarding any Gentile nation describe Tyre. In Ezekiel 26 the prophet speaks of two separate powers coming against the city. Initially Nebuchadnezzar, the "king of kings", would come down from the north (verse 7). Many of Tyre would be slain by him (verses 8,9). However a number would survive, in order for the rest of the prophecy to be fulfilled. This remnant had decamped from the mainland to the isle of Tyre, which stood half a mile from the coast. At the start of verse 12 the pronoun changes from "he" (Nebuchadnezzar) to "they". This describes the actions of the Greeks, led by Alexander the Great. It is here that we read:

> "And they shall make a spoil of thy riches, and make a prey of thy merchandise: and they shall break down thy walls, and destroy thy pleasant houses: and they shall lay thy stones and thy timber and thy dust in the midst of the water." (verse 12)

History and archaeology demonstrate the accuracy of these words. When Alexander reached Tyre, it appeared untouchable. The only way for him to enter this island fortress was to build a road through the sea – a causeway from the mainland to the island. In order to do this, building materials were needed, and the ruins of the old city were, very literally, laid in the water, as foretold by God through his prophet.

Materials for the temple in Solomon's day

In Solomon's day, the king requested of Hiram additional materials for the temple. The response of this Gentile ruler indicates that he was a man of great understanding:

> "And it came to pass, when Hiram heard the words of Solomon, that he rejoiced greatly, and said, Blessed be the LORD this day, which hath given unto David a wise son over this great people." (1 Kings 5:7)

As with other faithful Gentiles, the use of the Yahweh name, and an indication that a blessing should be ascribed unto Him, surely demonstrates a genuine understanding of the Truth. Other Gentiles heard great words of wisdom from Solomon, perhaps without realising or acknowledging that such things were God-given. Hiram knew that David's prayer for a wise son to reign on his throne had been heard, and that, under Solomon's guidance, the nation would prosper.

In the Chronicles record of these things, Hiram is recorded as stating that "because the LORD loved his people", he had given them Solomon as a king after David (2 Chronicles 2:11). These things were sent in letter form, so there could be no misunderstanding on the part of the king. He also stated that the Father was the maker of heaven and earth (verse 12). Once more, these are statements of great insight on the part of this man of Tyre.

The necessary timber was provided by Hiram for God's house:

> "And we will cut wood out of Lebanon, as much as thou shalt need: and we will bring it to thee in floats by sea to Joppa; and thou shalt carry it up to Jerusalem." (verse 16)

How apt that the wood should arrive at Joppa. It was in this very city that Peter would see the vision of the different clean and unclean animals, and be told:

> "... What God hath cleansed, that call not thou common." (Acts 10:15)

So Joppa was a link with the outside world. Imports and exports passed through the city. In Solomon's time the necessary items for the house for God's name were brought to Israel via Joppa. Many years later the greatest 'export' ever to leave Israel – the hope of Israel – would commence with Simon Peter being given a vision at this very same place.

Solomon's navy

Solomon had "a navy of ships" (1 Kings 9:26). Without the methods of navigation which exist today, it would be vital that his men were accompanied by those who were able to plot their routes successfully. Once more, Hiram was able to assist:

> "And Hiram sent in the navy his servants, shipmen that had knowledge of the sea, with the servants of Solomon."
>
> (verse 27)

There is an echo of the words of Moses to Hobab in these things (see Numbers 10:29-31 and chapter 7, Zipporah and her family).

Hiram's men had "knowledge of the sea". Historians have suggested that Tyrian mariners travelled further than many before them, often heading out across oceans rather than staying close to the shore. In these things the people of Israel benefitted, as their ships reached Ophir and brought four hundred and twenty talents of gold to Solomon (1 Kings 9:28). This is a further pointer forward to the reign of the Lord Jesus Christ (Psalm 45:12).

A covenant is made

As the relationship between the two nations strengthened, the two men made an agreement together:

> "And the LORD gave Solomon wisdom, as he promised him: and there was peace between Hiram and Solomon; and they two made a league together." (1 Kings 5:12)

"League" is the Hebrew word normally translated "covenant", as in Genesis 15:18, where the Father made a covenant with Abraham. This great oneness between the kings resulted in peace between their nations, as the men of the two countries worked together in preparing for the house that would be constructed (1 Kings 5:13-18).

Somewhat confusingly, we read of another Hiram of Tyre in 1 Kings 7. He was the son of a man of Tyre and a woman of the tribe of Naphtali (verses 13,14), and oversaw the preparation of a number of the items that were used in the temple (verses 15,40,45).

Solomon's proposed gift to Hiram

When the temple was complete, Solomon determined to express his gratitude to Hiram by offering to him an area in the north of Israel:

> "And it came to pass at the end of twenty years, when Solomon had built the two houses, the house of the LORD, and the king's house, (now Hiram the king of Tyre had furnished Solomon with cedar trees and fir trees, and with gold, according to all his desire,) that then king Solomon gave Hiram twenty cities in the land of Galilee." (9:10,11)

For each year of service Solomon offered a city. We are not told that this act was wrong on the part of Solomon. However, under the law we read that the land was a gift to Israel by the Father and was not to be sold (Leviticus 25:23). As such, it could be argued that the gifting away of any part of it could never be right. The response of Hiram to this proposed gift is particularly interesting:

> "And Hiram came out from Tyre to see the cities which Solomon had given him; and they pleased him not. And he said, What cities are these which thou hast given me, my brother? And he called them the land of Cabul unto this day." (1 Kings 9:12,13)

The margin for "pleased him not" indicates that "were not right in his eyes" is a better translation of the original Hebrew. The land was then called "Cabul", meaning "displeasing" or "dirty" (KJV margin). Strong's Concordance suggests that this means 'sterile'.

This may be the same sentiment expressed by the leaders in the days of the Master. Our lord was known as Jesus of Nazareth (Matthew 26:71); they therefore concluded that he could not possibly be the Messiah, who had to come from Bethlehem (2:1-6).

> "Others said, This is the Christ. But some said, Shall Christ come out of Galilee? … They answered and said unto him (Nicodemus), Art thou also of Galilee? Search, and look: for out of Galilee ariseth no prophet." (John 7:41,52)

Why was this gift refused by Hiram? Was it simply because the land was distasteful? Was the soil of poor quality? Were there no rivers or streams? We cannot be sure, although it is possible that Hiram meant something different. Could he have been (politely) reprimanding Solomon for trying to gift some of the land to him? Possibly he knew that, as all of the land was given to Israel by the Almighty, no part of it should have been given to any other nation. If this is what Hiram meant, we see a man of immense spirituality.

This same incident appears to be described in the Chronicles record:

> "And it came to pass at the end of twenty years, wherein Solomon had built the house of the LORD, and his own house, that the cities which Huram had restored to Solomon, Solomon built them, and caused the children of Israel to dwell there." (2 Chronicles 8:1,2)

Were these cities which Hiram had "restored" the twenty which he had refused to accept? Were they others, taken by former kings of Tyre which he realised he had no right to possess? Whatever this describes, we see an act of generosity on the part of Hiram. More than that, we see a man with an appreciation of the fact that the land belonged to Israel and that Gentile nations had no right to possess any part of it.

What a wonderful relationship was enjoyed between the kings of Israel and Hiram. Unlike other Gentile nations, there was peace between the two peoples and a feeling of love and trust which lasted throughout the lives of their kings. In these things we see a pointer forward to the righteous reign of the Master, when kings of the earth will bow before him, acknowledging his greatness, serving him in peace and love:

> "And again, Esaias saith, There shall be a root of Jesse, and he that shall rise to reign over the Gentiles; in him shall the Gentiles trust." (Romans 15:12)

20

The queen of Sheba

WITH the obvious exception of the Lord Jesus Christ, Solomon was surely the wisest man of all time. He had requested, and been granted, wisdom by God, that Israel might be judged acceptably (1 Kings 3:5-12). Other blessings were also given: riches and honour were bestowed upon him, so that Solomon's kingdom was unique (verse 13). It would be these two blessings, his astounding wisdom and unparalleled glory, which would prompt many from the nations round about to come and seek his favour. It seems that some of those who did so would also come to know of the God whom Solomon worshipped.

Blessings bestowed upon Solomon
When the Father determined to bestow the gifts of wisdom, wealth and honour upon the king, one further blessing was promised. There was, however, a crucial difference:

"And if thou wilt walk in my ways, to keep my statutes and my commandments, as thy father David did walk, then I will lengthen thy days." (verse 14)

The blessings of wisdom, riches and honour were given unconditionally. Yet length of days was conditional upon service. These things were repeated and amplified later in his reign (9:4-9). Similar things were said when the temple was built (6:12). If Solomon walked in God's ways as David had walked, then his life would be extended.

When God visited him in the dream and offered him whatever he asked, Solomon described himself as "a little child", knowing not how to "go out or come in" (3:7). His reign lasted forty years (11:42), which was more than many of those who came after him. Maybe he would have reigned for longer, had his reign not deteriorated so badly towards the end (1 Kings 11). Or perhaps the words of God speak of something else? Is this a pointer to the promise made to all who seek to serve the God of Israel? He will bestow many blessings upon His people, often unconditionally, yet length of days is totally dependent upon faithful service.

The call of the Gospel

We have, by grace, been made aware of "great and precious promises" (2 Peter 1:4). We receive wonderful blessings in this life. Many of these have been granted to us irrespective of whether we serve faithfully or not. Natural blessings are bestowed from the Father upon the just and unjust (Matthew 5:45). Yet the greatest blessing of all, length of days in the kingdom of God, is totally dependent upon our faithful service. Though we cannot earn salvation, for it is the gift of God, bestowed in grace (Ephesians 2:8), we must seek to serve to the best of our ability, believing that God is, and that He will reward those who seek Him diligently (Hebrews 11:6).

The wisdom of Solomon

The wisdom enjoyed by King Solomon was, therefore, totally unlike that of other kings. David was a wise man (1 Samuel 16:18), yet even his wisdom was eclipsed by his son. Solomon's desire, as we have already noted, was that he might judge Israel acceptably (1 Kings 3:9). This would have happened throughout the early part of his reign; however there is only one example of this taking place actually recorded for us. Two women appealed to the king, both claiming to be the mother of a living child (verses 16-27). When judgement was passed and the rightful parent identified, this was reported throughout the nation:

> "And all Israel heard of the judgment which the king had judged; and they feared the king: for they saw that the wisdom of God was in him, to do judgment." (verse 28)

There is an echo of this in the book of Proverbs. All sorts of symbols appear in the book; however one of the most common and most powerful themes is that of wisdom and folly, portrayed as two women (Proverbs 14:1). The two women who came to the king – one truthful and the other not, one who desired life and the other content with death – speak of the ways of truth and error. In the New Testament we read of the true ecclesia, which will be presented to the Master a "chaste virgin" (2 Corinthians 11:2), contrasted with the apostate church which is portrayed as a whore (Revelation 17:1).

Gentile nations serving Solomon

Solomon's reign was one of almost unbroken peace and prosperity. Towards the end of his days, as he descended into apostasy, he was troubled by various adversaries (1 Kings 11:14,23,26). There appears to be only one occasion where Israel did battle during the time of Solomon (see 2 Chronicles 8:3), for the nations round about Israel served and respected their king. For the most part Solomon enjoyed a time of great peace, reigning over many different lands (1 Kings 4:24). It was a time unlike any other, with God's people dwelling securely, in a type of the coming kingdom:

> "And Judah and Israel dwelt safely, every man under his vine and under his fig tree, from Dan even to Beersheba, all the days of Solomon." (verse 25)

Little wonder, then, that many Gentiles came before this great monarch:

> "And Solomon reigned over all kingdoms from the river unto the land of the Philistines, and unto the border of Egypt: they brought presents, and served Solomon all the days of his life." (verse 21)

What an amazing type of the kingdom of God, when Israel will inherit all the land promised to Abraham (Genesis 15:18), and kings will bow before Jesus Christ, with all nations serving him (Psalm 72:11).

"And there came of all people to hear the wisdom of Solomon, from all kings of the earth, which had heard of his wisdom."
(1 Kings 4:34)

The queen of Sheba

Of these Gentile monarchs who came before Solomon, only one is described in any detail:
"And when the queen of Sheba heard of the fame of Solomon concerning the name of the LORD, she came to prove him with hard questions." (10:1)

This was not merely inquisitiveness. She had heard that Solomon was rich and famous, however most monarchs are wealthy and are known beyond their own borders. Her wish was not simply to establish peace with a powerful neighbour. Rather she had heard of his fame "concerning the name of the LORD", and was moved to visit him and know more.

Names today are often of little importance. In Bible times, however, names often had real meaning. Sometimes new names were given or taken to indicate a particular change in a person's position (Abraham, Jacob, Simon Peter, etc.). The name of the God of Israel, Yahweh, has immense importance (Exodus 3:14,15; 6:3; 34:5-7). It indicates His promise to fill the world with glory by a race of redeemed, immortalised people, manifesting Him (Isaiah 11:9; Habakkuk 2:14). A Gentile queen, hearing of the fame of a king of Israel concerning the name of Israel's God, clearly teaches us two things:
1. Solomon was letting his "light shine before men" (Matthew 5:16).
2. The queen of Sheba had a genuine desire to know more of the God he served.

Sheba

The name Sheba appears first in Genesis 10:7. Sheba was one of the descendants of Cush, indicating an association with Africa, probably the areas of modern-day Ethiopia and / or Sudan. Other men called Sheba are named in Genesis 10:28 and 25:3. Whether the queen and her people were descended from any of these men it is impossible to say. Twice in the book of Job the name appears, once translated "Sabeans" (1:15), and once "Sheba" (6:19). The nation is listed amongst those who sold their wares in the markets of Tyre, selling spices, precious stones and gold (Ezekiel 27:22). A number of prophecies regarding the latter days make mention of Sheba, either being allied with the merchants of Tarshish (38:13), or bringing gifts to Israel or her king (Psalm 72:10,15; Isaiah 60:6).

Where precisely the queen of Sheba journeyed from is open to debate. Smith's Bible Dictionary suggests that she was from the area of Yemen, rather than Ethiopia, although there is little direct evidence to support this. The Lord Jesus taught that she came from "the south". All we can be sure of is that her land was a place of great wealth, and some distance from Israel, as the Master describes this as the "uttermost parts of the earth".

The queen's visit to Solomon
The queen of Sheba arrived at Jerusalem. Her intention was to prove Solomon with "hard questions" (1 Kings 10:1). This is one Hebrew word, elsewhere translated "riddle" (see Judges 14:12-19), "dark saying(s)" (Psalm 49:4; 78:2; Proverbs 1:6) and "proverb" (Habakkuk 2:6). She was, therefore, determined to ask him of "weightier matters" (Matthew 23:23). This was not simply a state visit to a far-off land to negotiate trade deals or sign a peace treaty. This Gentile queen wanted to know more of the God Solomon worshipped, and came to him with genuine questions regarding the things of Israel's hope.

> "And she came to Jerusalem with a very great train, with camels that bare spices, and very much gold, and precious stones: and when she was come to Solomon, she communed with him of all that was in her heart." (1 Kings 10:2)

The use of camels indicates that the journey was substantial, and that she had come from, or through, an area of desert. Arriving in Jerusalem she was welcomed by the king and spoke of "all that was in her heart". What, then, is in your heart, and mine? It is possible for us to project an appearance of spirituality so that others are convinced. It is even possible to deceive ourselves. However the Father knows us, and can see into our hearts and minds:

> "If thou sayest, Behold, we knew it not; doth not he that pondereth the heart consider it? and he that keepeth thy soul, doth not he know it? and shall not he render to every man according to his works?" (Proverbs 24:12)

One day we shall stand before the king, the all-wise Son of David, who will reign in righteousness from Jerusalem. He will look into our hearts and know whether we have followed him, longing for his coming. May we therefore seize the opportunity "while it is called today" (Hebrews 3:13) to ensure that our hearts "burn" for the things of the truth (Luke 24:32).

Solomon's response was similarly powerful:

> "Solomon told her all her questions: there was not any thing hid from the king, which he told her not." (1 Kings 10:3)

So all her questions were answered; she 'asked and it was given' (Matthew 7:7). There was nothing regarded as secret as far as Solomon was concerned. Presumably this means that no matter what she asked regarding the law or the promises, Solomon answered her. Some may have regarded these things as solely for Israel; however he was content to relay the wonderful truths of God to this Gentile ruler. Following this revelation, and the queen's consideration of Solomon's house, food, servants, their apparel and the king's ascent to the house of the Lord, she was truly moved:

> "… there was no more spirit in her. And she said to the king, It was a true report that I heard in mine own land of thy acts and of thy wisdom. Howbeit I believed not the words, until I came, and mine eyes had seen it: and, behold, the half was not told me: thy wisdom and prosperity exceedeth the fame which I heard. Happy are thy men, happy are these thy servants, which stand continually before thee, and that hear thy wisdom. Blessed be the LORD thy God, which delighted in thee, to set thee on the throne of Israel: because the LORD

loved Israel for ever, therefore made he thee king, to do judgment and justice." (1 Kings 10:5-9)

"No more spirit." We are reminded of the occasion when Jacob heard that Joseph was still alive and ruling Egypt. Initially "his heart fainted"; later, upon seeing the goods which his son had sent, he "revived" (Genesis 45:26,27). Surely this tells us that the queen, who must have been accustomed to wealth, honour and glory, was moved in a way which was highly unusual. The glory of other kingdoms, in comparison, left her completely cold. She had been told of Solomon's glory and wisdom, however she said the account of such things did not truly do them justice. The reality was that the kingdom in Israel was more than twice as glorious as she had been told. Similar things appear in Job:

"And that he would shew thee the secrets of wisdom, that they are double to that which is! ..." (Job 11:6)

The queen was not simply impressed by the glory of Solomon's kingdom and the contentment of his servants. Like Hiram before her (1 Kings 5:7), she blessed the Lord, and declared that it was because of His love for Israel that He had chosen Solomon to reign on David's throne. How marvellous to hear such things from a Gentile queen. We do not know what pagan deities she may have worshipped in her own land; however in the presence of Solomon she acknowledged that the only true God, the Almighty one of Abraham, Isaac and Jacob, loved, and will continue to love Israel "for ever" (see also Romans 11:1).

The queen departs from Solomon

We do not know how long the royal visit lasted. Gifts were bestowed from the queen: one hundred and twenty talents of gold (four and a half tonnes!), precious stones, and spices in a quantity never seen before (1 Kings 10:10). Prior to her return, we read of one final meeting between these two rulers:

"And king Solomon gave unto the queen of Sheba all her desire, whatsoever she asked, beside that which Solomon gave her of his royal bounty ..." (verse 13)

"All her desire ... beside that ... of his royal bounty." We can only surmise as to the meaning of this. Some have dared to suggest that Solomon had an intimate relationship with the queen. One of the most fanciful suggestions is that the king gifted the ark of the covenant to the queen of Sheba, and she took it home with her.

We need not waste time trying to disprove such fables. Had there been an inappropriate relationship between Solomon and the queen, then based on the content of 1 Kings 11, we would surely be told this. As to the releasing of the most holy item in the empire to a Gentile queen from a land at the extremities of the civilised world, even if such an act had been possible without the judgements of God being poured out (see 1 Samuel 5 and 2 Samuel 6), would it not be recorded for us?

As sons and daughters of the living God we are interested in facts. The Bible portrays for us a time of mental oneness between the king on David's throne, and a faithful, respectful Gentile queen who bowed before him. There was a genuine understanding between them. There was a love of God's word, His name, His plan and purpose. This took place in a time of unparalleled peace. Surely we see in these events a beautiful depiction of that time which is yet to come, when David's greater Son will sit upon his throne (Luke 1:32). In that great day his bride, many members of whom will have come from the lands of the Gentiles, will be gathered unto him (Ephesians 5:25-27).

As we read such things therefore, there is a challenge for every one of us. In the Master's day the leaders were condemned for knowing the truth without applying it. Jesus taught that they will be judged for their actions. And when that takes place, the queen of Sheba will be there, raised to stand before the one of whom Solomon was but a pale shadow. May we be privileged to be amongst the blessed in that glorious time!

"The queen of the south shall rise up in the judgment with this generation, and shall condemn it: for she came from the uttermost parts of the earth to hear the wisdom of Solomon; and, behold, a greater than Solomon is here."

(Matthew 12:42)

21

The widow of Zarephath

OF all the kings of Israel and Judah, Ahab was, without question, the worst. His father, Omri, had been worse than any who had gone before him (1 Kings 16:25), but Ahab plumbed new depths (verse 30). What was his worst act? Scripture leaves us in no doubt:

"And it came to pass, as if it had been a light thing for him to walk in the sins of Jeroboam the son of Nebat, that he took to wife Jezebel the daughter of Ethbaal king of the Zidonians, and went and served Baal, and worshipped him."

(verse 31)

A "light thing": this is a very literal translation of the original Hebrew word. By implication it means small, easy, trifling or vile (Strong's). The NKJV renders this "trivial". As if all the vile deeds performed by Ahab were not bad enough, he excelled himself by marrying Jezebel, because of her evil, pagan, selfish, Gentile ways which would influence him and the nation as a whole.

The Prophet Elijah's grand entrance

Without any introduction, Elijah appears on the scene (17:1), declaring that, for the sins of Ahab and his household, there would be no rain for three years. This was a direct fulfilment of a prophecy made in Deuteronomy 11:16,17. Indeed, had Ahab known his history, he would have realised that Solomon, whose heart was also turned away from the truth by "outlandish women" (1 Kings 11:1-8; Nehemiah 13:26), had also been given this same warning (1 Kings 8:35).

21 – The widow of Zarephath

Initially, the prophet went and lived by the brook Cherith, and was fed by ravens. Twice a day they brought him bread and flesh (17:4-6). This was a reminder of the Father's dealings with the nation in the wilderness (Exodus 16:8), and also of the twofold daily offerings that were to be made by Israel under the law (Numbers 28:4). However, the brook dried up and Elijah had to move on. As we have seen, the real problem in Israel was Jezebel; she was 'the power behind the throne', as demonstrated in 1 Kings 21, where Ahab desired Naboth's vineyard. She had come from the land of the Zidonians; she was the daughter of the king of Zidon. Yet it was to her homeland that Elijah was sent next:

"Arise, get thee to Zarephath, which belongeth to Zidon, and dwell there ..." (17:9)

Of all places, Elijah was sent to a town which belonged to Zidon. He was heading back to the very land where this queen had learned her evil ways, and where her family were probably still living. Yet there, in a land of sin and death, he would meet a very different kind of woman who would sustain him, and receive a blessing from Yahweh, Israel's God.

Zidon

Zidon (sometimes called Sidon) was an ancient, and at times wealthy, city of the Phoenicians. It was around twenty miles north of Tyre on the Mediterranean coast, as far north as Damascus. The name Zidon means 'fishery', an indication of the occupation of the original inhabitants of the area. The man Zidon was a son of Canaan, and a grandson of Ham (Genesis 10:15). Like other descendants of Ham, the Zidonians caused affliction for the people of Israel.

By the days of Ahab, Zidon was no great city; Tyre was of far greater importance. Hence for an ailing power, a political alliance with a more powerful nation, forged through marriage, would have been extremely advantageous. Israel had become seriously impoverished in Ahab's days, and not merely because of the drought which had caused most of the animals to perish

(1 Kings 18:5). Ahab's army was so small it is compared with "two little flocks of kids" (20:27). He needed all the allies he could get, and so a marriage with a king's daughter could prove greatly beneficial. Yet "the friendship of the world is enmity with God" (James 4:4), and Ahab and the nation would pay a heavy price for this act of folly.

Smith's *Bible Dictionary* says the following regarding Zidon:
> "... all that is known respecting (Zidon) during the epoch is very scanty, amounting to scarcely more than that one of its sources of gain was trade in slaves, in which the inhabitants did not shrink from selling inhabitants of Palestine."

The Zidonians were known for their thriving slave trade. Under the rule of Jezebel, we could describe Israel as being "sold under sin" (Romans 7:14). But in her homeland, in a town which "belonged to Zidon" was a woman of great faith.

The widow of Zarephath
As previously, the Father had not left his prophet destitute, for in Zidon he would be preserved:
> "... behold, I have commanded a widow woman there to sustain thee." (1 Kings 17:9)

There is a phrase which appears twice in the first few verses of this chapter: "I have commanded." Both the ravens (verse 4) and the woman (verse 9) had received a command from the Almighty one of Israel to feed His servant. But there was one major difference: the ravens had no choice. These unclean birds (see Leviticus 11:13,15) were clearly made to do so. Their minds were being controlled by the Lord so that they were unable to do anything but obey. This was, surely, not true for the woman. Our God does not make people do His bidding; He takes no pleasure in the obedience of robots. He calls for men and women to serve, blessing them, protecting them, guiding them, but (although He could) He does not *make* His people serve Him.

As Elijah approached the city, he met this widow for the first time and requested "a little water" (1 Kings 17:10), and "a morsel of bread" (verse 11). The language used by the prophet indicates the severity of the drought, which had clearly affected many of the lands bordering Israel. The woman's response demonstrates the terrible situation in which she found herself:

"As the LORD thy God liveth, I have not a cake, but an handful of meal in a barrel, and a little oil in a cruse: and, behold, I am gathering two sticks, that I may go in and dress it for me and my son, that we may eat it, and die." (verse 12)

Note that she acknowledged her Gentile state. She refers to the Lord as Elijah's God. She was unworthy to approach the one whom he worshipped. However, this situation was about to change. All she had was a handful of meal and a little oil. The Hebrew for meal is also used by Abraham when speaking to Sarah, who was to make cakes for the visiting angels (Genesis 18:6). Oil was used for cooking, anointing, and also to light the lamp in the tabernacle (Exodus 27:20). Here was a Gentile who had already received illumination from God, and would doubtless be taught yet more by Elijah in the days that followed.

Elijah's request of the widow

Despite the seriousness of her situation, Elijah had a request for this widow:

"Fear not; go and do as thou hast said: but make me thereof a little cake first, and bring it unto me, and after make for thee and for thy son. For thus saith the LORD God of Israel, The barrel of meal shall not waste, neither shall the cruse of oil fail, until the day that the LORD sendeth rain upon the earth."
(1 Kings 17:13,14)

Let us never underestimate the magnitude of this request. To give her last meal was one thing; to give up her son's last meal was something else. Yet like Abraham, who was willing to offer Isaac, believing in bodily resurrection (Genesis 22; Hebrews 11:19), and like Hannah, who offered Samuel as a "living sacrifice" (1 Samuel 1:11,24-28), she was willing to give what was demanded of her.

Perhaps most especially we are reminded of that greatest of all sacrifices, when "the only begotten of the Father, full of grace and truth" (John 1:14) laid down his life for his friends. In an offering of indescribable magnitude, the Lord God permitted His Son to die that we might live with him. Again, the suffering of Mary is rarely mentioned in our community. Simeon spoke of a sword piercing her own soul (Luke 2:35). Indeed, when we realise that she watched her beloved firstborn Son give his life (John 19:25), we appreciate the enormity of the offering made by this "mother in Israel".

Despite the doubts which would surely have filled the widow of Zarephath's mind, she showed her faith by her works (James 2:14-26), and was blessed accordingly:

> "And she went and did according to the saying of Elijah: and she, and he, and her house, did eat many days. And the barrel of meal wasted not, neither did the cruse of oil fail, according to the word of the LORD, which he spake by Elijah."
>
> (1 Kings 17:15,16)

What, then, do we make of this widow's actions? This was not simply blind obedience on her part. Rather this was an acceptance of the words of promise that a blessing would come, and that neither she nor her son would suffer as a result of her acts. Indeed, she was surely applying the Law of Moses which spoke of Israel giving the "firstfruits" to God (Exodus 23:19). Here the prophet spoke of making a cake for him "first", and promised a blessing if she responded in faith.

How might we have fared, faced with a similar demand? How does our faith compare with this Gentile woman, living in a land of idolatry and sin? In one sense, we are called upon to believe precisely the same thing. Elijah promised that the woman and her son would be sustained until rain was sent. We believe we will be cared for by God until His Son comes. How is the coming of Jesus portrayed in the Psalms? Like rainfall:

> "He shall come down like rain upon the mown grass: as showers that water the earth." (Psalm 72:6)

So Elijah was sustained, many miles from home. Perhaps as he fled from Jezebel he would have been moved to reflect on this very incident as an angel provided food and water for him:

"And he looked, and, behold, there was a cake (same Hebrew word as 1 Kings 17:13) baken on the coals, and a cruse of water at his head." (1 Kings 19:6)

In the days of the Master
There are perhaps three key incidents in the life of Jesus Christ which remind us of this widow and her faith. The most obvious is the Syrophenician woman (see chapter 34), who appealed for her daughter to be healed (Mark 7:26). She was, it seems, in precisely the same area as this faithful woman in Elijah's day (verse 24). Both cried to great prophets for the life of their children; both received a blessing because of their faith. The other two are the woman who gave two mites, and the widow of Nain.

As the Master beheld the people donating money to the treasury, we read the following:

"And there came a certain poor widow, and she threw in two mites, which make a farthing." (12:42)

The context here helps us to appreciate the significance of what was given. Jesus "knew what was in man" (John 2:25); he also knew what was in this woman's purse! Only he could tell that this was not some insignificant donation by one who could and should have given more; rather this was "all that she had, even all her living" (Mark 12:44). This is all the more amazing when we see that the Master had previously condemned the leaders for devouring widows' houses (verse 40). This woman could easily have refused to give anything to the treasury, as the leaders were the ones who had taken what she had, and they collected the money donated by the people. But just like the widow of Zarephath, who gave all that she had (enough for two small meals), this faithful widow gave everything to God (two small coins).

The initial meeting between Elijah and the widow had taken place in "the gate of the city" (1 Kings 17:10). The Master met a widow in the gate of the city of Nain (Luke 7:12). In both cases, the son of the widow was raised, causing great rejoicing and a realisation that the one who had performed the miracle was indeed sent by God (1 Kings 17:24; Luke 7:16).

The resurrection of a son

The woman, her son and Elijah were sustained "many days" by the divinely provided food (1 Kings 17:15). However, the son then died, and his mother approached Elijah, appealing for help:
> "And she said unto Elijah, What have I to do with thee, O thou man of God? art thou come unto me to call my sin to remembrance, and to slay my son?" (verse 18)

This was not a complaint on the part of this woman. Rather she was declaring to Elijah, 'I have nothing in common with you', as other uses of this same phrase in scripture prove (see 2 Samuel 16:10; 2 Kings 3:13; Mark 5:7). She was stating that, as a Gentile, she was unworthy to receive any blessing from Israel's God. However, just as in the life of Elisha, the son of this kind and caring woman would be raised. Indeed, of Elisha there are two resurrections recorded, as he had a "double portion" of Elijah's spirit (see 2 Kings 2:9; 4:32-35; 13:21). More especially, these things are a pointer forward to the ministry of the Master, when on three key occasions we have recorded beloved family members being raised to life again, and the Father being glorified as a result (Luke 7:14; 8:54,55; John 11:43,44).

> "And the woman said to Elijah, Now by this I know that thou art a man of God, and that the word of the LORD in thy mouth is truth." (1 Kings 17:24)

On the surface, we may not think there is anything particularly amazing about this woman's response. Surely anyone would act in the same way. However when a different kind of resurrection took place shortly afterwards, the other woman of Zidon behaved very differently. When Elijah prayed and rain fell for the first time in three and half years (James 5:17), the people of Israel were saved. Their crops would grow and their animals would live. We might term this a "national resurrection". And how did Jezebel respond? She determined that, for slaying the prophets of Baal, Elijah should die:
> "Then Jezebel sent a messenger unto Elijah, saying, So let the gods do to me, and more also, if I make not thy life as the life of one of them by to morrow about this time." (1 Kings 19:2)

Once again, what a contrast is recorded here. One woman of Zidon knew, loved and obeyed the truth. She cared for Elijah, feeding him in her own home. She appealed to him for help. She worshipped the Lord when her son lived. The other one hated everything Elijah stood for. Even when the nation began to come to life again, her mind was only focused on the death of her enemy.

The challenge for us from the widow of Zarephath

Bodily resurrection is absolutely central to the plan and purpose of Almighty God. It was clearly preached by Old Testament prophets (Daniel 12:2), and was an intrinsic part of the teaching of the Master (Matthew 16:21) and the apostles (Acts 2:24; 17:31). And yet, when Lazarus was raised from the dead by Jesus, how did the leaders respond?

"But the chief priests consulted that they might put Lazarus also to death; because that by reason of him many of the Jews went away, and believed on Jesus." (John 12:10,11)

Unlike the woman of Zarephath, these worldly men were untouched by resurrection – as they were by the teaching and other miracles of the Lord Jesus. No wonder, then, that the Master commented that:

"… If they hear not Moses and the prophets, neither will they be persuaded, though one rose from the dead." (Luke 16:31)

When the Master was raised, did they then accept the truth? Far from it – they retreated yet more into sin, propounding the lie that the body of Jesus had been stolen (Matthew 28:13), and persecuting those who dared to teach otherwise (Acts 5:40). Like Jezebel, they refused to see the hand of God at work. Yet the woman of Zarephath demonstrates the attitude which the Lord and His only begotten Son are seeking. Once enlightened, her life was one of self-sacrifice, love, belief, and praise. Truly, this faithful Gentile woman, coming from a land of sin and death, manifested and glorified Israel's God in a way which is an example to us all.

22

Naaman the Syrian

'TYPES and shadows' can be a tricky subject. Some see types lurking behind every number, place, name and incident. Everything, we are told, points to Jesus in some way or other. Others object to comparisons being drawn even when such things may seem obvious to everyone else. Whatever our attitude may be, the incident we are to consider in this chapter is, without question, a genuine type. The Master himself said this.

In Luke 4 we find our Lord at Nazareth. He read from Isaiah 61, and offended those who claimed to know him by expounding the chapter, saying it was being fulfilled before them (Luke 4:21). He then stated that no prophet is accepted in his own country (verse 24), and to prove this he quoted two Old Testament incidents:

1. The raising of the widow of Zarephath's son by Elijah (verses 25,26).
2. The healing of Naaman the Syrian by Elisha (verse 27).

So these two great acts, where Gentiles responded to the truth and were blessed, are symbols for the work of the Lord Jesus Christ and the blessings that can be enjoyed through him. Like the prophets of old, the Master was rejected by many of his people, but others came to God through him and were accepted. The lesson of Naaman the Syrian in his dealings with Elisha is that any can be blessed by Israel's God if they submit, in faith, to what is required of them. This is, surely, the same message the apostles preached after the ascension of the Master, when they went to the "uttermost part of the earth" (Acts 1:8).

Naaman the Syrian

Naaman had everything going for him. He was successful, rich, honourable, mighty and accepted by his king. However he had one major problem:

> "Now Naaman, captain of the host of the king of Syria, was a great man with his master, and honourable, because by him the LORD had given deliverance unto Syria: he was also a mighty man in valour, but he was a leper." (2 Kings 5:1)

Leprosy is a horrendous disease of the flesh which often leads, if not to death, to a lingering lifetime of suffering. Under the Law of Moses (Leviticus 13), there were different kinds of leprosy, some of which permitted contact with others. In other cases, the leper had to dwell "without the camp". A vile fleshly disease, causing suffering, separation and death: surely this speaks, in symbol, of sin.

Naaman's name means 'pleasantness'; it is the masculine form of the name Naomi (see Ruth 1:20). Yet this Syrian warrior was anything but pleasant, and his condition required a cure which only Israel's God could provide.

Syria

The name Syria means 'the highland' (see Strong). It is indeed a mountainous region. In 1967, during the Six-Day War, Israel took the Golan Heights from Syria, in anticipation of a time when the King of the North will descend upon "the mountains of Israel" (Ezekiel 38:8; 39:2).

Laban is termed a Syrian (Genesis 25:20). Jacob's dealings with his father-in-law were nothing if not challenging. Despite being blessed with wives, children, flocks and herds during his time in Laban's house, Jacob suffered great hardship whilst working for him (31:38-41).

As the nations of Syria and Israel shared a common border, there was much contact between them. Damascus, the chief city, is only seventy miles from the sea of Galilee. In David's day Israel held the upper hand, and garrisons were placed in Damascus (2 Samuel 8:6). However under Solomon, the Syrians began to wrest power away from Israel (1 Kings 11:23-25). Asa, king of Judah, made a league with Syria, fighting together against Israel; this was condemned by the Lord (2 Chronicles 16:7-9).

In Ahab's day, Israel won notable victories over the Syrians, but the king then spared Benhadad the Syrian ruler, and was judged for his actions by God (1 Kings 20:42,43). Later Hazael was appointed king of Syria at the direction of the Lord (19:15; 2 Kings 8:13), executing the Father's judgements against His wayward people (10:32; 13:3).

Throughout Elisha's days there was regular contact with Syria. Most notable is the occasion where an entire army of Syrian soldiers were blinded, led from Dothan to Samaria, had their sight restored, were fed with a great meal, and then sent back home (6:8-23; see chapter 23). As Elisha died, Israel was still doing battle with Syria (13:17). Later, in Jeremiah's time, the Syrians were still causing suffering for God's people (Jeremiah 35:11). In the Master's day Syria, like Judaea, had been incorporated into the Roman Empire (Luke 2:2).

The little maid

Sometimes, the solution to a problem comes from the most unexpected of sources. In one of Naaman's raids on Israel, a little maid had been taken captive. She waited on his wife:

> "And she said unto her mistress, Would God my lord were with the prophet that is in Samaria! for he would recover him of his leprosy." (2 Kings 5:3)

We are given no further information regarding this child. We simply know she was "little". Her faith, however, was immense. The phrase translated "Would God" is better rendered "O that". The RSV has "would that"; the NKJV renders this "if only". The same word is only used on one other occasion:

> "O that (same word) my ways were directed to keep thy statutes!" (Psalm 119:5)

We might say that God *had* directed her ways, to Syria; despite this she *did* keep the statutes of the Lord. Did she have in mind the beginning of the following section in this great Psalm?

"Wherewithal shall a young man cleanse his way? by taking heed thereto according to thy word." (verse 9)

This little girl knew that Naaman's cleansing would only be possible if he was to obey the word of Israel's God. Her attitude here is truly amazing. She wished no ill on the man who had captured her; rather she sought his salvation. Despite being taken captive to a foreign land, possibly without her parents, her faith in, and love for, the God of Israel was unshakeable. She believed that Naaman's leprosy would be cured, although there is no record of such a cure being afforded through Elisha or any other man up until this point. Leprosy was clearly a very common problem, as there were "many lepers in Israel" at this time (Luke 4:27); none were healed, except this Syrian. Yet this small child knew in her heart that such a rare and unlikely event would pose no problem for the Lord's prophet. What faith! What kindness! What a lesson, and a challenge for us all.

Naaman's return to Israel
Naaman was the most powerful Syrian warrior. Yet he had to head back to the land he had conquered, that he might enjoy freedom. The captor had to return to the land he had captured, in order to receive a gift. When the Master conquered sin, the greatest of all gifts was promised to his people:

"... When he ascended up on high, he led captivity captive, and gave gifts unto men." (Ephesians 4:8)

How unlikely it is, naturally speaking, that all these people (Naaman, his wife, the king and his men) should believe this little maid. Nonetheless, Naaman was sent to Israel, although her words appear to have been lost in translation somewhat. She said the *prophet* would effect a healing for Naaman, yet it was to the king of Israel he was sent (2 Kings 5:5,6). The king, suspecting that this was a trick on the part of the Syrians, rends his clothes, and then quotes scripture!

"... Am I God, to kill and to make alive, that this man doth send unto me to recover a man of his leprosy?" (verse 7)

Oh that he could have quoted – and believed – the end of the verse from which this quotation comes:

> "See now that I, even I, am he, and there is no god with me: I kill, and I make alive; I wound, and I heal: neither is there any that can deliver out of my hand." (Deuteronomy 32:39)

Elisha's instruction to Naaman

Realising what was taking place, Elisha sent a message to the king: "Let him come now to me" (2 Kings 5:8). This reminds us of the words of the Master, the one whom Elisha foreshadows so powerfully:

> "... If any man thirst, let him come unto me, and drink." (John 7:37)

What took place next appeared to Naaman to be a gross insult. Elisha refused to come to meet him, instead sending a message that he should wash in the Jordan seven times. Assuming Elisha was in Samaria, as the maid had said, Naaman would have needed to travel around twenty to twenty-five miles eastwards. In an age when good roads may have been rare, this could have meant a journey of many hours.

Clearly the act of washing, in itself, was nothing. It was the act of humility and faith which was of importance. Naturally speaking, baptism is nothing to do with actual cleansing; rather it is a demonstration of the faith of the one being baptized (1 Peter 3:21). Connections with baptism are made stronger by the location, for John baptized at the banks of the Jordan (Matthew 3:5,6). Similarly, the Master used the same phrase "go and wash" to the man born blind (John 9:7), prior to his healing.

Naaman was clearly unimpressed with the words of the prophet, asking two questions (2 Kings 5:12):

1. Weren't the rivers of Damascus better than all the rivers of Israel?
2. Could he not wash there and be clean?

On the surface, his complaints were perfectly logical. The rivers of his homeland were probably much better, cleaner, and nicer than Jordan. Yet the location of the washing was unimportant; it was the symbolism behind it that he was missing. We cannot come to God on our own terms. If adult baptism is demanded (Mark 16:16), then how dare man ignore this command altogether or invent some alternative (e.g., infant sprinkling), believing that this ought to be equally acceptable.

Naaman's servants, who clearly respected and loved their lord, wanted him to be healed:

"And his servants came near, and spake unto him, and said, My father, if the prophet had bid thee do some great thing, wouldest thou not have done it? how much rather then, when he saith to thee, Wash, and be clean?" (2 Kings 5:13)

"Some great thing". The Hebrew for "great" is the same as verse 1: Naaman was a "great" man. Yet great actions in this world count for nothing in the sight of our Heavenly Father. He requires acts of humility, and an acceptance that His plan and purpose will be fulfilled. We are saved, by grace, not by "works" (Ephesians 2:9), but through faith and obedience to the word of God. The servants' soft words turned away their lord's wrath (Proverbs 15:1), and he descended into the Jordan seven times:

"... and his flesh came again like unto the flesh of a little child, and he was clean." (2 Kings 5:14)

This mighty Gentile warrior had humbled himself and descended into the waters of Jordan in faith. When he arose the seventh time, his flesh was as a "little child". The word "little" is the same in the Hebrew and English as in verse 2: the "little" maid. Like a "little child" he had accepted the truth (as required by the Master, Matthew 18:3), and had responded accordingly.

Elisha meets Naaman

Like the one leper in Luke 17, Naaman returned to stand before Elisha. The other nine healed by Jesus had not glorified God; only one did, and he was a Samaritan (called a "stranger" by the Master in Luke 17:18).

Previously, Naaman had refused to obey the prophet's instructions because of pride. Elisha had insulted him by not coming to see him; and the rivers of Damascus were much better than Jordan. Personal and national pride had been offended. But note how, having been healed, these feelings of self-importance had vanished altogether:

> "Behold, now I know that there is no God in all the earth, but in Israel: now therefore, I pray thee, take a blessing of thy servant." (2 Kings 5:15)

There was no God in all the earth but Israel; nationalistic pride in Syria had gone. And how did he refer to himself in relation to the prophet? "Thy servant". No longer did he feel any sense of personal pride or self-worth. Surely this was the attitude of the little maid, and this is the state of mind the God of Israel seeks today. Naaman offered gifts to the prophet (verses 15,16), but like others before and after (Abraham especially, Genesis 14:23), Elisha refused. He then made a rather strange request of the prophet:

> "… Shall there not then, I pray thee, be given to thy servant two mules' burden of earth? for thy servant will henceforth offer neither burnt offering nor sacrifice unto other gods, but unto the LORD." (2 Kings 5:17)

Was this simply a reminder of the land of his healing? No: this was a reflection of what was said in Moses' law about altars:

> "An altar of earth thou shalt make unto me, and shalt sacrifice thereon thy burnt offerings, and thy peace offerings, thy sheep, and thine oxen: in all places where I record my name I will come unto thee, and I will bless thee." (Exodus 20:24)

Did Naaman know what the law taught? In *all* places? Was he heading back to Syria, desiring to continue to worship the mighty one of Israel, and to offer sacrifices as required under the law given through Moses? If so, we see a foreshadowing of the words of the Master to the Samaritan woman. Jesus spoke of worshipping the Father "in spirit and in truth" in any location (John 4:21-24). This is precisely what Naaman determined to do upon his return to Syria.

Naaman and Gehazi

Elisha's servant, Gehazi, had listened to this exchange with growing disbelief. Here was a wealthy man, offering his master all sorts of valuable gifts, and they had been refused. Perhaps he concluded that Naaman's wealth had been plundered from lands such as Israel and was, as such, fair game. There is even a degree of racial superiority in his attitude:

> "... Behold, my master hath spared Naaman this Syrian, in not receiving at his hands that which he brought ..."
> (2 Kings 5:20)

So once Naaman had departed, Gehazi followed him, and then lied to obtain the gifts which had been refused by his master, asking for a talent and silver and two changes of raiment.

> "And Naaman said, Be content, take two talents. And he urged him, and bound two talents of silver in two bags, with two changes of garments, and laid them upon two of his servants; and they bare them before him." (verse 23)

Everything was doubled. Here was a "double-minded man" (James 1:8). Indeed there are two lies recorded of Gehazi: one to Naaman (2 Kings 5:22), and one to Elisha, when he denied having been anywhere when asked to explain his absence (verse 25). Like Achan before him (Joshua 7), and Ananias and Sapphira afterwards (Acts 5), Gehazi grasped after the wealth of this age, and paid the price.

For his sin, the leprosy of Naaman was to cleave to Gehazi and his seed forever (2 Kings 5:27). This tragic incident reminds us that, just as the blessings promised to Abraham were received by faithful Gentiles such as Naaman, so Israelites, if shown to be unworthy, would receive only a curse. We are reminded of the words of the Master when speaking with a disciple who was beginning to waver:

> "No man, having put his hand to the plough, and looking back, is fit for the kingdom of God." (Luke 9:62)

Had not Gehazi done exactly this? He was "looking back"; indeed when he followed Naaman he was heading away from Israel, towards the lands of the Gentiles. Unlike his master (1 Kings 19:19-21), his hand had been removed from the plough. There was now only a longing for, and determination to obtain, the treasures of this world.

In our day, many seeking to follow the Lord Jesus are surrounded by the gold, silver and garments of this age. Many of these items may appear totally innocent; others can have a devastating effect on the life of a believer. How much, then, are we like Elisha and Naaman? How little are we like Gehazi? If we wish to be transformed, made like unto our lord, then we must seek to shun the wealth of this present world and look, in faith, to the coming of the one prefigured so wonderfully by Elisha:

"Lay not up for yourselves treasures upon earth, where moth and rust doth corrupt, and where thieves break through and steal: but lay up for yourselves treasures in heaven, where neither moth nor rust doth corrupt, and where thieves do not break through nor steal: for where your treasure is, there will your heart be also." (Matthew 6:19-21)

23

Elisha and the Syrian army

HAD the healing of Naaman meant nothing to those in Syria? Leprosy must have been an immense problem in Bible times, highlighted by the fact that the Master said there were "many" lepers in Israel (Luke 4:27). Presumably this applied to other lands also. Naaman must have been just one of a great number of Syrians suffering from this vile, unsightly disease. Yet he had travelled to Israel and returned perfectly whole. Would there have been an acknowledgement of this from the Syrian king? Would there be gifts bestowed, or at the very least a cessation of hostilities between the two countries? Tragically, this was not to be, for 2 Kings 6:8 commences with the phrase, "Then the king of Syria warred against Israel".

Maybe this was a different king from the one recorded in chapter 5? Maybe Israel had prompted this action by attacking Syria? Or maybe this is simply a case of a man of the flesh doing what so many men of the flesh do. The things of the truth, once neglected, are readily forgotten. Acts of mercy are rarely recalled by those in the world. The God of Israel, through His mighty prophet Elisha, had healed Naaman the Syrian, permitting him freedom from the affliction which had caused such suffering. Yet just a short while afterwards the Syrians desired to bring Israel into bondage.

These things were known to the prophet, and he relayed them to the king of Israel. In an act replicating the deliverance afforded in the cities of refuge (Numbers 35), this king was permitted to flee to a place of safety (2 Kings 6:9,10). This happened a number of times, leading the Syrian king to suspect there was a traitor in his ranks (verse 11). He was told by one of his servants – a man with astonishing insight – that there was no traitor; rather Elisha was revealing such things to the king in Israel. Plans were then made to try to capture the prophet of the Lord (verses 12,13).

The Syrians' efforts to capture Elisha

We marvel at the folly of this plan. If Elisha knew that there had been plans to take the king, would he not also be aware of the Syrians' intention to capture him? If he did know, then he manifested a great degree of faith in remaining in the place where he was, the city of Dothan (verse 13). The record speaks of the frightening sight which greeted Elisha's servant the following morning:

> "And when the servant of the man of God was risen early, and gone forth, behold, an host compassed the city both with horses and chariots. And his servant said unto him, Alas, my master! how shall we do?" (verse 15)

So all the might of Syria had been roused for one man. Like Jesus, men of violence came to take God's servant, for they were fearful of the power he possessed. Also like Jesus, the efforts to capture Elisha must have commenced at night (John 13:30). For this discovery to have been made "early" we can assume that the journey from Syria had (at least in part) been taken during the hours of darkness. Unless there was a particularly bright moon, torches would have guided the way as these men travelled south into Israel (see 18:3). This is relevant, as we shall see later.

The Syrians had come with "horses, chariots, and a great host". These same words are used in the very next chapter, where another Syrian attack is thwarted by their hearing a noise:

> "For the Lord had made the host of the Syrians to hear a noise of *chariots*, and a noise of *horses*, even the noise of a great *host*: and they said one to another, Lo, the king of Israel hath hired against us the kings of the Hittites, and the kings of the Egyptians, to come upon us. Wherefore they arose and

fled in the twilight, and left their tents, and their horses, and their asses, even the camp as it was, and fled for their life."
(2 Kings 7:6,7)

These three words are the same in the Hebrew and English. In these things we see a perfect demonstration of the words of the Apostle Paul:

"God is not mocked: for whatsoever a man soweth, that shall he also reap." (Galatians 6:7)

Note also that before the sun was up, these men fled, for their exodus took place "in the twilight". By this stage the men of Syria must have been accustomed to travelling in a state of darkness!

"There are more that be with us …"

As Elisha's servant beheld the great number of enemy soldiers encamped around the city walls, he turned to his master in despair. The prophet's response is beautiful and powerful:

"And he answered, Fear not: for they that be with us are more than they that be with them." (2 Kings 6:16)

We read similar words in 2 Chronicles 32:7 regarding the Assyrian invasion in Hezekiah's day, and in 1 John 4:4 concerning the antichrist. What a comfort it is to know that this truth remains unchanged to this very day.

In the context of this study, the next words of Elisha are particularly apt:

"And Elisha prayed, and said, LORD, I pray thee, open his eyes, that he may see. And the LORD opened the eyes of the young man; and he saw: and, behold, the mountain was full of horses and chariots of fire round about Elisha." (2 Kings 6:17)

There were things which only Elisha could see. His servant's eyes were blind to the immense multitude of angels which encamped not round about the city, but "round about Elisha". Could Elisha actually see them, or did he just know they were there? He had certainly seen them previously when horses and chariots of fire had taken Elijah away, leaving him to take up his mantle and continue the work (2:11-13). Possibly this is what the Lord Jesus had in mind when he spoke of the deliverance that could have been afforded him:

"Thinkest thou that I cannot now pray to my Father, and he shall presently give me more than twelve legions of angels?" (Matthew 26:53)

There were others in scripture unable to see what was in front of them. We think of Hagar (Genesis 21:19), and Balaam (Numbers 22:31). On both occasions we find angels at work, and we read that the Lord "opened the eyes" of those who were unable to see.

What a warning there is for us here! There are so many things in this world which can cause us to be distracted. We seek to "look unto Jesus" (Hebrews 12:2), walking in the light (Isaiah 2:5; 1 John 1:7); however too easily we can turn to the things of this age which, if unchecked, can cause us to leave the path leading to life. No wonder the Apostle Paul spoke of the people of this age being in a state of blindness:

"In whom the god of this world hath blinded the minds of them which believe not." (2 Corinthians 4:4)

The judgements of God on the Syrian army

Having prayed for his servant's eyes to be opened, Elisha then turned his attention to the enemy army:

"And when they came down to him, Elisha prayed unto the LORD, and said, Smite this people, I pray thee, with blindness. And he smote them with blindness according to the word of Elisha." (2 Kings 6:18)

Others suffered a similar fate. The men of Sodom (Genesis 19:11), Saul of Tarsus (Acts 9:9), and Elymas the sorcerer (13:11) were all blinded that the plan and purpose of God might be done, and that others might be saved.

Elisha then told the Syrian soldiers that they were in the wrong place, and led them to the city of Samaria (2 Kings 6:19). We can pass over this verse very quickly without considering the magnitude of what took place. Imagine leading one blind man a distance of a mile over rough terrain. From Dothan to Samaria is a distance of around fourteen miles. How then was Elisha able to guide an entire army? Surely the angels of God who were with the "horses and chariots of fire" were instrumental in leading these blinded men to their destination.

Job said that he had been "eyes to the blind" (Job 29:15); this is precisely what Elisha was for the Syrians. In using the phrase "follow me", the prophet was foreshadowing the work of the Master, who would use the same expression on a great number of occasions (see Matthew 4:19; 8:22; 9:9; 16:24; 19:21).

Is there an echo of these amazing things in Isaiah 42?

"I the LORD have called thee in righteousness, and will hold thine hand, and will keep thee, and give thee for a covenant of the people, for a light of the Gentiles; to open the blind eyes, to bring out the prisoners from the prison, and them that sit in darkness out of the prison house ... And I will bring the blind by a way that they knew not; I will lead them in paths that they have not known: I will make darkness light before them, and crooked things straight. These things will I do unto them, and not forsake them." (Isaiah 42:6,7,16)

Although this is unquestionably a messianic prophecy (see verses 1-3; Matthew 12:18-20), we are surely struck by the similarities in the life of the one who foreshadows the Lord Jesus so powerfully. Elisha and the angels had "held the hand" of the blinded Syrian warriors, bringing them by a way that they knew not. They led them in paths they did not know, that the mercy and truth of the God of Israel might be manifested unto them.

The Syrians' sight is restored

Having blinded the Syrians and led them to Samaria, the prophet then prayed to God once more:

"And it came to pass, when they were come into Samaria, that Elisha said, LORD, open the eyes of these men, that they may see. And the LORD opened their eyes, and they saw; and, behold, they were in the midst of Samaria." (2 Kings 6:20)

There is a further reminder of the work of the Lord Jesus here. Only he was able to open the eyes of a man born blind

(John 9:32). Indeed, when speaking with Pharisees (verse 40), he spoke of blinding men, that the truth might be accepted (verse 39). This would then take place in the life of one key Pharisee, Saul of Tarsus (Acts 9:9; 23:6). Yet Elisha stands as a remarkable type of the Master in restoring the sight of these Gentiles. Surely this also reminds us that one of the events which will take place in the kingdom age is the opening of blind eyes (Isaiah 35:5).

The king of Israel, upon seeing these enemy soldiers before him, requested permission from Elisha to execute the entire number. The prophet's response was particularly forthright:

> "And he answered, Thou shalt not smite them: wouldest thou smite those whom thou hast taken captive with thy sword and with thy bow? set bread and water before them, that they may eat and drink, and go to their master." (2 Kings 6:22)

So having been blinded, guided and then enlightened, these Syrian warriors were given food ("great provision", verse 23). What were they being shown, but that the God of Israel is merciful, gracious and longsuffering (Exodus 34:6)? What was Elisha doing but loving and feeding his enemies (Matthew 5:44; Romans 12:20)? In the Psalms we read of the work of our God:

> "[The LORD] … giveth food to the hungry … looseth the prisoners … openeth the eyes of the blind … preserveth the strangers." (Psalm 146:7-9)

All of these acts of love we see manifested in the actions of Israel towards these Syrian soldiers.

A symbol of the Gospel message

For an army to be blinded and guided a great distance is unusual, and for their sight to be restored upon the request of a man. That a great feast was laid before men (at a time when food was scarce, see 2 Kings 4:38; 6:25) is also surprising. Yet most remarkable of all, the beneficiaries of these things were Gentiles.

We can only imagine the effect this must have had upon these Syrian soldiers. As we have already seen, another Syrian invasion was to take place shortly after this (see verse 24), but how could any man who had experienced the events described above fail to have been moved by them? Might some have remained in the company of Elisha, desiring to know more of the God that he worshipped? Would others have sought out Naaman upon their return home and spoken of the amazing acts of love and mercy of which they had been the recipients?

The call of the Gospel is very clear. We have turned from the darkness of this age to behold the glorious light of the truth (Romans 13:12), manifested perfectly for us in Jesus Christ, the "light of the world" (John 8:12; 9:5). Having done so, we must now seek to show this in our lives (Matthew 5:14-16), shining as lights that those who are yet in darkness might see the hope that we have (1 Peter 3:15). Truly we can say, as the Syrian soldiers doubtless declared, and as the man born blind stated to the leaders of his day:

"... one thing I know, that, whereas I was blind, now I see."
(John 9:25)

24

Jonah and the mariners

THOSE who were privileged to attend Sunday school probably learned of Jonah when they were aged about five or six. He was the man who tried to run away from God and failed. In the process he was cast from the ship in which he was travelling, and swallowed by "a great fish". He survived, and then went to preach to the Ninevites as originally commanded. In this chapter we wish to look beyond this narrative to the reactions of those mariners who came into contact with him. As we shall see, his words and actions provoked a response amongst a large number of people. As far as we know, all of these were Gentiles.

Jonah's prophecy regarding Israel
When considering Jonah, we shall obviously concentrate on the events contained within the short book which bears his name. However he is mentioned elsewhere in the Old Testament. Jeroboam the son of Joash reigned over Israel for forty-one years (2 Kings 14:23). During this time he acted very much like his namesake, Jeroboam the son of Nebat, who had "made Israel to sin" (verse 24). Despite this, he achieved notable success in reclaiming land which had been lost to Syria. This had been foretold by the prophet Jonah:

> "He restored the coast of Israel from the entering of Hamath unto the sea of the plain, according to the word of the LORD God of Israel, which he spake by the hand of his servant Jonah, the son of Amittai, the prophet, which was of Gath-hepher."
> (verse 25)

Jonah was one of only a very small number of prophets to the northern, ten-tribe kingdom of Israel. Is this an indication as to his reluctance to preach to the Ninevites? It was not simply racial superiority. He would know what Assyria would do when the land of Israel was invaded. He loved Israel and wanted God's people to be saved. Did he conclude that if the judgements of God were poured out upon the principal city of Assyria, there could be no invasion of Israel? Regardless of his reasoning at this time, and his foolhardy actions in attempting to negate the purpose of God, two key points stand out from the above verse.

Firstly, he is called not only the prophet of the Lord God of Israel, but also His servant. Irrespective of what followed when he was commanded to preach to Nineveh, he had served the Almighty with faithfulness. We can never condone a man refusing to obey a direct instruction from the Father. However, we must never forget that prior to Nineveh being spared (and maybe even afterwards?) Jonah was a servant of the Lord.

Jonah, the Galilean

The second point relates to the city from which he had come. He was of Gath-hepher. This was in the area allotted to the tribe of Zebulun when the land was divided up. In Joshua 19:13 the same place is mentioned, although it is translated Gittah-hepher. This section of the land was within the overall area of Galilee. This area, inherited by two tribes Zebulun and Naphtali, is mentioned in relation to the Messiah:

"The land of Zabulon, and the land of Nephthalim, by the way of the sea, beyond Jordan, Galilee of the Gentiles; the people which sat in darkness saw great light …" (Matthew 4:15,16)

So this area was not simply called 'northern' by the rest of Israel. It was not just 'despised' by those in the south. It was termed "Galilee of the Gentiles". Inhabitants of a border town may be regarded as 'foreign' by others within the nation to whom they belong. This was certainly the case for the cities of Galilee. The leaders in the days of Jesus were desperate to find any reason to discredit him. They knew a little of his ancestry. They may even have known that he was born in Bethlehem, hence their vile sleight regarding his parentage (John 8:41). However, as he was known as a man from Nazareth in Galilee, they had reason to reject the claims of those who said he was the anointed of God: "They answered and said unto [Nicodemus], Art thou also of Galilee? Search, and look: for out of Galilee ariseth no prophet." (7:52)

No prophet? Was Jonah of Gath-hepher not a prophet? Perhaps they refused to acknowledge him because the beneficiaries of his work were Gentiles. There is no record of a prophecy made by Jonah being hearkened to by any in Israel. However, two separate groups of people responded to his words and they were both from the Gentile world.

The mariners heading towards Tarshish

When Jonah sought to flee from the presence of the Father he caught a boat at Joppa which was heading to Tarshish (Jonah 1:3). The location of this far-off country has been debated at length. Time does not permit us to consider all of the information regarding this place which is mentioned a number of times in the Old Testament. We do know that Jonah's intention was to travel west, heading up the Mediterranean Sea as far away from Israel as possible. Although we are not told the others in the vessel were Gentiles, there is clear indication in the record that this is the case.

Not long after setting sail a fierce storm descended. The key teaching in the book of Jonah is that of greatness. So the tempest was "mighty" and the wind "great" (verse 4). Initially the mariners cried unto their own gods, whilst all the time Jonah remained asleep below deck (verse 5). This teaches us that the men, despite having set sail from a port in Israel, were almost certainly not Israelites. They served their own gods. There is no indication that they cried unto Yahweh at this time. Even a man of Israel who had cast off true worship for the pagan deities of the nations would still, in desperation, call to the one the fathers of his nation had served.

Eventually lots were cast in an effort to determine the one who was responsible for the great storm having descended. When Jonah was identified, he was asked to explain his actions. His reply is particularly instructive:

> "And he said unto them, I am an Hebrew; and I fear the LORD, the God of heaven, which hath made the sea and the dry land." (verse 9)

Jonah called himself "an Hebrew". We saw previously how this is a title used to identify the people of God (see chapter 2, Abraham). The phrase often appears when distinguishing them from Gentiles. Sometimes it is used in a derogatory way by those of the nations. Potiphar's wife called Joseph "an Hebrew" when she accused him (Genesis 39:14). When Jonathan and his armour-bearer approached a Philistine garrison, the enemy spoke of the Hebrews coming out of their hiding places (1 Samuel 14:11). David's presence within the ranks of the Philistines caused consternation and the question was asked, "What do these Hebrews here?" (29:3).

By stating to the sailors that he was a Hebrew, Jonah was clearly acknowledging that he was a different nationality from them. Whether they had come from Tarshish, or were Phoenician sailors, we are not told. We do know that his declaration of the God he served, what His name was, and what He had done in creating the heaven and the earth, caused terror amongst these mariners:

> "Then were the men exceedingly afraid, and said unto him, Why hast thou done this? For the men knew that he fled from the presence of the LORD, because he had told them."
> (Jonah 1:10)

The men then asked Jonah what needed to be done that the sea might be calmed. He told them they would have to throw him into the raging ocean. In an act which was truly praiseworthy, they tried with all their might to bring the boat to land (verse 13). When this failed, they agreed to do as Jonah had said. Before this, however, they prayed to the God from whom Jonah had fled:

"Wherefore they cried unto the Lord, and said, We beseech thee, O Lord, we beseech thee, let us not perish for this man's life, and lay not upon us innocent blood: for thou, O Lord, hast done as it pleased thee." (verse 14)

These men displayed an attitude which was not only unusual, but also highly commendable. They accepted that the Lord had the power to destroy them, and prayed for mercy that the death of Jonah might not be held against them. They used the phrase "innocent blood". This appears a number of times in the law, where the importance of applying commands regarding life and death is stressed (Deuteronomy 19:10-13; 21:8,9).

Did they know what the Law of Moses said? As Gentiles, their wish to please Israel's God and avoid the death of a man is truly remarkable. Tragically, some within Israel did not share their high ideals. Manasseh filled Jerusalem with the blood of innocents (2 Kings 21:16). The leaders in the Master's day were content that innocent blood should be shed (Matthew 27:4). Yet these Gentile mariners were determined to do what was right.

The mariners' faithful response

As soon as Jonah was cast into the sea it became calm. Unsurprisingly, the sailors were moved by this:

"Then the men feared the Lord exceedingly, and offered a sacrifice unto the Lord, and made vows." (Jonah 1:16)

Three separate pieces of information are provided for us regarding the actions of these men:

1) They feared the Lord exceedingly

Here we have another of the great words of Jonah. The respect and awe of these mariners, who must have seen all sorts of things when out on the seas, was truly amazing. The words "feared" and "exceedingly" are exactly the same as in verse 10, when the men, learning of Jonah's folly, were "exceedingly afraid". These men were terrified when they were in peril, yet when the danger was past they did not shrug their shoulders and continue as if nothing had happened. Like the disciples of the Master (Mark 4:41), they remained fearfully respectful of the one who had calmed the sea.

2) They offered a sacrifice unto Him

Although they were Gentiles, they showed their faith in making an offering to the God of Israel. Under the law there were strict requirements as to the kinds of animals that could be offered. Saul was condemned for offering a sacrifice in place of Samuel, and he was an Israelite (1 Samuel 13:9-13). Here a group of Gentile mariners, who may have had very little knowledge of Israel's God offered sacrifices unto Him, and were accepted by Him.

3) They made vows

Were these just empty words of men who had escaped death? A man may promise all sorts of things at a time of great danger. As has been noted many times, we will never find an atheist in a lifeboat! However the danger had passed. When all was calm, these men expressed a genuine desire to seek and serve the one of whom Jonah had spoken.

We read of vows many times in scripture, especially in the Old Testament. The very first recorded example of one making a vow is Jacob after he left his family home (Genesis 28:20). Under the law vows could be made, as in the case of the Nazarite (Numbers 6). The importance of fulfilling the vow was stressed many times (see Numbers 30; Deuteronomy 23:21-23; Ecclesiastes 5:5). A number made vows and fulfilled them, despite what they may have wanted to do (Jephthah and Hannah).

Time and again in the book of the Psalms we read of the Psalmist, or the one of whom he was inspired to write, "paying his vows" (e.g., Psalm 22:25). Just like the faithful in Israel, the sailors made vows to the Lord and, as far as we know, they fulfilled them.

Whatever the future may have held for these men, we are surely struck by their faith and determination to serve the God of whom Jonah had spoken. In the book of Psalms we read of those at sea and the perils they face. We also read of the call of God to such people. His desire is that men should be like those mariners on the way to Tarshish who feared and praised Him, and vowed that they would serve faithfully:

> "They that go down to the sea in ships, that do business in great waters ... he commandeth, and raiseth the stormy wind, which lifteth up the waves thereof ... Then they cry unto the LORD in their trouble, and he bringeth them out of their distresses. He maketh the storm a calm, so that the waves thereof are still ... Oh that men would praise the LORD for his goodness, and for his wonderful works to the children of men!" (Psalm 107:23,25,28,29,31)

25

Jonah and the Ninevites

HAVE you ever been truly amazed by someone's response to the things of the truth? In the Western world we may be accustomed to a lack of interest, or even open hostility. Yet just occasionally we may meet someone possessing a genuine desire to know more. Around the time of her baptism one elderly sister said to me: "I'm seventy-five years old and I feel as though I've been waiting for this all my life."

We wonder how Jonah might have felt as he approached the city of Nineveh. Surely nobody here would respond? This will be a total waste of time. They have their own gods. Why should they believe that the God of Israel was about to destroy what was one of the best fortified and largest cities in the world?

We considered the prophet's initial reaction to the commands of God in chapter 24. We know how he was cast into the sea, yet survived almost certain death through divine intervention. In the belly of the fish he declared his willingness to fulfil his vow to serve, acknowledging that "salvation is of the LORD" (Jonah 2:9). He would almost certainly be anticipating a further instruction from the Father to call the Ninevites to repentance. In due course, that command came (3:1).

The Assyrian city of Nineveh

Nineveh was an ancient city built on the eastern bank of the river Tigris. The remains are in modern-day Iraq. It is first mentioned in Genesis 10:11. Asshur went out from Babel and established four cities, one of which was Nineveh. Asshur is the same name which is elsewhere translated Assyria (2:14). The original Asshur was therefore the ancestor of the Assyrians. Nineveh was the capital city of Assyria in the days of Sennacherib (2 Kings 19:36). Archaeology supports Bible teaching regarding the size and importance of the city. It is said that Sennacherib's palace had seventy-one rooms. Not surprisingly, evidence has also been unearthed indicating that the worship of numerous pagan deities was commonplace in the empire.

The Assyrians

The Assyrians were, therefore, an ancient, advanced and powerful people. Fittingly, it appears that the Pharaoh at the time of the exodus was an Assyrian (Isaiah 52:4). Like others who came after him, he saw evidence for the existence of Israel's God, yet refused to respond. In the days of the kings, Menahem ruled over Israel. Pul, the king of Assyria, invaded the land, and demanded payment. He promised to support Menahem as king of Israel if the required levy was paid. The wealthy of the nation were taxed heavily so that the required sum (a thousand talents of silver) might be raised (2 Kings 15:19,20). This would, however, be only a temporary reprieve. A few years later the Assyrians, under king Tiglathpileser, came down again. Many were taken captive, including those from Gilead and Galilee (verse 29).

In the days of Ahaz king of Judah the nations of Israel and Syria united against him. In desperation, he turned to the Assyrians for help, tragically declaring to Tiglathpileser:

"I am thy servant and thy son: come up, and save me out of the hand of the king of Syria, and out of the hand of the king of Israel, which rise up against me." (16:7)

As previously, the Assyrians were content to assist if the price was right. Silver and gold from the house of the Lord was taken and sent to the Assyrians, who then went and attacked Damascus, the chief city of Syria (verses 8,9). If only Ahaz had appealed to the Holy One whose house he had plundered, things might have been very different.

Back in the northern kingdom of Israel, Hoshea had begun to reign (17:1). His name speaks of salvation however his rule was a time of sin, suffering and death. He commenced by agreeing to pay the tax imposed by the Assyrians, yet later turned to the Egyptians for assistance. The king of Assyria learned of this and so Hoshea and all those left in Israel were carried away captive into Assyria (verses 4-6). There would be no way back for them. The return from captivity under men like Nehemiah and Ezra was from Babylon. Those who returned were originally of Judah. The ten-tribe kingdom of Israel was at an end:

> "... until the LORD removed Israel out of his sight, as he had said by all his servants the prophets. So was Israel carried away out of their own land to Assyria unto this day."
>
> (verse 23)

Around this time the Assyrian army swept into the south, seeking to destroy Judah. Hezekiah, the son of Ahaz was ruling from Jerusalem. All the fenced cities of Judah were taken by the enemy, and once more payment was demanded from God's people (18:13,14). The remaining treasures in the Lord's house and the gold which Hezekiah had used to overlay items in the temple was used to pay off the Assyrian king, Sennacherib (verses 15,16).

Later the king sent Rabshakeh, who led the Assyrian army encamping round the walls of Jerusalem. Promises were given by the enemy; threats were made. A letter was written, stating how resistance was fruitless (18:19-19:14). Naturally speaking, things could hardly have been any worse for the faithful in Judah. The enemy appeared about to breach the walls; food was failing. On top of this the king was seriously ill (20:1). However, just when it seemed there was no hope, the Father sent one angel who killed 185,000 Assyrian soldiers (19:35). When Sennacherib returned home he was murdered in the house of his god by two of his sons (verses 36,37).

This would be the turning point as far as the nations of Judah and Assyria were concerned. Never again would God's people be persecuted by the Assyrians. In due course the first major world power, Babylon, would arise. After prolonged warfare throughout the empire, the city of Nineveh fell in 612 BC.

There are two key points which demand our attention as we consider the prophet Jonah and the commission given to him by the Father. Firstly, the destruction and captivity of Israel by Assyria had been foretold by prophets of the Lord (17:23). Secondly, when the initial captivity took place, those in Galilee were amongst the first areas to suffer (15:29).

Can we imagine how Jonah, a prophet of Gath-hepher in Galilee (Joshua 19:13; 2 Kings 14:25) might have felt as he saw the might of Assyria increasing? As we noted in the previous chapter, this is very probably the reason why this servant of the Lord was so reluctant to preach to the Ninevites. If Nineveh was wiped out, then there could be no invasion of Israel and those who Jonah cared about most would be spared.

Disobeying the Father is never acceptable. Jonah had been given an instruction and he should have complied with it. However we can surely sympathise with this reluctant prophet. Like Paul, his heart's desire was that Israel might be saved (Romans 10:1). If only the rest of the nation had loved the things of the truth as much as Jonah, then perhaps there would have been no Assyrian invasion!

Jonah's preaching at Nineveh

Can we imagine the trepidation in Jonah's mind as he approached the city, with its immense gates and high walls? The size of the city is referred to in Jonah 3. As with so many things in this short book, the 'greatness' of Nineveh is emphasized:

> "So Jonah arose, and went unto Nineveh, according to the word of the LORD. Now Nineveh was an exceeding great city of three days' journey." (Jonah 3:3)

Whether this means it would have taken three days to walk from one side to the other, or three days to walk right round it, we cannot be sure. What we do know is that this was a city of monumental proportions. Jonah was, very possibly, the only Israelite in Nineveh. He entered the city and delivered the message of the God of Israel:

> "And Jonah began to enter into the city a day's journey, and he cried, and said, Yet forty days, and Nineveh shall be overthrown." (3:4)

There are many forty-day periods in the Bible. A number of these speak of judgement:

- In Noah's day, rain descended for forty days and forty nights (Genesis 7:4,12).
- Moses remained in the mount, receiving the law from the Lord for forty days and nights on more than one occasion (Deuteronomy 10:10).
- The spies searched out the land for forty days (Numbers 13:25). God's judgement on the nation was that they would wander in the wilderness for forty years, each day for a year (14:34).
- Ezekiel lay on his right side to represent the sins of Judah for forty days (Ezekiel 4:6).
- The Master fasted in the wilderness for forty days (Matthew 4:2).

These represent only some of the forty-day periods in scripture. What surely stands out is that God's word was spoken and His judgements seen. Both of these apply in the case of Jonah. The word of God stated clearly that His judgements would be poured out upon the city and its inhabitants at the end of this time period.

The Ninevites' response

Amazingly, all of the people hearkened to Jonah's words:

> "So the people of Nineveh believed God, and proclaimed a fast, and put on sackcloth, from the greatest of them even to the least of them. For word came unto the king of Nineveh, and he arose from his throne, and he laid his robe from him, and covered him with sackcloth, and sat in ashes."
>
> (Jonah 3:5,6)

Why was it that these Gentiles, from the king right down to the lowliest servant, believed the God of a foreign nation? For the most part the men and women of Israel refused to hearken to His words spoken through the prophets, so why did these Assyrians?

We cannot know for sure, although it is distinctly possible that news of the events of Jonah chapter 1 had reached the city. None would know that Jonah had survived. However, the account of the sea becoming calm as soon as he was thrown overboard would have spread like wildfire. What if, when he arrived at the city, one of the mariners had been there? Can we not picture the scene, as one by one his audience realise that they were listening to the very one of whom they had heard such incredible things? He was the man who had survived the most severe storm the sailors had ever witnessed. Added to this, it seems distinctly possible that his skin would have been bleached by the acid in the fish's belly. He would surely have been a very unusual sight.

Jonah: a type of Christ

The account of Jonah's survival in the belly of the "great fish" and the Ninevites' response to his preaching was quoted by the Lord Jesus Christ. The scribes and Pharisees had demanded of him a sign. He called them "an evil and adulterous generation", and refused their request (Matthew 12:38,39). He did, however, expound a passage of scripture in relation to him:

> "For as Jonas was three days and three nights in the whale's belly; so shall the Son of man be three days and three nights in the heart of the earth. The men of Nineveh shall rise in judgment with this generation, and shall condemn it: because they repented at the preaching of Jonas; and, behold, a greater than Jonas is here." (verses 40,41)

Once more we read of one who was great. This time scripture doesn't speak of an event in the life of Jonah, but of the one whom he typified. Truly Jesus was "greater" than all others.

The repentance of the Ninevites was real. Their words and acts of contrition reflected a genuine feeling of sorrow on their part, and an attempt to manifest their desire that the Almighty might relent. Based on the Master's words, there is a very clear indication that they will be accepted at the judgement seat when others (such as the leaders of his day) will be rejected.

What a sober warning this is for us. Although we live in very different times, with no inspired prophets amongst us, the call for every one is the same. We must believe that great judgements are coming on the earth, and modify our behaviour accordingly.

In Jonah's day the forthcoming destruction of Nineveh was foretold. In the Master's time the outpouring of the might of Rome in AD 70 was prophesied. We believe that great judgements will be seen upon the earth when the Master comes again. Earthquakes will shake the world; all buildings will fall. Many will be slain. A time of warfare, the like of which the world has never seen, will take place. Only then will the Son of God come, with all his holy angels and those who have waited for him, in patience and faith (2 Thessalonians 1:7-10). Although none can be sure, there are numerous signs which indicate to us that this time may well be at the door.

Who then are we most like? The (previously) ignorant Gentiles in Nineveh (Jonah 4:11), or the learned rulers in the Master's day? Lip service is no service at all. The leaders pretended to obey, but the Master could see right through their façade of spirituality. He knew what was in their hearts (Matthew 9:4). The men and women of Nineveh manifested a genuine, reverential belief that the God of Israel possessed the power to destroy and to forgive. They manifested this faith in their actions, and were accepted by Israel's God.

In the age to come there will, of course, be none of the things that divide man from man and nation from nation today. There is a strong indication that a universal language will be spoken in the Millennium (Zephaniah 3:9). One king will reign, instead of many different monarchs and governments (Zechariah 14:9). One set of laws will be applied throughout the earth (verse 16). All will concentrate their efforts on things which are peaceful (Micah 4:3). Even the borders, which are issues of such contention now, will mean nothing. In Jonah's day Assyrians in the city of Nineveh responded to his call. In the age to come these things will be repeated throughout the Middle East – indeed throughout the entire world:

"In that day shall Israel be the third with Egypt and with Assyria, even a blessing in the midst of the land: whom the LORD of hosts shall bless, saying, Blessed be Egypt my people, and Assyria the work of my hands, and Israel mine inheritance." (Isaiah 19:24,25)

The Rechabites

VERY few men have suffered for preaching the truth more than Jeremiah. As Jerusalem was surrounded by the Babylonians, he was condemned as traitor, beaten, imprisoned, and then sustained with the absolute minimal amount of food until the day that the city walls were breached by the enemy.

The task that our Heavenly Father called for Jeremiah to accomplish was an unenviable one: he had to serve the people of Judah with a 'final demand'. This was to be their last opportunity to serve the Lord, to cast off their idols and render unto Him the glory which is His due. As we know, generally speaking, these words went unheeded. There were, however, a few notable exceptions.

One faithful family
In Jeremiah 35 we read of a family descended from Jonadab, the son of Rechab. This family bore the name of the Rechabites, and they were commended by the Father through Jeremiah for their steadfast faith and obedience to their forefather's command. This is arguably one of the greatest ironies in scripture, for these people were Gentiles by their ancestry!

Jeremiah's work was to call Israel to reject the ways of the Gentiles and serve their God in truth. Who hearkened unto him? Who turned from the things of the world and walked as Abraham, Isaac and Jacob? A family who were not even of the house of Israel originally. Who rejected Gentile practices? A

Gentile family! Such tragedy – and irony – would surely not be lost on this great prophet, who would doubtless be comforted by the fact that at least some of his hearers understood and believed his words, and would therefore be saved as a result.

The Gentile ancestry of the Rechabites

Jeremiah 35 describes in detail the prophet's dealings with this family. Yet nowhere in this chapter do we read the word 'Gentile', or the name of any Gentile nation from which the forebears of these people had come. Our only indication is in verse 7, where the men of this family speak of dwelling as "strangers" in the land. One other passage, however, provides a vital link:

> "And the families of the scribes which dwelt at Jabez; the Tirathites, the Shimeathites, and Suchathites. These are the Kenites that came of Hemath, the father of the house of Rechab." (1 Chronicles 2:55)

This one verse puts a different complexion on Jeremiah 35: Hemath, the father of the Rechabites was a Gentile. He was a Kenite who had come to Israel and as other Gentiles such as Caleb, Rahab, Ruth and Uriah, had become incorporated into the nation.

Three families are listed here. Their names never appear again in scripture, nor do we read of Jabez, where they dwelt. However, the fact that they were scribes, or recorders, is surely of note. Here were men who presumably wrote out the law; more importantly, here were men who knew, loved and applied the law, unlike many round about them.

The Kenites

The nation of the Kenites, from which the Rechabites had come, is mentioned a number of times in the Old Testament. However, unlike other Gentile nations, they do not appear to have been openly hostile towards God's people:

- Jethro, Moses' father-in-law was Kenite (see chapter 7), though he lived in Midian (Judges 1:16).

- Some of his descendants lived among the Israelites (verse 16). Possibly they were the Rechabites' ancestors.
- Heber was a Kenite; he and his wife Jael (see chapter 12) had severed themselves from the nation (4:11,17).
- When Saul was about to attack an Amalekite city he gave the Kenites who dwelled there the opportunity to flee (1 Samuel 15:6), citing the kindness they had shown to Israel when they had come out of Egypt (see chapter 8).

God's covenant with Abraham

The very first occasion we read of this people in scripture demands our attention. In Genesis 15 we have the record of the covenant that the Father established with Abraham. Parts of animals were divided, and a smoking furnace and burning lamp passed between them. After this the Lord declared that He would give the land to Abraham's seed (verse 18); He then identifies the nations who would be dispossessed in order for this to take place:

"The Kenites, and the Kenizzites, and the Kadmonites, and the Hittites, and the Perizzites, and the Rephaims, and the Amorites, and the Canaanites, and the Girgashites, and the Jebusites." (verses 19-21)

The very first nation mentioned in this list is the Kenites. The Lord could not have been any more forceful in emphasizing those who would *not* inherit this land. According to His covenant with Abraham, the Promised Land should been have been cleared of Kenites. Yet in the days of Jeremiah, one faithful family, whose ancestors had come from this nation, dwelled therein. As we shall see they were more like Abraham than any from Israel. Truly, in their hearts, they were Abraham's seed.

Genesis 15 describes one of the most important incidents in Abraham's life: as well as the covenant being made, a promise was given regarding the seed being of Abraham's own bowels, and as the stars in the sky for multitude. These were established by the cutting of the pieces of the dead animals, and the amazing things that followed. The smoking furnace and burning lamp, surely a representation of Jesus Christ, the light of the world

(John 8:12), passed between the parts. This pattern is only mentioned once more in scripture, and this forms the background to Jeremiah 35.

In Jeremiah 34, we read of events in the days of Judah's last king, Zedekiah. Families who had servants also of Judah made a covenant, under which these men and women were given their freedom (verses 8-10). They even emulated the events of Genesis 15, cutting animals in two and walking between the parts (Jeremiah 34:18). However, this promise was broken very quickly:

> "But afterward they turned, and caused the servants and the handmaids, whom they had let go free, to return, and brought them into subjection for servants and for handmaids."
>
> (verse 11)

In their actions they sought to replicate the events in the life of Abraham; in their hearts they could not have been less like him. As a result of their inconsistency and hypocrisy in proclaiming freedom but delivering bondage, they, along with their king, would be taken by the Babylonians and either slain or carried away captive (verses 19-22).

The timescale of Jeremiah 34 and 35

We now move back to consider chapter 35, and are faced by something rather unusual in the very first verse. Chapter 35 steps back in time, from the reign of Zedekiah (Judah's last king) in chapter 34 (34:2), to the days of Jehoiakim, who had reigned a short time before, in chapter 35 (35:1). Why is this the case? Surely it is to draw a contrast between those in chapter 34 who made a covenant and broke it almost immediately, and those in chapter 35 who were obedient to the commandment of their ancestor over many years.

Jeremiah was instructed by the Lord to take the family of the Rechabites into the temple, and give them wine to drink. The prophet's invitation was greeted with steadfast refusal on the part of these men:

> "But they said, We will drink no wine: for Jonadab the son of Rechab our father commanded us, saying, Ye shall drink no

wine, neither ye, nor your sons for ever: neither shall ye build house, nor sow seed, nor plant vineyard, nor have any: but all your days ye shall dwell in tents; that ye may live many days in the land where ye be strangers. Thus have we obeyed the voice of Jonadab the son of Rechab our father in all that he hath charged us …" (verses 6-8)

Jonadab, the father of the Rechabites
Who then was Jonadab, and why did he command his descendants to act in such a way? It is in 2 Kings 10 that we read of events in the life of this man.

In the dark days following the reign of Ahab, Elisha sent a man of the sons of the prophets to anoint Jehu as king of Israel (9:1-3). Once this had taken place, Jehu wasted no time in purging the nation of the sins of Ahab's house. He oversaw the killing of:
- Joram (also called Jehoram), the king of Israel (verse 24).
- Ahaziah, the king of Judah (verse 27).
- Jezebel, the power behind the throne (verse 33).
- The seventy sons of Ahab in Samaria (10:7).
- Ahaziah's forty-two brothers (verse 14).

His work was not yet complete, however, for having purged the monarchy, he turned his attention to the corrupt religious leaders: the prophets of Baal. As he was en route to exact this further act of judgement, he met a man coming towards him. That man was Jonadab (rendered here Jehonadab), the father of the Rechabites:

"And when he was departed thence, he lighted on Jehonadab the son of Rechab coming to meet him: and he saluted him, and said to him, Is thine heart right, as my heart is with thy heart? And Jehonadab answered, It is. If it be, give me thine hand. And he gave him his hand; and he took him up to him into the chariot. And he said, Come with me, and see my zeal for the LORD. So they made him ride in his chariot."
(2 Kings 10:15,16)

Jehu's question for this man was very clear: is your heart right? Do you believe truth as I do? Will you apply that truth in your life? When a positive answer was received, Jonadab was welcomed into the chariot to share in the work of purification.

These events find a parallel in our own lives. Having declared that we believe "the things concerning the kingdom of God, and the name of Jesus Christ" (Acts 8:12) we are given the "right hand of fellowship" (Galatians 2:9), and permitted to travel in the vessel – the ecclesia. In Old Testament times, "giving the hand" was a symbol for establishing a covenant (see Ezekiel 17:18).

Why was Jonadab on his way to meet Jehu? The king, as we know, was about to kill the worshippers of Baal; perhaps Jonadab was to be a witness to these events, to ensure that everything was done correctly. The law required that if any man was to be put to death two or three witnesses were required (Deuteronomy 17:6), so Jonadab went into the house of Baal with Jehu, probably to confirm that only worshippers of Baal were present (2 Kings 10:23).

The failings of Jehu's reign

Whatever the reason for Jonadab's presence that day, we can imagine that the things he saw would have left an indelible impression on his mind. He would never have forgotten those scenes of horror; perhaps more importantly he would have remembered how Jehu failed to live up to the high standard he had shown at the commencement of his reign.

This may be one of the reasons why Jonadab was so opposed to the drinking of wine. Did Jehu have a drink problem? We know he was a man who did everything with all his might: he rode a chariot as he lived his life – "furiously" in 2 Kings 9:20 (literally with "craziness": this Hebrew word only appears in two other places in the Old Testament, and is translated "madness" in Deuteronomy 28:28 and Zechariah 12:4). What did Jehu do when Jezebel was thrown down?

"And when he was come in, he did eat and drink ..."

(2 Kings 9:34)

Maybe eating – and more particularly drinking – permitted this new king the freedom to indulge his own personal preferences. It could be that Jonadab knew that it was drinking to excess that had caused Jehu to be swayed from the path upon which he had originally set his feet (10:29-31). Hence Jonadab commanded all his descendants to avoid this terrible scourge.

Jonadab's command for all his household

We have seen what Jonadab didn't want for his family. What did he want for them? As we already noted, he wanted them to live in the land promised to Abraham, the land where he acknowledged they were but "strangers" (Jeremiah 35:7).

His commands were stringent indeed: avoid alcohol, don't build houses, own fields or vineyards, and live all your days in tents. Do this, said Jonadab, and you will live in the land for many years. Whose example did Jonadab want his children to emulate? Ask the youngest Sunday school scholar at your ecclesia to name a man who lived in a tent, and he or she will surely answer: Abraham. The connections between these two men are unmistakable:

"For I know him, that he will command his children and his household after him, and they shall keep the way of the LORD, to do justice and judgment; that the LORD may bring upon Abraham that which he hath spoken of him." (Genesis 18:19)

Jonadab's role model was Abraham: both men commanded their households after them to keep the way of the Lord. Both households obeyed these instructions, dwelling in tents in a land that was not theirs, in faith (see Hebrews 11:9).

There is, in fact, a remarkable connection in the Law of Moses with the actions and words of Jonadab:

"Honour thy father and thy mother: that thy days may be long upon the land which the LORD thy God giveth thee."

(Exodus 20:12)

The Rechabites *did* honour their father, their days *were* prolonged, and they *did* dwell many years in the land. Once again, we are surely struck by how unusual this is: Gentiles keeping Israel's law, following the example of the ancestor of the nation, and serving Israel's God, whilst all the time they were surrounded by Israelites acting as the Gentile nations!

A life of steadfast service

How the Rechabites survived throughout the ages, without fields to plant, we are not told. Possibly they gleaned, or did manual labour. We know that they were scribes, so they could have made a living by copying out the law. What we do know is that all Jonadab's children obeyed; his grandchildren obeyed and great-grandchildren – indeed approximately 250 years elapsed between 2 Kings 10 and Jeremiah 35, and the descendants of this man remained obedient to his commands. With snow on the ground, they still lived in tents, refusing to own land or buildings, and refusing any alcoholic drink.

We are left in no doubt as to how their faithfulness was regarded by our Heavenly Father:

> "Thus saith the LORD of hosts, the God of Israel; Go and tell the men of Judah and the inhabitants of Jerusalem, Will ye not receive instruction to hearken to my words? saith the LORD. The words of Jonadab the son of Rechab, that he commanded his sons not to drink wine, are performed; for unto this day they drink none, but obey their father's commandment: notwithstanding I have spoken unto you, rising early and speaking; but ye hearkened not unto me."
>
> (Jeremiah 35:13,14)

Surely this is why chapter 35 appears where it does. Chapter 34 describes the faithlessness of the nation of Judah, how a covenant was made and broken. Chapter 35 presents to the nation of Israel – and to us – the contrast between those who denied their God, and those who served Him year after year, keeping the covenant their father had imposed upon his house, "steadfast, immovable", for 250 years.

The Lord's promise to the Rechabites

At the end of our chapter the Father blesses this family:

"And Jeremiah said unto the house of the Rechabites, Thus saith the LORD of hosts, the God of Israel; Because ye have obeyed the commandment of Jonadab your father, and kept all his precepts, and done according unto all that he hath commanded you: therefore thus saith the LORD of hosts, the God of Israel; Jonadab the son of Rechab shall not want a man to stand before me for ever." (verses 18,19)

We can perhaps imagine the great prophet Jeremiah delivering these words with an ironic smile. All around him were faithless Jews; yet this family of faithful Gentiles were to dwell in the land "for ever"! Once again, we are being directed back to the man in whose footsteps Jonadab sought to walk: Abraham.

The phrase "shall not want" in verse 19 is better rendered "there shall not be cut off". That Hebrew word appears almost 300 times in the Old Testament, and is normally translated "cut", "cut off" or "make". The second use in scripture takes us to Genesis 15 once again:

"In the same day the LORD made (literally, 'cut'; same Hebrew as 'shall not want') a covenant with Abram ..."

(Genesis 15:18)

The Father said to Abraham that He was 'cutting', or 'making' a covenant with him, part of which involved the 'cutting off' of the Gentiles. As we saw previously, the very first nation which should have been cut off were the Kenites (verse 19). Yet some Kenites were not cut off. Jonadab, his sons and his daughters followed the pattern of the life of Abraham to perfection, and were therefore grafted in to the nation of Israel because of their faith, enjoying Israel's hope.

A Psalm sung by the Rechabites

The final two references to Rechabites in scripture emphasize this principle yet further.

The headings to the Psalms often give us insight into the mind of the Psalmist or the circumstances he may have experienced in his life. There is no heading to Psalm 71 in the KJV, but in the Septuagint version we read the following:

"A Psalm sung by the sons of Jonadab and the first that were taken captive."

It is a beautiful, powerful, moving Psalm, speaking of the certainty that the Father will save His people. If indeed this Psalm was sung by Jonadab's house, then perhaps they sang one verse with particular feeling:

"Now also when I am old and grayheaded, O God, forsake me not; until I have shewed thy strength unto this generation, and thy power to every one that is to come."   (Psalm 71:18)

This is exactly what Jonadab did! He showed his children what was to come, and through their love and respect for him, and their faith in the God they served, they were obedient to his command.

The Rechabite who returned from captivity

The last occasion we read of this family is in Nehemiah 3. The Babylonian captivity had taken place, and then in Nehemiah's day the opportunity to return presented itself to those living under Persian rule. One who chose to return was a Rechabite. Despite being taken out of Judah, back into the Gentile world from which his ancestors had come so many years before, he remained a son of Abraham in his heart, and desired to return to Jerusalem when the opportunity came.

"But the dung gate repaired Malchiah the son of Rechab, the ruler of part of Bethhaccerem; he built it, and set up the doors thereof, the locks thereof, and the bars thereof."

(Nehemiah 3:14)

Surely when people dispersed around the city walls and selected a part or gate to repair, Malchiah would have been on his own! The "dung gate" means exactly that: the place where the refuse was removed from the city. Malchiah the Rechabite was willing to do this most menial job. Yet he was a "ruler": his name means 'king of Yah'. We are reminded of our ruler – our king appointed and anointed by Israel's God, who humbled himself and performed the most menial, degrading task, that of laying down his own life, that he might be exalted in due course and that we may be exalted with him, by grace.

Malchiah was the ruler of Bethhaccerem: it means 'the house of the vineyard'! Even if vines grew there, and even if wine was produced, it is unlikely that this man ever tasted of it. His faithfulness to Jonadab's command made 350 years previously, would surely have been manifested to all who were around him.

"Written for our learning"
What, then, are the lessons for us from this faithful family? The Rechabites were obedient to the words of their forefather. The word of God records for us the words and works of our ancestors, those who have trodden the path before us – men and women whose example we seek to emulate. Are we as obedient to our Heavenly Father as the Rechabites were to Him, and to Jonadab? Do we maintain our stand, regardless of what those round about us may do and say? Do we seek to walk in the footsteps of Abraham, as strangers and pilgrims, acknowledging that here we have no continuing city, but we seek one to come (Hebrews 13:14)? Do we follow the example of our Lord and Master, performing the degrading jobs, the tasks that others may shy away from?

If only we can remain true to the promise that we made at baptism, shunning the things of this age, and looking with the eye of faith to the kingdom that is yet to come, then when Abraham rises from the dust to inherit the land, with Jonadab and his children, then we shall be there as part of that great seed, united with our Lord for ever.

27

Ebed-melech the Ethiopian

HOW terribly so many of the servants of our God have suffered in ages past. They were mocked, scourged, laid in bonds and in prison. They were stoned, dismembered, tempted or put to the sword. They had no home to call their own and wandered, wearing the most basic of clothing, being "destitute, afflicted, tormented" (Hebrews 11:36,37). Of these great, courageous, resilient men and women, the writer was inspired to say "the world was not worthy" (verse 38). Such a man, without question, was Jeremiah.

Jeremiah was called upon to deliver what was, for the nation of Judah, a 'final demand'. Serve the Lord acceptably, put aside your idols, and you will be blessed (Jeremiah 18:11). His words went largely unheeded, and for daring to relay the message of the Almighty to the people of Jerusalem he was mocked, beaten and starved. Finally, he was lowered into a vile, stinking pit, sinking into the mire which lay at its bottom.

Yet, just when it seemed things couldn't possibly get any worse and all hope was lost, help arrived. Jews had caused his suffering, acting in the most Gentile of ways, but an Ethiopian, by the name of Ebed-melech, one of the king's servants, came to his aid. This great irony would not have been lost on the prophet. Outside the walls of Jerusalem the Gentile armies were gathering. Inside, surrounded by Jews acting in the most worldly of ways, one faithful Gentile risked his life to save the prophet of the Lord.

The background to the appearance of Ebed-melech

Josiah, arguably Judah's greatest king, had died in battle. His death was mourned by all, but most especially by Jeremiah (2 Chronicles 35:24,25). A number of his descendants reigned after him; all were pale imitations (2 Kings 23:30,34; 24:6). Last of all came Zedekiah, his third son to sit on the throne that his father had once graced (verse 17). This, for the nation of Judah, was the beginning of the end, and Jeremiah knew it.

As in AD 70 (see the Master's words in Mark 13:14 about the people fleeing when the Romans came), the army of the Chaldeans retreated from the city (Jeremiah 37:5). In due course they would return, as foretold by Jeremiah. During this short time of apparent ease, Jeremiah tried to leave the city. In doing so he was wrongly condemned as a collaborator, arrested and taken to the princes. They beat and imprisoned him (verses 13-16).

Shortly afterwards the king came to see him and he was permitted to remain in "the court of the prison", sustained by one piece of bread per day until the city walls were breached (verse 21). Jesus encouraged his disciples to pray for their "daily bread" (Matthew 6:11). For Jeremiah, this was a reality. Like the Master, who was arrested and accused of "perverting the nation" (Luke 23:2), Jeremiah suffered at the hands of the leaders of the nation simply for speaking the truth.

Jeremiah: the suffering servant

Tragically, this time of relative respite for the prophet was not to last. His enemies approached the king, stating that his constant assertions that the Babylonians would take the city were bad for morale. He should be punished. He had to be silenced. The king's response was almost unbelievable:

> "Then Zedekiah the king said, Behold, he (Jeremiah) is in your hand: for the king is not he that can do any thing against you."
> (Jeremiah 38:5)

Just like Pilate (Matthew 27:23,24), this spineless, cowardly man knew what was right and yet, for fear of those who were baying for blood, claimed that his hands were tied. Jeremiah was at the mercy of his enemies once again:

> "Then took they Jeremiah, and cast him into the dungeon of Malchiah the son of Hammelech, that was in the court of the prison: and they let down Jeremiah with cords. And in the dungeon there was no water, but mire: so Jeremiah sunk in the mire." (Jeremiah 38:6)

Why did they not stone him, as required by the law? Why did they not throw him into the mire head first? Very simply, they wanted him to suffer. Drowning in mud would have been 'too good for him'; they were determined that this should drag out.

This dungeon may well have been some sort of well. The same Hebrew word is translated "well" in 2 Samuel 23:15, where David longed for water from the well of Bethlehem. So what should have been life-giving in fact became a place of suffering and death. Was there water in this well? If the Lamentations are a commentary on this time of agony, it seems so:

> "They have cut off my life in the dungeon, and cast a stone upon me. Waters flowed over mine head; then I said, I am cut off." (Lamentations 3:53,54)

During this most horrendous of times, Jeremiah prayed (Lamentations 3:55) and, unsurprisingly, he wept. Yet his tears were not of self-pity; rather they were shed for the people of Jerusalem, and the agony which would come upon God's people:

> "Mine eye runneth down with rivers of water for the destruction of the daughter of my people." (verse 48)

What a remarkable man he was, and a type of the Master: for Jesus also wept, not for the suffering that he knew would come upon him, but for all that would happen to the city and people of Jerusalem in AD 70 (Luke 19:41).

We are reminded of the words of David in Psalm 40, who also spoke of being in "miry clay" (verse 2). "Clay" is the same Hebrew word as "mire" in Jeremiah 38:6. David was also lied about (Psalm 40:4) yet, like Jeremiah (Jeremiah 20:9), God's law was within his heart (Psalm 40:8).

Ebed-melech the Ethiopian

We do not know how long Jeremiah was entombed in that place of death. What we do know is that deliverance came from a man who, naturally speaking, had no association with the people of Israel:

> "Now when Ebed-melech the Ethiopian, one of the eunuchs which was in the king's house, heard that they had put Jeremiah in the dungeon ... Ebed-melech went forth out of the king's house, and spake to the king, saying, My lord the king, these men have done evil in all that they have done to Jeremiah the prophet, whom they have cast into the dungeon; and he is like to die for hunger in the place where he is ..."
> (Jeremiah 38:7-9)

Ebed-melech appears to be a title rather than a name. It means 'servant of a king', and indeed he was – however the king he served and feared was the one who dwells in heaven. As a servant, or probably a bondslave, of Zedekiah, he would have had no rights. Daring to question the king's judgements could have resulted in his death. Siding with Jeremiah when all the princes had determined that he was worthy of such punishment was a brave, some might say foolhardy, move. It would have been normal for any man who declared sympathy for the one in the mire to have been made to join him. Yet Ebed-melech was a brave man, and the God of Israel blessed him for his courage and faith.

We see that he was a eunuch. Just like the man who met Philip in Acts 8:26-39, this Ethiopian was unable to father children. Some might have described him as 'dead'. His family line could continue no further. Yet the promises to Abraham speak of life, fellowship and a family for any who choose serve the Father in truth (Genesis 12:3), regardless of their nationality. Indeed, in the prophecy of Isaiah we find words of power and comfort regarding eunuchs:

> "Neither let the son of the stranger, that hath joined himself to the LORD, speak, saying, The LORD hath utterly separated me from his people: neither let the eunuch say, Behold, I am a dry tree. For thus saith the LORD unto the eunuchs that keep

my sabbaths, and choose the things that please me, and take hold of my covenant; even unto them will I give in mine house and within my walls a place and a name better than of sons and of daughters: I will give them an everlasting name, that shall not be cut off." (Isaiah 56:3-5)

How beautifully these words describe the faithful eunuch in Jeremiah's day, Ebed-melech the Ethiopian.

Ethiopia

This nation is mentioned many times in the Old Testament. Its people were often hostile towards Israel. The original name is "Cush"; this is occasionally left untranslated in scripture (as in Genesis 10:6). As with many of the enemies of Israel, these people were descended from Ham; Cush was his firstborn son and the father of Nimrod (verse 8).

Prior to Jeremiah's day, the Assyrians had taken many Ethiopians captive, as foretold in Isaiah 20:3-5. In the days of Esther the land was incorporated into the Medo-Persian Empire (Esther 1:1; 8:9).

At the time of the end Ethiopia will be allied with the King of the North (Ezekiel 38:5; Daniel 11:43). After the Master has been manifested upon the earth and the Millennium commences, Jews will flock to Israel having come from, amongst other lands, Ethiopia (Isaiah 11:11; Zephaniah 3:10).

There is one key passage which is particularly apt as we consider the actions of this faithful Ethiopian:

"Can the Ethiopian change his skin, or the leopard his spots? then may ye also do good, that are accustomed to do evil."

(Jeremiah 13:23)

The second of these rhetorical questions has made its way into our own language. A leopard never changes its spots. What this teaches is that some people are simply unchangeable. They act in the worst possible ways. No matter what is done or said by anyone else, no matter what the consequences of their actions may be or the punishments which are meted out upon them, they refuse to amend their ways.

Leopards do not change in appearance, and neither do Ethiopians. A man from Ethiopia, whose skin is very dark, is virtually unaffected by the sun. Yet a man with very light and sensitive skin will need to be extremely careful when the sun is strong, as his skin will burn very easily. At the end of a day in the sun such a man will look very different from at the beginning!

What was our Heavenly Father saying to the people of Judah? Was it not that they were, quite simply, beyond repentance. It is as though they were so steeped in sin, so used to doing wrong, that they had reached the point where they were unable to stop, even if they had wished to. The events in Jeremiah 37 and 38 support this; their minds were set only on sin. They were beyond change. Yet an Ethiopian showed them how they should have been acting in his love extended toward God's faithful prophet.

Jeremiah is raised from the dungeon

At last Zedekiah appeared to grasp the seriousness of the situation. Ebed-melech's appeal was accepted and, with thirty men, he went to the mouth of the dungeon. Cords were lowered down and the prophet was raised (Jeremiah 38:13). We can picture this Gentile's hand being extended in love towards Jeremiah, who was raised up from what had almost become his grave. The words of Isaiah are particularly appropriate here:

> "I the LORD have called thee in righteousness, and will hold thine hand, and will keep thee, and give thee for a covenant of the people, for a light of the Gentiles; to open the blind eyes, to bring out the prisoners from the prison, and them that sit in darkness out of the prison house." (Isaiah 42:6,7)

As Jeremiah reached the mouth of the dungeon, Ebed-melech held his hand, and he came out of the darkness and into the light. This Gentile man had truly been enlightened, and he responded to what he knew by rescuing the faithful prophet.

What exhortation there is in the example of this faithful Gentile servant. He went to Jeremiah in prison. He ministered to him, bringing comfort and joy. This is what the Master said we should do, for in caring for each other we are, in symbol, caring for him (Matthew 25:36). May we be found at the judgement seat having been willing to care for our fellow members of the ecclesia, emulating the example of those faithful men and women who have gone before us.

The blessing of Ebed-melech by Israel's God

The commencement of Jeremiah 39 describes the time the prophet had foretold. The walls of Jerusalem were breached. The king saw the enemy and fled, only to be captured in the plains of Jericho. Many of the people were killed; others were carried away captive into Babylon, and only the poorest of the land remained (verses 1-10). It was, surely, one of the saddest days in the long history of this unique nation. God's people had refused the call to be separate. They had worshipped idols. As a result they would be carried away to a land which was absolutely full of idols. They had lusted after the things of the world. The Father determined that they should be taken to the most worldly place of all.

Yet during this time of sorrow, two remarkable things are recorded. Firstly, Jeremiah was cared for. At the instruction of Nebuchadnezzar himself, and possibly at the instigation of Daniel, the prophet was not to be mistreated; rather he would be given the freedom to dwell where he chose (verses 11-14).

Secondly, we read words of power and comfort regarding Ebed-melech. Verses 15-18 of chapter 39 step back in time to when Jeremiah had been raised and the armies were still outside the city:

> "Now the word of the LORD came unto Jeremiah, while he was shut up in the court of the prison, saying, Go and speak to Ebed-melech the Ethiopian, saying, Thus saith the LORD of hosts, the God of Israel; Behold, I will bring my words upon this city for evil … But I will deliver thee in that day, saith the LORD: and thou shalt not be given into the hand of the men of whom thou art afraid … thy life shall be for a prey unto thee: because thou hast put thy trust in me, saith the LORD."
>
> (verses 15-18)

So this man who had saved Jeremiah would reap the rewards of his bravery. He would be delivered. Of whom was he afraid? Was it the men of Jerusalem, who had sworn revenge on him for the kindness he showed to Jeremiah? Was it the men of Babylon? Was it both? We are not told; all we do know is that this man was to be spared because he conquered his fear. Unlike Zedekiah, who was afraid and permitted that terror to conquer him (38:19), Ebed-melech acted as he did despite his fear, and was blessed by the mighty one of Israel.

As a reward for the love shown to Jeremiah, Ebed-melech's life was to be granted unto him as "a prey". This means 'booty'; the Hebrew word is normally translated "spoil":

"Behold, the day of the LORD cometh, and thy spoil (same word) shall be divided in the midst of thee." (Zechariah 14:1)

While the Babylonians were helping themselves to the spoils of war, this servant's life was spared, and he was granted his freedom. He had heard the words of truth from the prophet of the Lord, and had responded. Regardless of what others may have done or said, he determined to associate himself with the suffering servant of God, and was blessed for his faith.

The lesson of the life of Ebed-melech for us

We live in very different times from those described in scripture. The challenges we face are, surely, nothing like the ones faced by the inhabitants of Jerusalem as the Babylonians encamped outside. It is unlikely we shall ever face the kind of horrors endured by the faithful at that time, or that we shall have to endanger our own lives by seeking to rescue someone who has been wrongly imprisoned. We have no prophets living amongst us who are able to speak the words of the Lord. Rather, we have His inspired word of truth, from which we can, and must, learn. Yet the attitude of Ebed-melech to the issues of his day, his courageous response to the needs of the prophet and the words of the Father to him through Jeremiah, do connect with our own lives of service.

Much as we cannot 'earn' salvation, for it is a free gift, through grace (Ephesians 2:8), our God demands that we seek to bring forth fruit unto Him (Colossians 1:10), shinning as lights whilst the world around us is dark (Matthew 5:14). Our Heavenly Father has called us to great things and promised us that, despite the problems and dangers of this age, we shall never be left or forsaken (Romans 8:31-39).

If we are willing, like the faithful of old, to put our trust in Him, we shall be blessed with life. As Ebed-melech was granted freedom – his life was given him as a gift – so we hope and pray that the gift of eternal life will be granted to us, when the Master comes again. May it be our privilege in that great day to meet with those faithful Gentiles of old, as the world is transformed under the righteous rule of our beloved Master.

> "And in that day there shall be a root of Jesse, which shall stand for an ensign of the people; to it shall the Gentiles seek: and his rest shall be glorious." (Isaiah 11:10)

In the days of Daniel

HOW easy it is for us to form the wrong impression. How often have we thought we knew what was going on and why, only to realise afterwards that our assumptions were totally incorrect? It is certainly possible for us to do this with the word of God. Prayerful, careful, regular reading is absolutely essential if we are not to miss the true message.

During the captivity some of the Jews achieved positions of great responsibility. Daniel was one of the most powerful men in Babylon. Esther and Mordecai were similarly mighty under the kings of the Medes and Persians. Jeremiah had written to those in captivity telling them not to expect an early return. Rather they were to build houses, settle down and seek the peace of the nation in which they dwelled (Jeremiah 29:1-7).

Based upon passages such as these, it would be easy for us to build up a picture of a people in complete contentment. They were living in peace. They were part of a mighty and powerful empire. Opportunities were open for them to enjoy what the world of their day had to offer. As we know from the prayer of Daniel in chapter 9, this was not the case. Daniel prayed every day facing the city of Jerusalem (6:10). When he read the words of Jeremiah regarding the desolation of the city and the timescale thereof, he mourned greatly. Despite his undoubted position of wealth and privilege in Babylon, he never regarded himself as a Babylonian. In the book of the Psalms we are left in no doubt as to the mindset of many of the faithful in the time of their captivity:

> "By the rivers of Babylon, there we sat down, yea, we wept, when we remembered Zion ... How shall we sing the LORD's song in a strange land? If I forget thee, O Jerusalem, let my right hand forget her cunning. If I do not remember thee, let my tongue cleave to the roof of my mouth; if I prefer not Jerusalem above my chief joy." (Psalm 137:1,4-6)

Others doubtless were content to embrace everything that city life had to offer in Babylon. The faithful of Judah refused these things. This was demonstrated by the refusal of Daniel and his three fellow Jews to comply with Babylonian laws which contradicted those of Israel. Separation was essential (2 Corinthians 6:14-18). The difference between the holy and profane had to be maintained (Ezekiel 44:23). In the land of their captivity, those who loved the things of the truth sought to manifest this to those Gentiles round about them. On a few key occasions, this difference was noted.

Daniel's arrival in Babylon

From the moment captives arrived in the city, they were left in no doubt as to their new status. They were now Babylonian. This is highlighted by the fact that the four young men who had come from Jerusalem were given new names:

> "Unto whom the prince of the eunuchs gave names: for he gave unto Daniel the name of Belteshazzar; and to Hananiah, of Shadrach; and to Mishael, of Meshach; and to Azariah, of Abednego." (Daniel 1:7)

Daniel's response was clear: he "purposed in his heart" not to be defiled (verse 8). The word translated "purposed" is a very common Old Testament word, meaning 'to put'. It is the same as "gave" in verse 7. So the rulers in Babylon sought to put a new name on their captives. A new way of thinking was imposed on the minds of those from other lands. Daniel deliberately and consciously put the things of the truth on his heart, symbolically clothing himself in that which spoke of Israel.

Like Joseph before him (Genesis 39:1-6), Daniel was blessed in his place of captivity:

"Now God had brought Daniel into favour and tender love with the prince of the eunuchs." (Daniel 1:9)

This man was genuinely concerned for his own, and Daniel's, well-being. When Daniel refused to eat of the king's meat he expressed his doubts. If their requested diet of pulse resulted in their looking ill, then questions would be asked. Daniel asked that they be permitted to eat pulse for a trial period of ten days, after which a decision would be made:

"And at the end of ten days their countenances appeared fairer and fatter in flesh than all the children which did eat the portion of the king's meat. Thus Melzar took away the portion of their meat, and the wine that they should drink; and gave them pulse." (verses 15,16)

What took place was surely a miracle. A diet of vegetables would never result in someone being "fatter in flesh" than others who ate meat. Daniel's bodily frame reflected his faithfulness. He sought that which was holy and true, and he was blessed with a body of unnatural healthiness and vigour.

Others were similarly blessed. Moses was one hundred and twenty and yet as strong as he had been when he was young, with 20/20 vision (Deuteronomy 34:7). Samson was not strong because he had immense muscles. If he looked like some modern-day bodybuilder, why would Delilah have asked where his strength came from (Judges 16:6)? He was strong because the spirit of the Lord moved him (13:25; 14:6). In all of these examples, we are reminded of things yet to come. The promise of immortality is of a nature no longer afflicted by the weakness of the flesh. We shall, by grace "run and not be weary ... walk, and not faint" (Isaiah 40:31), being made "partakers of the divine nature" (2 Peter 1:4).

This miraculous, abnormal degree of health would have been noted by the prince of the eunuchs. Whether he was moved to ask of the God whom Daniel served, we are not told. What we do know is that he witnessed the result of God's blessing in the bodies of these faithful young Jewish men. They were physically and mentally superior to others who stood in the presence of the king, and he knew why.

Before Nebuchadnezzar
It is hard for us to imagine what life must have been like in the courts of a man like Nebuchadnezzar. He was a dictator, in the fullest sense of the word. When the meaning of the dream of the image was revealed to him he was told, "Thou art this head of gold" (Daniel 2:38). What the king said, went; he was not hamstrung by the laws of the land, as were the kings of the Medes and Persians. Yet even in his presence, these faithful captives were careful not only to do the right thing, but to make sure the reasons for their actions were known.

When the command went forth regarding the king's dream, Daniel requested time that he and his companions might take the matter to God in prayer. When the Father revealed the dream and its meaning, Daniel made a point of thanking God first before approaching Nebuchadnezzar (verses 20-23). It is the words of Daniel before the king which demand our attention, however. Nebuchadnezzar asked Daniel whether it was really true that he could reveal the dream and its meaning. This great man of faith was careful to explain that alone he could do nothing. Only because of the blessing of his God was he able to reveal the matter:

> "Daniel answered in the presence of the king, and said, The secret which the king hath demanded cannot the wise men, the astrologers, the magicians, the soothsayers, shew unto the king; but there is a God in heaven that revealeth secrets, and maketh known to the king Nebuchadnezzar what shall be in the latter days …" (verses 27,28)

When the dream and its meaning were revealed, the king was truly moved:

> "The king answered unto Daniel, and said, Of a truth it is, that your God is a God of gods, and a Lord of kings, and a revealer of secrets, seeing thou couldest reveal this secret." (verse 47)

Here we have the most powerful man on earth praising the God of Israel. Although Babylon had taken captives from many nations, the king, at least at this stage, appears to acknowledge that all his pagan gods were nothing. He realised that only someone blessed by the mighty one of Abraham, Isaac and Jacob had been able to reveal the dream and its meaning.

The fiery furnace

We need not dwell long upon the events of Daniel chapter 3. We know how a new law was passed, insisting that all bowed down to Nebuchadnezzar's golden image. Previously he had been told that he was the head of gold. This, for the king, was insufficient. He wanted his empire to continue for ever. Only part of an image was not enough.

Daniel's three companions refused to bow before the image of the king. When they were challenged regarding this, they stated very clearly the reason for their actions. The king gave them opportunity to reconsider, daring to state "… who is that God that shall deliver you out of my hands?" (Daniel 3:15).

Had he remembered nothing from the events recorded in chapter 2? Could a God able to reveal and interpret dreams not save from a furnace? The response of these three men spelled out the facts to the king:

"Shadrach, Meshach, and Abednego, answered and said to the king, O Nebuchadnezzar, we are not careful to answer thee in this matter. If it be so, our God whom we serve is able to deliver us from the burning fiery furnace, and he will deliver us out of thine hand, O king. But if not, be it known unto thee, O king, that we will not serve thy gods, nor worship the golden image which thou hast set up." (3:16-18)

Just like Daniel in chapter 1, they stated with clarity and power the reason for their actions. They were not anarchists. They were not disobeying simply because they wanted a change of government. They refused to keep the king's law because it would have necessitated their breaking the laws of their God. The truth was not solely something they believed; it was something they preached and manifested (John 3:21).

They were saved from the furnace by a "son of God", whose brightness outshone all that was around him (Daniel 3:25). This prompted the king to make a decree which echoed his words at the end of chapter 2:

"… every people, nation, and language, which speak any thing amiss against the God of Shadrach, Meshach, and Abednego, shall be cut in pieces, and their houses shall be made a dunghill: because there is no other God that can deliver after this sort." (3:29)

This great and mighty ruler had been shown once more that there is only one true God, and that He can and will save His people. Although Nebuchadnezzar appeared very slow to comprehend this message, he could never have claimed that he was not given sufficient evidence.

Nebuchadnezzar and the vision of the tree

In Daniel chapter 4 we read of yet another dream which puzzled the king. A great tree was cut down at the instruction of God. The stump was left in the ground, with a band of iron and brass round it. A voice from heaven then spoke of the heart of the one of whom the tree speaks being changed from a man's to a beast's, for a set period. The king summoned his wise men, yet none could interpret the dream for him. Eventually Daniel was called. Manifesting a spirit of genuine compassion and kindness, the prophet began by stating that the dream foretold evil things for the king. The tree represented Nebuchadnezzar himself, who would be deposed for a time. These things would take place as judgements from Israel's God for the king's refusal to give Him the glory (verses 24-27).

Two key points stand out for us. Firstly, Daniel acknowledged that the interpretation of the dream had come from God alone. Never did he claim to have any special ability. As in chapter 2, he was able to declare things hidden from other men simply because the God he worshipped had revealed them to him.

"This is the interpretation, O king, and this is the decree of the most High, which is come upon my lord the king." (4:24) Secondly, whilst others in Babylon may have rejoiced that a dictator such as Nebuchadnezzar would be, albeit temporarily, removed, Daniel showed genuine concern for this man:

"Wherefore, O king, let my counsel be acceptable unto thee, and break off thy sins by righteousness, and thine iniquities by shewing mercy to the poor; if it may be a lengthening of thy tranquillity." (verse 27)

What was Daniel encouraging the king to do but to embrace the standards of Israel? A cessation of sin, followed by acts of righteousness and showing mercy to the poor are all things which abound in the history of Israel. They are encouraged throughout the law given through Moses. Daniel manifested the Lord in the courts of this Gentile ruler, and called for the king to emulate his high standards so that the judgements which had been foretold might be avoided. Of course, this was not to be. The king continued to act as he had previously, marvelling in his greatness and the city which he had built. Like Herod, who also revelled in his position of authority and power (Acts 12:21-23), Nebuchadnezzar would be judged by the Almighty. As foretold in the vision of the tree, he was driven from his palace and lived as an animal for seven years (Daniel 4:33). It was when his sanity returned that he finally accepted the truth of Daniel's words:

"And at the end of the days I Nebuchadnezzar lifted up mine eyes unto heaven, and mine understanding returned unto me, and I blessed the most High, and I praised and honoured him that liveth for ever, whose dominion is an everlasting dominion, and his kingdom is from generation to generation ... now I Nebuchadnezzar praise and extol and honour the King of heaven, all whose works are truth, and his ways judgment: and those that walk in pride he is able to abase." (verses 34,37)

All this from one of the most powerful Gentile rulers this world has ever seen.

Nebuchadnezzar and the prophet Jeremiah

It may be because of these things that the king did all he could to save the prophet Jeremiah. Jerusalem was besieged by the Babylonians, and captives taken on (at least) three different occasions:

- In the days of king Jehoiakim (2 Kings 24:1) the Babylonians swept into the land. This was the occasion that Daniel was taken captive (Daniel 1:1,6).
- Jehoiachin, the son of Jehoiakim, reigned for just three months. During this time Nebuchadnezzar came again, and many were carried away, together with the treasures of the house of the Lord (2 Kings 24:8-12). There is a strong indication that it was on this occasion that the prophet Ezekiel was taken (Ezekiel 1:2).
- Zedekiah was Judah's last mortal king. In his days the city was destroyed by the Babylonians and almost every man, woman and child was either killed or taken captive (2 Kings 25:1-12).

During this last assault Nebuchadnezzar gave very specific instructions to the captain of his army regarding one man. Of all those left in Judah the prophet Jeremiah was to be spared, and granted his freedom:

"Now Nebuchadrezzar king of Babylon gave charge concerning Jeremiah to Nebuzaradan the captain of the guard, saying, take him, and look well to him, and do him no harm; but do unto him even as he shall say unto thee. So Nebuzaradan the captain of the guard sent ... and took Jeremiah out of the court of the prison, and committed him unto Gedaliah the son of Ahikam the son of Shaphan, that he should carry him home: so he dwelt among the people."   (Jeremiah 39:11-14)

How unlikely is this! What a task for the captain of the guard. One man, of all those in the city, was to be spared. Was Jeremiah known by one of the captives, who was carried back to the city to identify him? However he may have been found, we know that this strict instruction from the king was kept. The "captain of the guard" was, in fact, the chief of the executioners or slaughtermen (as indicated in the KJV margin). Here he was given the task of saving a life. Why was it that Nebuchadnezzar insisted on sparing just one man? Had Daniel appealed to him? Was it because of the events recorded in Daniel 4? Whatever his reasons, this Gentile king, who had seen many foreign lands taken and an immense number of people slain, ensured that the faithful prophet Jeremiah was spared.

The writing on the wall

Daniel chapter 5 describes the reign of Nebuchadnezzar's 'son', Belshazzar. In one of his feasts he decided to bring out the golden vessels which had been taken from the temple of the Lord in Jerusalem (verse 3). As his guests drank from them, a man's hand appeared (verse 5). The words "mene, mene, tekel upharsin" were written (verse 25). As before, wise men were summoned (verse 8). As before none could interpret, and so Daniel was called (verse 13). And exactly as before, Daniel not only revealed the meaning behind what had been seen, but attributed his knowledge to God alone.

"And thou his son, O Belshazzar, hast not humbled thine heart, though thou knewest all this; but hast lifted up thyself against the Lord of heaven; and they have brought the vessels of his house before thee, and thou, and thy lords, thy wives, and thy concubines, have drunk wine in them; and thou hast praised the gods of silver, and gold, of brass, iron, wood, and stone, which see not, nor hear, nor know: and the God in whose hand thy breath is, and whose are all thy ways, hast thou not glorified ..."   (verses 22,23)

These words had little effect on the king. That very night the city of Babylon fell to the Medes, and Darius began to reign. However a number of simple, basic, beautiful truths – things we read so many times in scripture – were declared to Belshazzar by Daniel. The only true God is in heaven, and He is the giver of life to all. The idols of the Gentiles are nothing. Those who ignore Him will eventually be judged and punished. As he did before Nebuchadnezzar, Daniel, like a man on a watchtower

(Ezekiel 33:7; Habakkuk 2:1), proclaimed the truth to any who would listen.

The lions' den

In our day such a thing would surely be unthinkable. If a government is ousted, either by losing an election or through more forceful methods, a leading light in the previous administration would not be kept on by the new regime. Yet this is precisely what happened in the case of Daniel. He had been one of the most trusted men under the Babylonian kings. When the Medes took the city he was installed in a position of similar authority. Surely we are being told that in eyes of those in the world of his day, Daniel was valued and respected.

In due course his popularity and ability made him enemies. As a result of his "excellent spirit", Darius was minded to set him over the whole realm (Daniel 6:3). The other rulers hated him for this. Like Joseph before him, and the Lord Jesus Christ afterwards, his enemies plotted his downfall. A new law was passed which made the petitioning of any god a capital offence (verse 7). The response of Daniel, who would have known that he was being watched, was truly wonderful:

> "Now when Daniel knew that the writing was signed, he went into his house; and his windows being open in his chamber toward Jerusalem, he kneeled upon his knees three times a day, and prayed, and gave thanks before his God, as he did aforetime." (verse 10)

Daniel was "steadfast, immovable" (1 Corinthians 15:58). His attitude was echoed by Peter so many years later. When the Jewish leaders reminded him that he had been told not to preach about Jesus, we read:

> "Then Peter and the other apostles answered and said, We ought to obey God rather than men." (Acts 5:29)

What lessons there are for us in these examples of faith and courage. The world is forever changing. New laws will be passed, some of which may impinge on the lives of the followers of the Lord Jesus. Right from the formation of our community, in times of conscription we have stood apart, refusing to comply with those who would have us take up arms and fight. If the laws of the land in which we dwell demand of us something which is contrary to scripture, then we must seek to obey God, no matter what the consequences may be.

The king tried hard to save Daniel. He was, however, restricted by the fact that the law could not be changed (Daniel 6:15). Such is the folly of man-made legislation! However as the man of God was sent to his (supposed) death, the king made a bold declaration:

"Thy God whom thou servest continually, he will deliver thee."
(verse 16)

The absolutely certainty in the mind of this Gentile monarch is truly remarkable. He did not declare that Daniel's God "could" deliver him, although this would have been a statement of truth. Rather he believed that Daniel "would" be delivered. In the morning he hastened to the mouth of the lions' den:

"And when he came to the den, he cried with a lamentable voice unto Daniel: and the king spake and said to Daniel, O Daniel, servant of the living God, is thy God, whom thou servest continually, able to deliver thee from the lions?"
(verse 20)

His doubts were soon dispelled:

"Then said Daniel unto the king ... My God hath sent his angel, and hath shut the lions' mouths, that they have not hurt me ..." (verses 21,22)

As previously, all that Daniel achieved he attributed to God. Never did he claim any special authority, or that he had accomplished anything in his own might. His deliverance from the lions' den is symbolic of the Master's conquering of sin. In 1 Peter 5:8 the devil is compared to a "roaring lion". So we see in Daniel's descent into and ascension from a place of death, a foreshadowing of the death and resurrection of Jesus. Surely this great prophet, with his astounding knowledge of the plan and purpose of the Father, would recognise these things and rejoice at the thought of the one who was to come.

As we have seen time and again, Daniel never hid his light under a bushel (Matthew 5:15). He was ready to give an answer to those who asked of the hope that was within him with meekness and fear (1 Peter 3:15). There would have been many men and women from different Gentile lands in Babylon. None who encountered Daniel could have failed to notice that he was different. In that place of spiritual darkness, he shone like a beacon, manifesting the High and Holy One of Israel. He let his "light shine":

> "I have even heard of thee, that the spirit of the gods is in thee, and that light and understanding and excellent wisdom is found in thee." (Daniel 5:14)

Truly his life is both an example and a challenge to every one of us.

In the days of Esther

THE book of Esther is unique. As has been noted many times, there is no use of the name or any of the titles of the Father here. What we do see, however, is the hand of God at work throughout the entire book.

The primary message of the book of Esther is that the Lord loves Israel and seeks their salvation, with their enemies being cursed and ultimately destroyed. When we look closely, however, we see that a number of Gentiles throughout the Medo-Persian Empire were very supportive of the Jews, against whom their enemy had devised such terrible things. Indeed on one key occasion a number chose to renounce their Gentile ancestry and embrace the hope of Israel.

Haman the Agagite
We need not consider the king's rejection of Vashti or his choosing of Esther as her replacement (chapters 1 and 2). What we know is that at the start of chapter 3 we are introduced to a man who sought the annihilation of every Jewish man, woman and child throughout the empire.

Haman the son of Hammedatha was an Agagite (Esther 3:1). Agag was the king of the Amalekites (1 Samuel 15:8). The Father had declared that He would be, through His people, at war with the Amalekites "from generation to generation" (Exodus 17:16). In chapter 8 we saw the reasons for this, and Saul's failure to comply with the instructions of God to wipe out these people and their king.

In an act very typical of so many in the world, and reminiscent of Nebuchadnezzar when the golden image was made (Daniel 3), Haman, with royal ascent, commanded that all bow down before him (Esther 3:2). One man, however, refused to do so:

"... but Mordecai bowed not, nor did him reverence. Then the king's servants, which were in the king's gate, said unto Mordecai, Why transgressest thou the king's commandment? Now it came to pass, when they spake daily unto him, and he hearkened not unto them, that they told Haman, to see whether Mordecai's matters would stand: for he had told them that he was a Jew." (verses 2-4)

Mordecai was Esther's uncle (2:7). When he refused to bow before Haman he made a point of stating that he was unable to do so because he was Jewish. His fellow servants appeared to want him to do as they did. This is not unusual. The servants of God will regularly be put under pressure to conform by those with whom they work. This will often cause unrest:

"Wherein they think it strange that ye run not with them to the same excess of riot, speaking evil of you ..." (1 Peter 4:4)

Like others before and after him, Mordecai's life was in danger because of his stance. Similar things are spoken of elsewhere:

"Yea, truth faileth; and he that departeth from evil maketh himself a prey ..." (Isaiah 59:15)

Mordecai, just like Shadrach, Meshach and Abednego, did not choose to disobey the law because he felt he was better than those who bowed before Haman. Nor was he a revolutionary. He refused to obey because such an action would have meant sinning against his God, and he ensured that others knew the reason why he had acted as he did.

There is a strong indication that Mordecai, and indeed the Jewish population in the empire as a whole, were highly regarded by those round about them. When Haman persuaded the king to pass a law which permitted their slaughter on a set day, we read of the state of mind of many in the city:

"... but the city Shushan was perplexed." (Esther 3:15)

Others knew what Haman refused to acknowledge. Despite their differences, those who had come from Judah were no danger to the Medo-Persian Empire. In fact they were of great benefit. At the end of chapter 2 we read of the plot to assassinate the king which had been made. This was known to Mordecai and he revealed this to Esther. The king was spared and a record made of Mordecai's actions. Mordecai had preserved life, yet Haman wanted him and all his people killed.

Esther's preparation for her appeal to the king
Mordecai realised that the only way for this law to be repealed was for Esther to petition the king, but she had not been summoned for thirty days, making this a matter of great seriousness. Any who approached Ahasuerus in his inner court, without being called for, could be put to death. This was, however, the only course of action open to them, and so Esther requested that all the Jews in Shushan be gathered together to fast for her. She then made a comment which tells us a great deal of her faith:

> "… I also and my maidens will fast likewise; and so will I go in unto the king, which is not according to the law: and if I perish, I perish." (4:16)

Apart from her bravery in appearing before a man who could have had her executed immediately, there is one further thing which stands out. She and her maidens were to fast. There is no indication that her maidens were Jewesses. Some may have been, although we are not told that this was the case. More likely they were Gentiles, and Esther was calling for them to embrace the practices of Israel. When the Master spoke to his disciples about their inability to perform a miracle, he said that which was impossible normally can be accomplished, with God's blessing:

> "Howbeit this kind goeth not out but by prayer and fasting." (Matthew 17:21)

The insight of Haman's wife and friends
How Haman must have rejoiced as his plan appeared to be coming together. The law was passed permitting all Jews to

be killed (Esther 3:12,13). Never again would his authority be undermined by Mordecai. All would bow before him. For a while everything seemed to be going as he had planned. However things began to turn against him, as recorded in Esther chapter 6. When he, mistakenly, thought Ahasuerus wanted to glorify him, he suggested that someone with whom the king was pleased should be placed on the royal horse and led round the city by a mighty man in the empire. The man would have to declare that this is how the king treats someone whom he delights to honour. We can imagine his feeling of utter revulsion when he was instructed to do precisely this for his nemesis, Mordecai (6:6-11). He returned home in deep disgrace, having his head covered (verse 12). Perhaps seeking solace, he relayed these things to his wife and friends. They responded with insight:

"And Haman told Zeresh his wife and all his friends every thing that had befallen him. Then said his wise men and Zeresh his wife unto him, If Mordecai be of the seed of the Jews, before whom thou hast begun to fall, thou shalt not prevail against him, but shalt surely fall before him."

(verse 13)

What an amazing comment! These things appear to manifest an understanding of the promises to Abraham:

"And I will bless them that bless thee, and curse him that curseth thee: and in thee shall all families of the earth be blessed." (Genesis 12:3)

How did they know such things? These "wise men" were wise indeed! Details of the history of the nation of Israel appear to have been known. Perhaps they knew of the decimation of Egypt when the children of Israel departed. Maybe they had heard of the people's survival in the wilderness for forty years and of the mighty nations of the land, with their strong cities, being destroyed. Did they know something of Israel under David and Solomon? Or men like Hezekiah and Josiah?

Even in the days of their captivity the unique history of this remarkable people struck fear into the hearts of their enemies. The Father had said to Israel in the wilderness, "I will send my fear before thee" (Exodus 23:27). Presumably the Jews who dwelt in the empire had revealed these wonderful truths to others. Haman's family accepted what he refused to believe: that those who dare to set themselves against God's people would fall. One verse sums up the book of Esther very well:

> "No weapon that is formed against thee shall prosper; and every tongue that shall rise against thee in judgment thou shalt condemn. This is the heritage of the servants of the LORD, and their righteousness is of me, saith the LORD."
> (Isaiah 54:17)

How remarkable it is that these wonderful truths appear to have been believed by Haman's wife and friends!

Haman's death

In due course Haman's plot was revealed to the king and he was executed. In comments made by one of the servants of Ahasuerus at this time, we see just how highly Mordecai was regarded by those with whom he worked:

> "And Harbonah, one of the chamberlains, said before the king, Behold also, the gallows fifty cubits high, which Haman had made for Mordecai, who had spoken good for the king, standeth in the house of Haman. Then the king said, Hang him thereon." (Esther 7:9)

This man knew how Mordecai had saved the king. He would also have been aware of the reason Haman desired his destruction. In choosing to inform Ahasuerus that there was an (unused) gallows, prepared initially for Mordecai by Haman, this man was clearly suggesting that the Jews' enemy should be executed thereon. The king agreed and Haman was destroyed. Harbonah ensured that there no misunderstanding: Mordecai was the man who had "spoken good for the king". As we read in the book of the Proverbs 26:27 and 28:10 and Ecclesiastes 10:8, those who dig a pit fall into it. In saying what he did, this man was clearly manifesting his desire to be allied with Mordecai and the Jewish people.

The Jews fight back, and increase in number

The original law could not be repealed, so a further law had to be made. This gave the Jews the freedom to fight back when attacked (Esther 8:11). It resulted in a great number of their enemies being put to death, including Haman's ten sons (9:5,10). A further incident took place at this time, however, and this is surely of equal importance:

> "And in every province, and in every city, whithersoever the king's commandment and his decree came, the Jews had joy and gladness, a feast and a good day. And many of the people of the land became Jews; for the fear of the Jews fell upon them." (8:17)

So what had commenced as an attempt to exterminate all Jews concluded with the very opposite taking place. Not only did the Jews survive, but many Gentiles, presumably scattered throughout the empire of the Medes and Persians, embraced the Jewish faith. They beheld the actions of the Jews in their midst. They noted how they responded to the needs of one another. More especially they came to know the God of the Jewish people. They worshipped Him, and embraced the hope which He offers to those who are His.

As we have seen in the preceding chapters, there were a number of faithful Gentiles who chose to embrace the truth and be associated with God's people. However, when did a number such as this "become Jews"? Is this the largest Gentile conversion under the Old Covenant? With the possible exception of the people of Nineveh in Jonah's day (see chapter 25), there is surely no other record of such an amazing event taking place in the Old Testament.

Many in the Household of Faith today are Gentiles by their ancestry. In coming to an understanding of the truth, they have done precisely what was done by this great number in the days of the Jews' captivity. Recognising that the things of the world are nothing, they have embraced the one true hope of Israel. Surely this great Gentile conversion foreshadows this. However it also points forward to that time when the Master will be here, when all will glorify Israel's God and yet more Gentiles will do what was done in the days of Esther:

> "Thus saith the LORD of hosts; In those days it shall come to pass, that ten men shall take hold out of all languages of the nations, even shall take hold of the skirt of him that is a Jew, saying, We will go with you: for we have heard that God is with you." (Zechariah 8:23)

30

The return from captivity

THE captivity of Judah was surely the saddest time for God's people since their ancestors had suffered in the land of Egypt. The history of Israel is littered with times of tragedy. Despite all of the Father's warnings, His people refused to repent and serve Him. So Nebuchadnezzar the king of Babylon came, the city of Jerusalem was destroyed and the people taken captive (2 Kings 25). For seventy years they would remain in the lands of the Gentiles (Jeremiah 29:10), with the faithful mourning their loss (Psalm 137:1-6).

Evil-merodach
As we saw in chapters 28 and 29, some of the Jewish captives rose to positions of great authority and privilege in the land of their captivity. Daniel and Mordecai, amongst others, were elevated to rule over great numbers. Others, doubtless, were not as privileged. We read nothing of King Zedekiah after he was carried away by Nebuchadnezzar, except that he remained in prison until the day of his death (Jeremiah 52:11). However one of the kings of Judah was treated very differently by his captors:

"And it came to pass in the seven and thirtieth year of the captivity of Jehoiachin king of Judah … that Evil-merodach king of Babylon in the year that he began to reign did lift up the head of Jehoiachin king of Judah out of prison; And he spake kindly to him, and set his throne above the throne of the kings that were with him in Babylon; and changed his prison garments: and he did eat bread continually before him all the days of his life. And his allowance was a continual allowance given him of the king, a daily rate for every day, all the days of his life." (2 Kings 25:27-30)

Why did the king of Babylon act in this way? Why was one former king of Judah elevated above all the other kings? Could it be that the prophet Daniel had appealed to Evil-merodach for him? Perhaps Jehoiachin had manifested a spirit of repentance. We know that king Manasseh had been more evil than any other during the early part of his reign. When he was taken captive he repented of his sins, and was forgiven (see 2 Chronicles 33:9-13). Maybe Jehoiachin had responded to his affliction in the same way. What we do know is that a Babylonian ruler chose to bless a man of Judah, raising him from his prison cell, speaking kindly to him, and caring for him all his days.

Cyrus

Cyrus was a king of Persia (Daniel 10:1). He ruled over the empire in the days of Daniel (1:21; 6:28). Many years before he was born, the prophet Isaiah was inspired to speak of his reign:

"That saith of Cyrus, He is my shepherd, and shall perform all my pleasure: even saying to Jerusalem, Thou shalt be built; and to the temple, Thy foundation shall be laid. Thus saith the LORD to his anointed, to Cyrus, whose right hand I have holden, to subdue nations before him; and I will loose the loins of kings, to open before him the two leaved gates; and the gates shall not be shut ..." (Isaiah 44:28-45:1)

Very few people in the Bible are mentioned by name before their birth. Of those that are, Cyrus is the only one not descended from Abraham:
- Ishmael (Genesis 16:11).
- Isaac (17:19).
- Solomon (1 Chronicles 22:9).
- Josiah (1 Kings 13:2).
- Cyrus (Isaiah 44:28).
- John the Baptist (Luke 1:13).
- Jesus Christ (Matthew 1:21; Luke 1:31).

In this we see an indication of the greatness of this man. Israel's God spoke of this Gentile ruler by name around one hundred years before his birth. Clearly we are being told that the work he was to perform was of immense importance. Indeed when we look more closely, we see there are significant types of the work of the Master:

Cyrus	Reference	Jesus Christ	Reference
"My shepherd"	Isaiah 44:28	"My shepherd"	Zechariah 13:7
"shall perform all my pleasure"	Isaiah 44:28	"This is my beloved Son, in whom I am well pleased"	Matthew 3:17
"saying to Jerusalem, Thou shalt be built"	Isaiah 44:28	"When the LORD shall build up Zion, he shall appear in his glory"	Psalm 102:16
"… and to the temple, Thy foundation shall be laid"	Isaiah 44:28	"Because of thy temple at Jerusalem shall kings bring presents unto thee"	Psalm 68:29
"Cyrus, whose right hand I have holden"	Isaiah 45:1	"For I the LORD thy God will hold thy right hand"	Isaiah 41:13
"to subdue nations before him"	Isaiah 45:1	"Thou shalt break them with a rod of iron"	Psalm 2:9
"to open before him the two leaved gates"	Isaiah 45:1	"Open to me the gates of righteousness: I will go into them"	Psalm 118:19
"the gates shall not be shut"	Isaiah 45:1	"the gates of it shall not be shut"	Revelation 21:25

How amazing it is that a Gentile king should be spoken of in such a way, and how unlikely that this Persian should be very similar to the Lord Jesus in so much of his work.

2 Chronicles … Ezra

The end of the second book of Chronicles and commencement of the book of Ezra are identical. Both speak of the return from captivity which took place in the days of Cyrus:

"Now in the first year of Cyrus king of Persia, that the word of the LORD by the mouth of Jeremiah might be fulfilled, the LORD stirred up the spirit of Cyrus king of Persia, that he made a proclamation throughout all his kingdom, and put it also in writing, saying, Thus saith Cyrus king of Persia, The LORD God of heaven hath given me all the kingdoms of the earth; and he hath charged me to build him an house at Jerusalem, which is in Judah. Who is there among you of all his people? his God be with him, and let him go up …"

(2 Chronicles 36:22,23; Ezra 1:1-3)

The Father "stirred up the spirit of Cyrus", so that right throughout the Medo-Persian Empire, Jews were offered the opportunity to return. We see that Cyrus was quick to acknowledge that all that he had was from the Lord. He also declared that he had been given a direct commission from Israel's God to make the rebuilding of the temple a possibility. This ties in with the words of Isaiah 44 (see above).

Can we imagine a ruler of a nation saying such things today? What would be said if a British Prime Minister stood up in the House of Commons and declared similar things? Cyrus ensured that everyone knew precisely why he was acting as he did. He genuinely believed that the God of Israel had raised him up that His plan and purpose might be fulfilled.

Had he received instruction from Daniel? We are not told, but we do know that a man of Gentile ancestry, ruling over the then-known world, worshipped and served Israel's God, and made provision for His people to return to His holy city and build His temple. This foreshadows the greater return in the age yet to come when the Son of God will rule from Jerusalem. In that wonderful time, a further regathering of Jews will take place (Isaiah 43:6), and a greater, more glorious, longer lasting temple will be built.

"He shall build an house for my name, and I will stablish the throne of his kingdom for ever." (2 Samuel 7:13)

The commandment of Darius

The work of rebuilding the temple had been commenced, but it was not quickly completed. Gentiles living round about the city did everything possible to hinder the work, and it stalled. In due course, under the influence of the prophets Haggai and Zechariah and men such as Zerubbabel and Jeshua, the people were motivated to recommence the building work (Ezra 5:1,2). Once more there was Gentile opposition (verse 3), and a letter was written to King Darius (verses 6-17). He made a search, realised all that the decree of Cyrus had said, and commanded that the Jews' enemies were to do nothing to hinder the work (6:1-7). His instructions regarding how the Jews were to be treated were truly amazing:

- Expenses incurred by the Jews were to be covered by the tribute money paid to the king (verse 8).
- All that was needed for sacrifices should be provided (verse 9).
- If the enemies dared to disobey they were to be punished by being hung from a rafter of their own house (like Haman, Esther 7:10). Their houses would then be turned into a dunghill (Ezra 6:11) – a punishment which was only applied at this time (see Daniel 2:5; 3:29).

Why this Gentile ruler responded in such a way we are not told. Surely we see the hand of Israel's God at work, guiding events so that His people might be blessed.

It is in the seventh chapter of Ezra that we are finally introduced to the man after whom the book is named (Ezra 7:1). It appears that there is quite a gap between the end of chapter 6 and the commencement of chapter 7 of Ezra. Some commentators suggest that the events described in the book of Esther took place during this time. Although we cannot be certain as to the precise timing, Ezra chapter 7 introduces another Gentile king called Artaxerxes. Ezra, the descendant of Aaron and "ready scribe in the law of Moses" had requested permission of the king to return to Jerusalem. This was granted, and he departed for "the city of the great King". He was not alone: accompanying him were priests, Levites, singers, porters and Nethinims (Ezra 7:7). Ezra carried a letter of authority from Artaxerxes with him:

> "Artaxerxes, king of kings, unto Ezra the priest, a scribe of the law of the God of heaven, perfect peace, and at such a time. I make a decree, that all they of the people of Israel, and of his priests and Levites, in my realm, which are minded of their own freewill to go up to Jerusalem, go with thee."
>
> (verses 12,13)

The contents of this letter are truly remarkable.

- The king made mention of the law of the God whom Ezra served (verse 14).
- He instructed that silver and gold which had been given by the king and his counsellors should be carried to Jerusalem (verse 15).
- He mentioned other offerings of silver and gold, presumably made by Jews throughout the empire; he even quoted the Law of Moses by using the phrase "freewill offering" (verse 16). The only uses of this phrase outside the law are in the book of Ezra.
- He made mention of those things that would be necessary for use as sacrifices (verses 17,22).
- He excused those returning from having to pay custom (verse 24).
- He offered further financial support, to be bestowed out of the king's treasure house (verse 20).
- He decreed that any who would not obey these instructions should be punished, either by having their goods confiscated, being imprisoned or executed (verse 26).

As if these declarations were not amazing enough, some of the terminology used by this king indicates that he was a man of spiritual insight. He called the God of Ezra "the God of Jerusalem" (verse 19), and "the God of heaven" (verse 23). He made mention of the wisdom of God which Ezra possessed (verse 25). He even implied that there would be wrath against his kingdom and royal house if he did not comply with the requests of the Jews (verse 23).

What made this king behave in such a way? Was Esther still queen in the empire? Was she the mother of this man? Whatever the reasons for these actions, we can clearly see the hand of the Father at work as His people returned to His holy city, as decreed by the prophets.

Rebuilding the walls in the days of Nehemiah

A further return would take place shortly after this. Those who knew their prophecies would have accepted that the time would come when God's people would retrace the steps of their forefather Abraham (Daniel 9:2). They would return from the lands of the east, and the nation would be re-established in the land promised to the fathers of old.

Nehemiah was one of the many Jews living in the Medo-Persian Empire. He had risen to the position of cup-bearer to the king Artaxerxes (Nehemiah 1:11). Having heard of the plight of the people of God he appealed to the king, and was granted permission to return (2:5-8), in fulfilment of the promises which had been made through Jeremiah (see above).

> "And the king said unto me, (the queen also sitting by him,) For how long shall thy journey be? and when wilt thou return? So it pleased the king to send me; and I set him a time."
>
> (verse 6)

Again, there are suggestions that the queen was Esther. We cannot be sure, but we do know that, with the Father's blessing (Nehemiah 2:8), Nehemiah was granted permission to travel to "the city of the great King". Letters were provided, allowing him free passage through the different territories. The necessary materials for repairing the city (timber especially) were provided. A secure, prosperous city would have been of great benefit to the empire. Was this simply a commercial decision? Whatever the reasons may have been, sending a large number of Jewish captives back to the city of their ancestors was an amazing act on the part of Artaxerxes. It may well be that he knew of the prophecies which had been made and was determined to play his part in permitting the city to be rebuilt.

The response of the Gentiles to the Jews' return

Initially, everything appeared to be going well. However as soon as Nehemiah and those who had chosen to return with him arrived in the land, there was opposition:

> "When Sanballat the Horonite, and Tobiah the servant, the Ammonite, heard of it, it grieved them exceedingly that there was come a man to seek the welfare of the children of Israel."
>
> (verse 10)

This opposition of Sanballat and his allies continued throughout Nehemiah's life. They began by being grieved. This developed into mocking (verse 19; 4:1-3). When the wall was completed they were "very wroth" (verse 7). Then Sanballat suggested that he and Nehemiah meet outside of the city (6:1,2). On four further occasions the same request was made in writing (verse 4). Clearly he was planning to attack Nehemiah, believing that without his influence the work would cease. A further letter was sent, accusing Nehemiah of desiring to be a king over the Jews (verses 5-7). Later still they hired a man of Israel to tell Nehemiah to hide in the temple (verses 10-12).

The end of the book records the tragic incidents which occurred in Nehemiah's absence. Amongst the sins which had taken place we read of Tobiah the Ammonite being given a chamber in the courts of the temple (13:7,8). In addition to this, a family member of Eliashib the High Priest had married Sanballat's daughter (verse 28). Nehemiah had done so much to restore the glory of Jerusalem. In permitting these Gentiles free entry to the city and access even to the temple itself, it was as though all his work had been undone.

Faithful Gentiles in Jerusalem with Nehemiah

Based on the above description of the actions and words of these Gentiles in Nehemiah's day, it would be easy for us to build up a picture of the Jews as a very insular group. Under the law separation from the Gentiles and their practices was stressed (Leviticus 18:24; Deuteronomy 18:9). Having suffered so much in captivity, it was clearly essential for the Jews that the division between the "holy and profane" was maintained. Yet, despite all that we have seen regarding the sins of the people round about them, there appear to have been some Gentiles who chose to become allied with Israel. In chapter 5 we read of those who ate with Nehemiah:

"Moreover there were at my table an hundred and fifty of the Jews and rulers, beside those that came unto us from among the heathen that are about us." (Nehemiah 5:17)

Similar things are recorded in Ezra 6:21. Who were these people? Were they Jews? This seems unlikely, as almost all had been carried away to Babylon under Nebuchadnezzar. Some were left in the land; however a number of these, against the instructions of Jeremiah, had travelled to Egypt and died there (Jeremiah 43:7). These people could have been descendants of the few Israelites who had remained in the land, but it seems more likely that they were Gentiles.

Throughout the history of Israel, from the times when they were slaves in Egypt, some from the nations came to be associated with them. Could it have been that the rebuilding of the walls, which took only fifty-two days (Nehemiah 6:15), prompted some from Gentile lands to seek to become united with God's people? Was it the unity of the workers, or the failure of their enemies which moved these people to come to the city? Most likely it was the hope of Israel, which was manifested so powerfully by the people of the Lord, which was behind their actions.

There is a vital lesson for us in these things. What do the people of the world see when they look at us? They may be somewhat bemused by our practice of meeting together as we do, remembering the Master every week and studying God's word. Maybe the way we dress and speak is so out of step with many in the world that we are regarded as strange. However, the way we act – especially towards each other – should be a demonstration that we have the truth. The Master said this:

> "By this shall all men know that ye are my disciples, if ye have love one to another." (John 13:35)

Some years ago a brother in Christ was in hospital. A close relative of his, who had been particularly antagonistic regarding the truth and all we stand for, had a great deal of contact with brethren and sisters during this time. As a result of this he made a comment which caused astonishment amongst the family, stating "Aren't Christadelphians lovely people". The truth, as we have seen time and again, is not something which must just be known or even loved; it has to be lived:

> "And every man that hath this hope in him purifieth himself, even as he is pure." (1 John 3:3)

What times these were! Under men like Zerubbabel, Ezra and Nehemiah God's people were gathered to His holy city of Jerusalem. The temple and the city walls were rebuilt. Jews and Gentiles appear to have been amongst the faithful. Times of joy, unlike anything that had been witnessed for hundreds of years, followed.

Surely in these things we can see a foreshadowing of that greater time of rebuilding at Jerusalem, when a greater temple will stand. In that day an immense number of faithful ones, from many different lands, will be called to share in those things. Jews and Gentiles will be united together as Jerusalem finally becomes a city of peace. No longer will there be division; no more tension between nations; no more racial hatred. There will just be one holy people, serving and manifesting the only true God forever.

> "... for mine house shall be called an house of prayer for all people." (Isaiah 56:7)

31

Wise men from the east

FOR around four hundred years, there had been darkness over the earth. Not literal darkness, as recorded in Genesis 1; rather the light of God's revelation to man had ceased. This had been foretold by the prophet Micah:

"Therefore night shall be unto you, that ye shall not have a vision; and it shall be dark unto you, that ye shall not divine; and the sun shall go down over the prophets, and the day shall be dark over them." (Micah 3:6)

However that darkness was to be dispelled by the coming of one man. He was the one who would in time be called "the light of the world" (John 8:12; 9:5), and "a light to lighten the Gentiles" (Luke 2:32). How apt, then, that just after his birth men from a Gentile land should be guided to him by a great light. A star appeared in the sky, pointing the way, and these men came before the Son of God, and worshipped him:

"Now when Jesus was born in Bethlehem of Judaea in the days of Herod the king, behold, there came wise men from the east to Jerusalem, saying, Where is he that is born King of the Jews? for we have seen his star in the east, and are come to worship him." (Matthew 2:1,2)

Wise men from the east
What, then, do we know of these "wise men"? The Greek word is *magos*. Often they are referred to as Magi, which is the Latin plural form of the word. Our English word 'magic' is derived from the same source. Strong's Concordance states that the word

implies "a magician, i.e., an Oriental scientist". The same word is used in Acts 13:6 of a sorcerer by the name of Elymas, also called Barjesus.

The original word is derived from a title used in the days of the Babylonian Empire:

"And all the princes of the king of Babylon came in, and sat in the middle gate, even Nergalsharezer, Samgarnebo, Sarsechim, Rabsaris, Nergalsharezer, Rabmag, with all the residue of the princes of the king of Babylon."

(Jeremiah 39:3)

"Rabmag": at first glance this appears to be a name of one of the Babylonian princes. However, it is in fact the title of the man called Nergalsharezer: it means chief soothsayer. The courts of Pharaoh, Nebuchadnezzar and Darius were full of such "wise men" (Genesis 41:8; Exodus 7:11; Esther 1:13; Daniel 1:20; 2:2; 4:6; 5:7).

Shortly after the birth of Jesus these wise men came "from the east". This is a fairly general phrase, however based on the contact that God's people had with those from "the east", it seems most likely that they had travelled from the areas known in the Old Testament as Assyria or Babylon.

Of course, the children of Israel had a great number of dealings with such people. The northern, ten-tribe kingdom of Israel was taken into captivity in Assyria (2 Kings 17:6). Judah, in the south, was carried away to Babylon (25:11). In the days of the Medes and Persians some returned under men like Zerubbabel (Ezra 2:1,2), Ezra (Ezra 7:6) and Nehemiah (Nehemiah 2:11). Others would have remained in the land of their captivity: could they have been the ancestors these Magi?

Daniel: a wise man in the east

When lands were conquered by nations such as Babylon, the wisest of all men were taken to serve their king. In Daniel chapter 1 we have a record of this practice. Daniel was one of the men chosen. So he was a wise man, in the east. Indeed, he stands as a symbol for these Magi that came before the Son of God:

- He worshipped towards Jerusalem (Daniel 6:10); they travelled to that same city.
- He refused to obey the law of the Medes and Persians (verse 10); they refused to return to Herod.
- He was guided by God's word (9:2); they were guided by a star and in a dream sent by God.
- He saw the day of the Son of God, with the eye of faith (7:13); they were privileged to see him as a child, and worship him.

Had Daniel met with men of like mind, and spoken of the coming of the Messiah? Was there a group, like those in Malachi's day who talked of these things (Malachi 3:16)? Were the wise men their descendants? Were they Gentiles? All we can be certain of is that they came from a Gentile land, seeking to see and worship the one "born King of the Jews". In due course they were rewarded for their faith.

There is one further connection with Babylon. The prophet Ezekiel was also amongst those of Judah taken captive by the Babylonians (Ezekiel 1:1). So like Daniel, he was also a "wise man in the east". During the revelation of the glorious temple which is to be built in the age to come, we read the following:

"He brought me to the gate, even the gate that looketh toward the east: And, behold, the glory of the God of Israel came from the way of the east: and his voice was like a noise of many waters: and the earth shined with his glory." (43:1,2)

The record goes on to say this was similar to what the prophet had seen at the commencement of his work (verse 3). Surely it is appropriate that when a manifestation of the God of Israel appeared to the prophet (who was, by now, in spirit in Jerusalem, see 40:2), it approached from the east. Later wise men from the same area were guided by another light to kneel before the only begotten Son of God.

The journey of the wise men

Assuming that we are right, and these men came from the area of ancient Babylon, they would have taken the same journey as many before them. Nehemiah and Ezra, returning to Jerusalem from the Persian Empire had taken exactly this journey. However, the more obvious connection is surely Abraham. We know that, leaving Ur, he would have travelled up through the "fertile crescent", crossed the river Euphrates and entered the land from the north. The very first promises made by the Father to him are of particular relevance:

> "Now the LORD had said unto Abram, Get thee out of thy country ..." (Genesis 12:1)

These things *had* been said, presumably when he was still in Ur. He was a "wise man in the east". The call had been very clear: 'Leave the land, travel to a place I will show you, and you will be blessed.' And at this time, the promise was made that we have considered a number of times already, that "all families of the earth" would be blessed in him (verse 3). Later, the promise of the seed was made for the first time (verse 7).

So the wise men copied the actions of Abraham in their journey. They did, in reality, what we are called to do in symbol:

> "... and the father of circumcision to them who are not of the circumcision only, but who also walk in the steps of that faith of our father Abraham, which he had being yet uncircumcised." (Romans 4:12)

Guided by the star

In coming to the land of Israel, they had followed a star. This was no ordinary star. Meteors or shooting stars move across the sky; however stars do not appear "over" a house, as this one did (Matthew 2:9). It was a miracle. Indeed this was one of a whole series of miracles which would take place over the next few years. Naturally it is impossible for a virgin to conceive, yet this is exactly what had taken place (Luke 1:34,35). Some have suggested that an incredibly unusual solar event took place at this time. We need not examine the apparent 'evidence' for such things. The Bible says a star appeared, and we believe this to be true. In symbol, stars speak of rulers:

"I shall see him, but not now: I shall behold him, but not nigh: there shall come a Star out of Jacob, and a Sceptre shall rise out of Israel, and shall smite the corners of Moab, and destroy all the children of Sheth." (Numbers 24:17)
In the book of Revelation, the word "star" appears a number of times; one of these connects with the events in Matthew 2:

"... I am the root and the offspring of David, and the bright and morning star." (Revelation 22:16)
Jesus is the "morning star", and in seeking him the wise men followed a star. How appropriate, then, that when the Master was born a star should appear.

We know how the words of the wise men caused consternation for Herod. After consulting with the chief priests and scribes (Matthew 2:4), he was told that Bethlehem would be the birthplace of the Messiah, based on Micah 5:2. He then requested of the wise men that they return to him when they had met this one special child, expressing a desire to worship him also (Matthew 2:8). Of course, these words were the lies of an evil, greedy man who would stop at nothing in his efforts to secure his position as ruler.

The wise men bow before God's Son

The star which they had seen, which had probably disappeared from view for a time, became visible again:

"When they had heard the king, they departed; and, lo, the star, which they saw in the east, went before them, till it came and stood over where the young child was. When they saw the star, they rejoiced with exceeding great joy. And when they were come into the house, they saw the young child with Mary his mother, and fell down, and worshipped him: and when they had opened their treasures, they presented unto him gifts; gold, and frankincense, and myrrh." (verses 9-11)

This is surely an echo of the events in the exodus, when the children of Israel were given light, whilst the Egyptians remained in darkness (Exodus 14:19,20). Herod, like Pharaoh and his men, remained in darkness, and God's children (see Matthew 2:15) were enlightened and saved.

The gifts of the wise men

What then of the gifts that were presented before the Master? Three items were brought: gold, frankincense and myrrh. These appear together in two other passages in God's word: Exodus 30 and Song of Solomon 3. Let us consider each item and the spiritual lessons behind them.

Gold is the most precious of materials. It was used extensively in the tabernacle and in Solomon's temple. Some items were overlaid with gold (Exodus 25:11), while others, such as the mercy seat (verse 17), were solid gold. What does gold signify? There is a strong connection between gold and faith:

> "That the trial of your faith, being much more precious than of gold that perisheth, though it be tried with fire, might be found unto praise and honour and glory at the appearing of Jesus Christ." (1 Peter 1:7)

Naturally speaking, gold is one of the least perishable of materials. Yet Peter is speaking of the things of this world, when contrasted with those of the truth. The wealth of this world passes away; our faith speaks of things eternal. If we have faith, it is counted as righteousness by our God (Romans 4:3,5). Truly this is something beyond price.

Gold, then, represents faith and the outworking of it. It speaks of the faithful character that our Father requires. It is precious, as are those with whom the Father is well pleased (Malachi 3:17).

Frankincense points back to the law. Unsurprisingly, the word that is translated "frankincense" (as in Exodus 30:34) is elsewhere rendered "incense" (Isaiah 43:23). It was a vegetable resin obtained from certain trees, produced by cutting into the bark, and came out as a gum. It was white in colour, and gave off a beautiful odour. What then does incense represent? David answers this question for us:

"Let my prayer be set forth before thee as incense; and the lifting up of my hands as the evening sacrifice." (Psalm 141:2) When incense is burned, it 'ascends'. This is true of prayer, for heaven is portrayed as being "above" the earth (Deuteronomy 4:39). Just as incense smells beautiful, so the content of our prayers should be beautiful, giving the Father pleasure.

The Greek word for myrrh is *smyrna*. It is the same as the name of the ecclesia in Revelation 2:8. Under the law it only appears once. In Exodus 30:23 it is described as being mixed with other items (cinnamon, calamus, cassia, olive oil), and used in the process of anointing. The tabernacle, the items therein, Aaron and his sons all had to be anointed. In the case of a priest or king, this normally indicated the commencement of his work (1 Samuel 10:1).

So if we list the three gifts, we see there is real significance behind each item:
- Gold is of great value. It speaks of endurance, faith, trial and righteousness.
- Frankincense depicts prayer, praise, and the giving of glory to God.
- Myrrh indicates anointing. It speaks of the setting apart of certain items / people for a particular work.

Surely we are being told that the wise men did not solely present gifts they thought might be appreciated. Their wares were not simply items of great value. They had a comprehension of the Mosaic law, and understood the importance of prayer and faith. They knew that the one before whom they were to bow would be special, anointed by God. Only in him would faith be counted as righteousness. Only through him would immortality be possible, and prayer be made. They knew he would be the Messiah as portrayed in the Old Testament scriptures.

The departure of the wise men
Having presented their gifts and worshipped the only begotten of the Father, the time came for the wise men to head home. They

had been guided by a star. Further guidance was afforded them in a different way before their departure:

> "And being warned of God in a dream that they should not return to Herod, they departed into their own country another way." (Matthew 2:12)

Later in this same chapter, Joseph was guided in the same way on two separate occasions (verses 19,22).

In these things there is a reminder of the fundamental truth of the Gospel message. A faithful association with Jesus Christ brings salvation. The wise men spent time in the presence of God's Son and were then saved. Had Herod known what they had done (he is recorded as having been "mocked" of them in verse 16), they would most certainly have been put to death. Yet by taking heed to God's word, they were saved. We read the same things in the life of the prophet Elisha. The king of Syria wished to capture the king of Israel, and Elisha warned him of the enemy's intention. There was a place of sanctuary to which the king was able to go, and he did so, in obedience to the prophet's words (2 Kings 6:8-10). Surely this is the call of the Gospel to which all of God's children hearken: 'Go my way – and live' (Isaiah 30:21; Matthew 8:22).

We are given no further information regarding these wise men. Did they head back to the east and preach the Gospel message there? Did they return to Israel later and meet with John, Jesus or the apostles? In all of these things the word of God is silent. We are simply left with the picture of faithful men, who came before the Son of God and brought offerings to him in faith and love. They were guided by a star sent specifically for them, and obedient to the instructions given them by the God of Israel. They are, like many other faithful Gentiles, wonderful examples for us as we look to that day when the "Sun of righteousness" will come and the earth will be transformed (Malachi 4:2).

Do we, like the wise men, sacrifice self that God might be glorified? Do we see in Christ a beautiful fulfilment of the types and shadows under the law? Do we long for the day of his coming? Are we obedient to God's word as they were? These are the challenges for every one of us from the lives of these faithful and courageous "wise men from the east".

"I beseech you therefore, brethren, by the mercies of God, that ye present your bodies a living sacrifice, holy, acceptable unto God, which is your reasonable service. And be not conformed to this world: but be ye transformed by the renewing of your mind, that ye may prove what is that good, and acceptable, and perfect, will of God." (Romans 12:1,2)

John the Baptist

WITH the obvious exception of Jesus Christ, who was the greatest man of all time? Noah? Melchizedek? Abraham? Moses? David? All were giants of faith, and served with the kind of courage, devotion and selflessness which would, doubtless, put every one of us to shame. The greatest man of all? There is a case to be made that this was John the Baptist. It was Jesus himself who said this:

> "Verily I say unto you, Among them that are born of women there hath not risen a greater than John the Baptist: notwithstanding he that is least in the kingdom of heaven is greater than he." (Matthew 11:11)

Maybe this refers to John as the greatest prophet (as implied in Luke's record, Luke 7:28). Or maybe John's greatness related to the fact that he did not merely speak of the Messiah. He wasn't like Abraham who "rejoiced to see [Christ's] day" (John 8:56), or David, who spoke of God having revealed the future of his house "for a great while to come" (2 Samuel 7:19). He didn't simply declare, 'The Messiah will come one day'; rather he said: 'Here he is!'

> "The next day John seeth Jesus coming unto him, and saith, Behold the Lamb of God, which taketh away the sin of the world ... and looking upon Jesus as he walked, he saith, Behold the Lamb of God!" (John 1:29,36)

The people's response to the preaching of John

When John began his ministry God's people had been starved of any real spiritual nourishment. Even the leaders, in a statement which is self-condemnatory in the highest degree, described the nation as "people who knoweth not the law" (7:49). A class of capable, willing yet ignorant pupils is a sign of an utterly useless teacher! When John arrived, therefore, the common people embraced his words like a man finding an oasis in the desert. At last, here was someone they could understand, someone who made the word of God live. No wonder many flocked to hear him:

"Then went out to him Jerusalem, and all Judaea, and all the region round about Jordan, and were baptized of him in Jordan, confessing their sins." (Matthew 3:5,6)

When scripture says all people came out to listen to John, it really does mean all. The despised of society loved and revered him (21:32). The common people regarded him so highly that the leaders were afraid to speak against him for fear of being stoned (Luke 20:6). Even Gentiles loved John. The Master said that John was "a burning and a shining light" (John 5:35). Truly he let that light shine before all.

In describing the work of John, Luke records how this was a fulfilment of a section of Isaiah chapter 40:

"As it is written in the book of the words of Esaias the prophet, saying, The voice of one crying in the wilderness, Prepare ye the way of the Lord, make his paths straight. Every valley shall be filled, and every mountain and hill shall be brought low; and the crooked shall be made straight, and the rough ways shall be made smooth ..." (Luke 3:4,5)

What does verse 5 mean? Is this describing the landscape of Israel? A careful consideration of the context provides the answer for us:

"And all flesh shall see the salvation of God." (verse 6)

So verse 5 is not referring to the topography of the land, but the people therein. "All flesh" seeing God's salvation reminds us of the promise made to Abraham that we have considered many times:

"... and in thee shall all families of the earth be blessed." (Genesis 12:3)

Luke 3:5 depicts four geographical areas or items, which relate to John's audience very precisely:

Every valley shall be filled	Those lowly, in need of encouragement and building up	The common people (verse 10)
Every mountain and hill shall be brought low	Those lifted up in their own eyes and needing to be humbled	The leaders (verse 7, see Matthew 3:7)
The crooked shall be made straight	Those whose ways were "crooked" and in need of rectification	The tax collectors (verse 12)
The rough ways shall be made smooth	Those who were hard; those untouched by the things that affected others	The Roman soldiers (verse 14)

The Roman soldiers

All people came to hear John. All desired to be baptized. Of the four groups listed above, three asked the same question: "What shall we do"? His answer to the Roman soldiers was particularly powerful:

"And the soldiers likewise demanded of him, saying, And what shall we do? And he said unto them, Do violence to no man, neither accuse any falsely; and be content with your wages."

(verse 14)

Three very specific instructions were given:
1. They were to do no violence.
2. The were not to accuse anyone falsely.
3. They were to be content with their wages.

The second and third of these commands should have posed no great problems for these men. Lying was unacceptable. The word of a soldier, in the case of accusations being raised by locals, would surely have stood. The God of whom John spoke had revealed Himself to Moses as being "abundant in goodness and truth" (Exodus 34:6). He demands that His people are similarly truthful.

Desiring to obtain additional payment by any unlawful means was also wrong. Roman soldiers had a number of deductions taken out of their salaries at source. One of these was a pension contribution. It is possible that some demanded payment from the people as a bribe to permit certain activities to go unchecked. John stated that such actions were incompatible with the life of a disciple. They were to be "content". This appears to be regarded as a weakness by some in the world today. Some years ago a brother in Christ went for an interview for a job and was told in no uncertain terms that his lengthy service in his previous position manifested a lack of ambition. The world demands that we strive for more. John was teaching the simple Bible truth that "godliness with contentment is great gain" (1 Timothy 6:6).

What of his first instruction to these men? They were to "do no violence". On the surface this appears to be demanding something which no soldier could give. Surely all soldiers fight, or at the very least must be willing to do so. The Greek word rendered "violence", according to Strong, means 'to shake thoroughly; figuratively, to intimidate'. The NKJV uses the word "intimidate". The KJV margin suggests "put no man in fear". Maybe John was saying that these men should never terrorize those over whom they ruled. Very few Roman soldiers would see active service. Most were involved in tasks of civil administration. During their work, if a non-Roman citizen was beaten or even killed, there would have been few if any repercussions as far as the soldier was concerned. Such an attitude demanded a serious rethink on the part of those before John.

Nonetheless we are still faced with the question: was John demanding that soldiers seek to resign their commissions? What would we say if a soldier wanted to be baptized today? Surely we would expect a change of occupation. It seems that it was possible for Roman soldiers to buy their way out of the army, although the cost would have been very high. A refusal to obey the commands of a superior officer would have been a serious matter indeed. Some Roman soldiers, in seeking to obey John's instructions to refuse violence, may even have faced execution.

None of these men would have been Jewish. Auxiliary soldiers were enrolled, but never posted back to their native land.

The Roman leaders were not fools: why train and equip a man so that he can turn and fight against you? We are not told where these Gentile men were from. What we do know is that they, along with the common people in Israel and the tax-collectors, came to John with a genuine desire to serve the God of Israel acceptably.

John's message to the leaders
In John's comments to the leaders of the nation, we read some of the most hard-hitting and condemnatory remarks in the whole of scripture:

> "Then said he to the multitude that came forth to be baptized of him, O generation of vipers, who hath warned you to flee from the wrath to come? Bring forth therefore fruits worthy of repentance, and begin not to say within yourselves, We have Abraham to our father: for I say unto you, That God is able of these stones to raise up children unto Abraham …"
> (Luke 3:7,8)

Matthew's record makes it clear that the "multitude" was, in fact, a multitude of rulers. These were Pharisees and Sadducees (Matthew 3:7). They had come, presumably, because so many of the people had been baptized and were daring to question their authority. They were not like the tax collectors or harlots, nor were they like the Roman soldiers – they were not Gentiles. John left them in no doubt as to what they were truly like. They claimed to be Abraham's children. He called them a "generation of vipers", or the seed of the serpent (Genesis 3:15). As if that wasn't enough, he explained that God could make children of Abraham out of "stones".

Why did John choose this particular symbol? He could have referred to any number of items which surrounded him in the wilderness. He might have spoken of plants, trees or animals. Why stones? A stone is dead; it has never lived, not will it ever do so. Was John saying that God can cause the dead to rise, as "living", or "lively" stones (1 Peter 2:5)? Possibly so, but there was a further vital lesson that he was seeking to expound to those who had "ears to hear".

We know that, initially at least, John worked at the banks of the Jordan. This is where the above words were spoken, and where, shortly afterwards, Jesus was baptized (Matthew 3:5,6,13). We read of him preaching at Bethabara (John 1:28), and Aenon, near to Salim (3:23). Bethabara means 'ferry house' (Strong). Thayer's Lexicon says it means 'place of crossing'. Some have connected this with Bethbarah in Judges 7:24, where Gideon encouraged the men of Ephraim to capture the Midianites. We know that Israel had crossed the Jordan to enter the land under Joshua. Was this the same place? It would certainly be a fitting location to preach of the greater Joshua who would come. What is baptism but a 'crossing over' from death to life?

As the nation crossed the Jordan, Joshua took twelve stones out of the river, and set them up as a pillar (Joshua 4:3,8,20). Another twelve stones were placed *in* the river at the same time (verse 9). Were any of these stones still visible in John's day? Were they the stones to which John was referring?

There is one other place where stones are spoken of which demands our attention. In Isaiah 5 we read of all that the Father had done for Israel when they came into the land:

"... My wellbeloved hath a vineyard in a very fruitful hill. And he fenced it, and gathered out the stones thereof, and planted it with the choicest vine, and built a tower in the midst of it, and also made a winepress therein ..." (Isaiah 5:1,2)

Some of these symbols are easily identifiable. The vineyard speaks of the house of Israel, and the vine the people of Judah (see verse 7). What do the stones represent? What (or, more correctly, who) was gathered out of the land that Israel might inherit? There is only one answer: the Gentile nations (Exodus 34:24). They were the "stones" in Isaiah's parable of the vineyard.

Surely John was referring to this when he said that God could make stones into children of Abraham. He was saying that even spiritually dead Gentiles – men like the Roman soldiers – could be baptized and embrace Israel's hope. In due course this prophecy came true to the letter. After the Master's ascension to heaven the word of God would indeed be preached to "the uttermost part of the earth" (Acts 1:8).

Around three and a half years later the Master used the same symbol. When the people sang praises to God as he entered the city of Jerusalem, the leaders demanded that they be silenced. His reply also picked up the language of Isaiah 5:

> "And he answered and said unto them, I tell you that, if these should hold their peace, the stones would immediately cry out." (Luke 19:40)

If Israel doesn't glorify God, then Gentiles will! What a sombre warning for the leaders. Yet for the most part, they paid absolutely no heed to these words.

"We have Abraham to our father"

John's condemnation of the attitude of the leaders was unmistakeable. They gloried in their 'roots'. They took delight in claiming that their family tree enabled them to trace their lineage right back to Abraham. Such things, said the great forerunner, are an abomination to God. Surely the fact that it was John who taught this is worthy of particular note. Who more than John had a right to claim that his family was the mightiest? Who more than John could speak of his great and noble relations? Did he do so? Did he say, 'There is one coming after me (Matthew 3:11) ... and he just happens to be my second cousin'? Far from it. Indeed when Jesus came to be baptized, John declared himself unworthy to perform this task (verse 14).

A man or woman's ancestry means nothing to the Lord. It is what a person is like, not what his or her family is like, that matters. Even Gentiles were accepted by John. Hardened Roman soldiers, doubtless regarded by so many as the enemy, bowed before him and sought his guidance. And throughout time men and women from all races have come to the word of God, seeking to serve the high and holy one of Israel, asking exactly the same question: "What shall we do"?

33

The centurion at Capernaum

JESUS had concluded his glorious address on the mount. As he descended, great multitudes followed him, hanging on his every word (Matthew 8:1). As he reached the bottom a leper met him, stating his unquestioning belief that, if Jesus wished to, he had the power to cleanse him. One touch from God's Son was sufficient. The healed man was told to present himself to the leaders with the offerings required by the Law of Moses "as a testimony unto them" (verse 4). As if this was not enough to emphasize the horrendous state of the majority of the Jewish leadership, the very next incident would hammer home the point. A centurion – a despised Roman soldier with authority over a great number of men – was to manifest the kind of faith which would put even those of Israel to shame.

Capernaum
Capernaum was a city on the western shore of the sea of Galilee. It is mentioned many times in the Gospels. It had its own synagogue where Jesus taught on a number of occasions (Mark 1:21; John 6:59). It seems likely that this had been built by the centurion mentioned above. One of the occasions when the disciples disputed as to who was the greatest took place at Capernaum (Mark 9:33). When the Master walked on the sea, the disciples were heading for this port (John 6:16-21). A nobleman of the city, whose son was sick, came to Jesus when he was in Cana, pleading for the life of his child. The Master healed the boy, and the man and all his house became believers as a

result (4:46-54). The city was clearly of some importance to the Roman authorities, indicated by the fact that tribute money was collected there (Matthew 17:24).

The most significant fact regarding the city is that, for a time, this was the home of the Lord Jesus:

> "And leaving Nazareth, he came and dwelt in Capernaum, which is upon the sea coast, in the borders of Zabulon and Nephthalim ..." (4:13)

We saw in chapter 24 how Matthew's record goes on to describe the whole area as "Galilee of the Gentiles". Jesus Christ was synonymous with this despised, northern region. Having moved from Nazareth (possibly because of the hostility of the leaders there, see Luke 4:16,29) he made his home in the neighbouring city of Capernaum (verse 31).

For some time God's only begotten Son remained in that place, teaching and healing, correcting and guiding. We might think that he would look back on his time there with memories of a people who were, on the whole, faithful and receptive. In fact, the very opposite was true:

> "And thou, Capernaum, which art exalted unto heaven, shalt be brought down to hell: for if the mighty works, which have been done in thee, had been done in Sodom, it would have remained until this day." (Matthew 11:23)

What a terrible thing to read! Even the men of Sodom, who were surely some of the most evil in the history of the world, would have responded had Jesus been in their midst. Yet the inhabitants of Capernaum, despite having witnessed "mighty works" performed by the Master, remained in a state of sinful self-exultation. It took a Roman centurion to manifest the kind of faith and humility with which God is pleased.

Centurions

Centurions have been described as "the backbone of the Roman army". They were legionaries and were easily identifiable by a transverse crest worn on their special helmets, and more ornate harness. They carried a short vine-wood staff as a symbol of rank;

this was also used as a weapon. A centurion would have worked his way up the ranks as a soldier, having been rewarded for his dedication and courage. Unsurprisingly, such men received far greater pay than the others in the army. It has been suggested that this would have been more than twenty times the salary of the average foot soldier, amounting to about 5,000 denarii per year.

Unlike his men, a centurion would have had a large, well equipped and more comfortable tent all to himself. This would be pitched at the head of his men's tents, and made from leather. He would also have slaves to look after him.

Within any legion there would be a hierarchy of centurions. Each would earn promotion until they reached the rank of Primus Pilus, or 'centurion of the first'. He would hold that rank for only one year before being promoted to a senior rank. At this point all the others would move up.

Centurions would have witnessed all sorts of things in the course of their service. On the battlefield they may have been accustomed to the kinds of sights and sounds which would, doubtless, fill each of us with horror. As an occupying force in a land there might have been uprisings which would need to be quelled. Taxes would have to be raised. Roads and buildings would need to be constructed or repaired. And, of course, the Roman method of execution was crucifixion, over which it appears a centurion was stationed (Matthew 27:54).

Centurions were battle-hardened warriors, normally impervious to the things that would touch other men. Yet one came before Jesus in great need, with genuine desire that one whom he loved might be blessed.

The centurion's request of the Lord Jesus
News of the Master's works travelled fast. When those who had family members sick heard that he was in the midst, many were moved to present their loved ones to him. When he came to Capernaum, one man acted in precisely this way:

"And a certain centurion's servant, who was dear unto him, was sick, and ready to die. And when he heard of Jesus, he sent unto him the elders of the Jews, beseeching him that he would come and heal his servant." (Luke 7:2,3) Matthew's record reads slightly differently, as the man appears to converse with Jesus. We have no problem with this. The conversation took place, albeit through intermediaries. The reason for this becomes apparent later in the record.

Even before we consider the events that followed, the fact that this man desired the healing of his servant is of particular importance. The Greek word rendered servant means 'slave', or 'bondslave'. We might wonder why this man, who was clearly wealthy and may have had a number of slaves, should have been so concerned about just one.

The above quotation says that the man was "dear unto him". This is the same word that is rendered "precious" in 1 Peter 2:6, describing Jesus Christ. The centurion was therefore a man of great compassion. He loved his servant and was grieved at his illness. Regardless of the fact that another such slave could have been obtained, he wanted this one to be healed. We get some indication as to the severity of the situation in Matthew's record:

"... my servant lieth at home sick of the palsy, grievously tormented." (Matthew 8:6)

The Greek for "palsy" implies paralysis. A man who was "grievously tormented" was clearly in great discomfort. Without the modern-day painkillers or medication which may have eased this man's suffering, it is easy to see the reason for his master's distress.

The appeal to the Master – via the Jewish leaders

Why then did the centurion not approach Jesus personally? There are two possible reasons for this. Firstly, he had a very close relationship with the Jews amongst whom he dwelt. Their willingness to approach Jesus on his behalf was not because he represented the might of Rome and they dared not refuse. They did so because of their respect for him, as their words to the Master demonstrate:

> "And when they came to Jesus, they besought him instantly, saying, That he was worthy for whom he should do this: for he loveth our nation, and he hath built us a synagogue."
>
> (Luke 7:4,5)

Secondly, the centurion felt unworthy to approach Jesus. His humility and awareness of his own sinfulness prompted him to ask others to seek the Master on his behalf.

We see how highly this man regarded the Jews. They said that he "loved" the nation: the Greek here is *agape*. This is the self-sacrificial, godly love which all true disciples of Jesus are called upon to manifest. Interestingly, the Master had used the same word in his discourse on the mount when talking about our attitude towards others:

> "But I say unto you, Love your enemies, bless them that curse you, do good to them that hate you, and pray for them which despitefully use you, and persecute you ... For if ye love them which love you, what reward have ye?" (Matthew 5:44,46)

This centurion is surely a classic example of one who applied this very command. The Jews, naturally speaking, might have been regarded as his enemies. To many Jews (e.g., people such as the Zealots), Roman centurions would most definitely have been treated as enemies. Yet this Gentile man loved God's people, and manifested that love by financing the construction of a synagogue at Capernaum.

I am not worthy ... he is worthy

There is a contrast between the opinion of the Jews regarding this man, and how he saw himself. The leaders had said that "he [the centurion] was worthy for whom he [Jesus] should do this" (Luke 7:4). As Jesus approached this man's house, the centurion sent messengers to him, stating:

> "... Lord, trouble not thyself: for I am not worthy that thou shouldest enter under my roof." (verse 6)

Was he worthy? Was he unworthy? In truth, we could correctly argue that both attitudes were wrong! No one is truly "worthy" to stand before Jesus Christ: all have sinned and come short of the glory of God (Romans 3:23). At best, when we have done all that is commanded, we are still "unprofitable servants" (Luke 17:10). Yet no one is too sinful to make forgiveness impossible. All can come to God through Christ and be saved by grace (Romans 7:24,25), if the truth is believed and accepted, and repentance of past sins is true and absolute (Proverbs 28:13).

The centurion's acceptance of the authority

In the words of this centurion, delivered via his friends to the Lord Jesus, we see the true spirit of this man:

"... but say in a word, and my servant shall be healed. For I also am a man set under authority, having under me soldiers, and I say unto one, Go, and he goeth; and to another, Come, and he cometh; and to my servant, Do this, and he doeth it."
(Luke 7:7,8)

He knew that Jesus possessed power which enabled him to heal from a distance with just a word. This Gentile soldier accepted what many from Israel seemed to struggle to comprehend: distance was no object for the Son of God.

When a nobleman, also in Capernaum, appealed to Jesus for the life of his son, the Master made a statement which summed up the nation (its leaders especially) vey well:

"Except ye see signs and wonders, ye will not believe."
(John 4:48)

Even some of his disciples seemed to struggle to see with the eye of faith. Thomas refused to accept the testimony of the ten that Jesus had been raised:

"... But he said unto them, Except I shall see in his hands the print of the nails, and put my finger into the print of the nails, and thrust my hand into his side, I will not believe." (20:25)

Yet a Gentile man put these Israelites to shame. He knew that Jesus could heal his servant with just one word. There is an echo of these things in Psalm 107:

"He sent his word, and healed them, and delivered them from their destructions." (verse 20)

There is one further comment which demonstrates the astounding insight possessed by this centurion. He knew that Jesus was a man "under authority". In other words, he knew that the power that Jesus possessed was that of his Heavenly Father. Once more, this displays an attitude which could not have been less like that of so many of the rulers. After entering Jerusalem for the final time, Jesus cast the traders and animals out of the temple. This prompted angry accusations by his foes:

> "And when he was come into the temple, the chief priests and the elders of the people came unto him as he was teaching, and said, By what authority doest thou these things? and who gave thee this authority?" (Matthew 21:23)

The authority of Jesus was that of his Father. The Jewish leaders knew that this was what Jesus claimed, yet refused to accept the claim. Those embracing the doctrine of the trinity, making Jesus "co-equal and co-eternal" with his Father, have a similar attitude. Others, such as John the Baptist, and this Roman centurion, accepted the simple, beautiful, powerful truth. Jesus stated this very clearly in one of the (many) discussions with the leaders in John's Gospel:

> "For as the Father hath life in himself; so hath he given to the Son to have life in himself; and hath given him authority to execute judgment also, because he is the Son of man." (John 5:26,27)

The Master marvels at the centurion's faith

Such was the power of this man's words, that Jesus was moved to comment:

> "When Jesus heard these things, he marvelled at him, and turned him about, and said unto the people that followed him, I say unto you, I have not found so great faith, no, not in Israel." (Luke 7:9)

Oh that such things might be said of us! For the Son of God to "marvel" at a man's faith was truly remarkable. What did he mean by not finding such faith "in Israel"? This cannot imply that none in Israel manifested this degree of trust and belief in

God. John the Baptist was still alive at this stage, and his faith surely eclipsed that of all others around him. Perhaps Jesus meant in Capernaum, or that particular area of Israel?

What we do know is that there is only one other occasion recorded in God's word where Jesus "marvelled". In Mark 6:1 we read that he came into his "own country", taught in the synagogue, and was rejected by his hearers:

> "And he marvelled because of their unbelief. And he went round about the villages, teaching." (verse 6)

He marvelled at the faith of a Gentile, and marvelled at the lack of faith of Jews!

What manner of persons ought we to be?

This unnamed centurion manifested his faith in the Son of God, accepting that his beloved servant could be healed with just a word. In our day we have no spirit-inspired leaders, able to perform miracles through the power of God. We do have God's holy word, which is able to build us up (Acts 20:32). As we read the Bible we are called upon to believe what this centurion accepted: that a transformation of our nature is possible (1 John 3:2). His servant was sick; we also suffer from a great sickness: mortality. As the Master afforded healing for all sorts of diseases in his ministry, the greatest 'illness' of all was conquered when he laid down his life, providing the way for us to live with him (2 Timothy 2:11).

When we stand before the Lord Jesus at his judgement seat (Romans 14:10), what will he say to us? Will he marvel at our faith, as he did with this Roman centurion? Will he say, "Well done, thou good and faithful servant" (Matthew 25:21)? Will he reject us for our failure to see beyond the things of this age? What manner of people should we be (2 Peter 3:11)? Surely we should be like this faithful Gentile man, who appealed to the Son of God at Capernaum, and was blessed.

34

The Syrophenician woman

THE Scribes and Pharisees were on the warpath. They had followed Jesus from Jerusalem, desperate to catch him out. In due course they would accuse him of breaking "the tradition of the elders". They were rightly condemned by the Master for their blatant rejection of the commands of God (Matthew 15:1,2). They were the hypocrites of whom Isaiah had written, honouring God with their lips, but not in their hearts (verses 8,9). The leaders were "offended" by this, and no wonder. They were also depicted as fruitless plants which would be dug up and cast away. They were the blind men, trying to lead other blind men, heading only for the ditch (verses 13,14).

At this time Jesus made the decision to travel north, out of Israel, into the Gentile world. This was a journey full of significance. The leaders had refused to hearken to God's words spoken through His Son. Ultimately they would instigate his arrest, trial and execution. So, as if in judgement, the Master headed far away into the lands of the Gentiles "into the coasts of Tyre and Sidon" (verse 21).

The Scribes and Pharisees refused to hearken to Jesus, but in a foreign land he would meet one woman who did. Indeed she could not possibly have been less like the leaders of the Jews in her acceptance of the Master and her faith in Israel's God.

Tyre and Sidon
Tyre and Sidon (sometimes called Zidon) were to the north-west of Galilee, on the Mediterranean coast. They were principal cities

of the ancient kingdom of the Phoenicians. We have already considered the people of Tyre (in chapter 19) and Zidon (in chapter 21).

The Phoenicians were a seagoing race. In Old Testament times they were a powerful, wealthy and influential people. The children of Israel had much contact with Tyre. Some of this was positive, as in the days of David and Solomon, some not so. By the days of the Master the ancient city of Tyre, having been decimated by Alexander the Great, had recovered some of its former glory. In Smith's Bible Dictionary we read the following:

"Strabo gives an account of [Tyre] at that period, and speaks of the great wealth which it derived from the dyes of the celebrated Tyrian purple. The accounts of Strabo and Pliny have peculiar interest in this respect, that they tend to convey an idea of what the city must have been, when visited by Christ. It was perhaps more populous than Jerusalem ..."

These words imply that Jesus visited the city of Tyre, although careful reading of the records does not support this. What we do know is that in the general area of Tyre and Sidon, Jesus met a Gentile woman of great faith.

The coasts of Tyre and Sidon

Having left Israel, Jesus and his disciples arrived in "the borders of Tyre and Sidon" (Mark 7:24). Matthew's record is even more specific – it was into the coasts of Tyre and Sidon that he journeyed (Matthew 15:21).

The word "coasts" can simply imply 'area'. As both cities were on the Mediterranean coast, it seems very likely that the Master was in a coastal town, somewhere in the region of (possibly even in between) the cities of Tyre and Sidon. One glance at a Bible map shows us that there was one town between these two cities. In the New Testament this is called Sarepta. In the Old Testament it was known as Zarephath. In chapter 21 we considered the widow who lived in Zarephath, and her dealings with the prophet Elijah. She fed the prophet in a time of famine, and was rewarded by the Lord in the provision of food whereby she, her son, and Elijah were sustained. Later her son died and was raised to life again through the work of the prophet. We can be sure that as the Master entered this area, he would have had this incident in mind.

The Syrophenician woman

As we have seen, Jesus was a long way from Israel. Yet even here he "could not be hid" (Mark 7:24). We are reminded of the call for all true disciples of Jesus:

> "Ye are the light of the world. A city that is set on an hill cannot be hid." (Matthew 5:14)

So it was that in this Gentile town, far from Jerusalem and the leaders who desired his destruction, a Gentile woman came before him:

> "And, behold, a woman of Canaan came out of the same coasts, and cried unto him, saying, Have mercy on me, O Lord, thou Son of David; my daughter is grievously vexed with a devil." (Matthew 15:22)

> "The woman was a Greek, a Syrophenician by nation; and she besought him that he would cast forth the devil out of her daughter." (Mark 7:26)

This woman was of mixed race. She is termed a "Greek". This does not necessarily mean someone from Greece. The term is used to describe Gentiles in New Testament times. We read, "there is no difference between the Jew and the Greek" (Romans 10:12), and "there is neither Jew nor Greek" (Galatians 3:28). The phrase "Syrophenician" tells us that one of this woman's parents was of Syria, and one of Phoenicia. Matthew's record describes her as a woman of Canaan. This was the name of the Promised Land before it was taken (and renamed) by the Israelites (Exodus 6:4).

What this tells us is that she could have appealed to any number of people for help. She might have turned to the religious leaders and pagan deities of Syria, or those of Phoenicia. Maybe she had done so, without success. Finally she came to realise that there was only one hope for her daughter. Only the God of Israel, through his Son Jesus Christ, would be able to effect a healing.

We get some indication of the mindset of this woman in Matthew's record, where we read of her addressing Jesus as "thou son of David" (Matthew 15:22). Yet, despite her heartfelt pleas, the Master appeared to ignore her cries:

"But he answered her not a word. And his disciples came and besought him, saying, Send her away; for she crieth after us." (verse 23)

She was clearly in a state of some desperation. The word translated "crieth" means 'to croak as a raven, scream' (Strong). This again reminds us of Elijah who, prior to meeting the woman of Zarephath, was fed at the brook Cherith by ravens (1 Kings 17:4-6).

When the disciples asked Jesus to send her away, he responded by saying that he was sent solely to "the lost sheep of the house of Israel" (Matthew 15:24). Was he thinking of the people in the days of the prophet Jeremiah?

"My people hath been lost sheep: their shepherds have caused them to go astray, they have turned them away on the mountains: they have gone from mountain to hill, they have forgotten their restingplace." (Jeremiah 50:6)

What a terrible picture of the children of Israel. They were without guidance or leadership from those who should have taught them God's word. Interestingly, the previous verse reminds us of the mindset of this woman:

"They shall ask the way to Zion with their faces thitherward, saying, Come, and let us join ourselves to the LORD in a perpetual covenant that shall not be forgotten." (verse 5)

Like so many other faithful Gentiles, this was the desire of the Syrophenician woman. She longed to be "joined to" God's people, and to enjoy their spiritual privileges. In due course, as a result of her faith, she would indeed be the recipient of these wonderful blessings.

The message of the Master for the woman

Initially, the Master appeared not to notice her. Maybe he was in a state of exhaustion, or perhaps he was testing her faith. She fell at his feet (Mark 7:25), worshipped him and pleaded for help (Matthew 15:25). His response to her heartfelt appeals seems, at first glance, somewhat unusual:

> "But Jesus said unto her, Let the children first be filled: for it is not meet to take the children's bread, and to cast it unto the dogs." (Mark 7:27)

Although we are not told this was a parable, the Master was clearly speaking symbolically. What did he mean?

There are two different groups described here: children and dogs. The picture is of a young family sitting at the dinner table, about to commence eating. How wrong it would be for youngsters to go hungry while dogs were fed. Under the law, casting items to dogs was permitted, but only what was not to be eaten by man (Exodus 22:31).

In Bible times dogs were not the domesticated animals we know today. They were scavengers – demonstrated by the fact that the body of Jezebel was consumed by dogs when left on the ground (1 Kings 21:23; 2 Kings 9:35,36). The term "dog" was an insult. It is used throughout scripture, both by Jews and Gentiles. In Psalm 22:16 the enemies of the Master are portrayed as a pack of dogs, compassing him. Often dogs are portrayed as being 'outside'. In Psalm 59:6,14 we read of the enemy making a noise like a dog "… round about the city". This symbol is also used in Revelation:

> "For without are dogs, and sorcerers, and whoremongers, and murderers, and idolaters, and whosoever loveth and maketh a lie." (Revelation 22:15)

Dogs were outside. As far as Israel were concerned, Gentiles were the same. They were outside the camp of Israel, and therefore not permitted to enjoy the blessings of the things of God.

The woman's faithful response

How might we respond to such things? Some might be terribly offended by the words of Jesus. To be called a "dog", unworthy of the blessings which the God of Israel had chosen to bestow upon His (often rebellions) people, might have been regarded as an insult. Some, doubtless, would have walked away. Not this woman:

> "And she answered and said unto him, Yes, Lord: yet the dogs under the table eat of the children's crumbs." (Mark 7:28)

She understood the language of the Lord Jesus perfectly. She acknowledged her state, as a Gentile "dog", whilst expressing her earnest longing for something better. Her desire was for "the children's crumbs", or something which has fallen from the table. Those of us who have had small children will know that a number of such items fall with great regularity!

Was this woman of Syrophenicia saying to Jesus that she could see what so many of the Jews were blind to? Many Israelites, especially the Scribes and Pharisees, rejected their Messiah. Psalm 118:22 describes him as "the stone which the builders refused": both the Master and Peter quoted this (Matthew 21:42; 1 Peter 2:7). The Lord Jesus Christ was rejected by the greatest number of the Jews, but loved by this Gentile woman.

She made reference to what is left over after a meal. It is surely significant that this incident appears directly between the two (recorded) occasions when great numbers were fed. In both instances the "fragments that remained" were gathered up (Matthew 14:20; 15:37). These remnants represent what was unwanted by the Jews. Jesus Christ was refused by so many within the nation, yet was accepted by tax-collectors and sinners (9:10), and by people like this Gentile woman.

In the actions of Jesus Christ towards her, we see an echo of one of his great forefathers. When the Moabitess Ruth met with Boaz, he commended her for her love in having travelled to the land of Israel with Naomi. He then acted in outstanding kindness:

> "And when she was risen up to glean, Boaz commanded his young men, saying, Let her glean even among the sheaves, and reproach her not: and let fall also some of the handfuls of purpose for her, and leave them, that she may glean them, and rebuke her not." (Ruth 2:15,16)

As in the Master's day, "handfuls of purpose" were permitted to fall from the table of Israel that a faithful Gentile might be blessed. In due course the Moabitess Ruth would be welcomed into the family of Boaz and would become one of the ancestors of David and Jesus.

"Great is thy faith"

The reaction of Jesus in response to her words is truly wonderful:
> "Then Jesus answered and said unto her, O woman, great is thy faith: be it unto thee even as thou wilt. And her daughter was made whole from that very hour." (Matthew 15:28)

The Greek word translated "great" is *megas*, from which we get our English prefix "mega" (as in megaphone). Her faith was above and beyond the norm.

Note also the concluding remarks of the Master: "Be it unto thee even as thou wilt." Mark's record is similarly powerful:
> "... For this saying go thy way; the devil is gone out of thy daughter." (Mark 7:29)

Jesus was indicating that because of her faith, she would receive what she really desired. He said the same thing to two blind men who wanted to see (Matthew 9:29). And he says the same thing to every one of us. If we are willing to seek first the kingdom of God, and His righteousness, we shall be recipients of a place therein, by grace (6:33). If we "look for" him, as this woman did, longing to be blessed, we shall receive our heart's desire (Hebrews 9:28).

Psalm 45 describes a bride appearing before her husband. Much as this may be reminiscent of marriages in Israel in the days of the Psalmist, in truth it can only ever be a depiction of our Lord and his immortal bride. Interestingly, we are given the location from which some of those who are to be united with the Son of God will have come:
> "And the daughter of Tyre shall be there with a gift; even the rich among the people shall intreat thy favour."(Psalm 45:12)

This woman from the coasts of Tyre had indeed forgotten her own people, for she recognised they could never help her. She bowed in faith before the one she knew possessed the power to heal her child. This verse appears to describe the daughter of Tyre giving a gift to Jesus. However "shall be there" is in italics, and is therefore not part of the original record. Could this be speaking of the Gentiles receiving a gift from him? It would certainly fit the context of the Psalm, and would make the faithful woman who appealed to Jesus a type of faithful Gentiles.

The woman's daughter was healed (Mark 7:30); the thing she had longed for – a crumb of comfort falling from the table of Israel – had been received. Truly her faith was counted as righteousness, and just like the believing woman of Zarephath, she had come to know and love the God of Israel and His faithful servant.

The Ethiopian eunuch

HAVE you ever noticed how sometimes, in the plan and purpose of God, the very opposite of what someone may have intended actually takes place? Haman had determined that all the Jews should be killed, leaving him free from the annoyance of Mordecai, and able to sit at the king's right hand unchallenged. In due course not only was Mordecai elevated to take his place, but the Jews were saved and he (Haman) was executed. God's hand was at work, and no man, no matter how great, was able to withstand Him.

We read a further example of just this pattern of events at the commencement of Acts chapter 8. The leaders of the Jews had determined that the disciples had to be silenced. No more must they speak of Jesus of Nazareth and his resurrection, or of the Gospel being preached to other nations. They would stop at nothing to ensure this. Stephen, a man full of the Holy Spirit, faith and power (Acts 6:3,8) was executed for daring to oppose them (7:58-60). More persecution followed, and all but the apostles were scattered (8:1).

However, the result of this was precisely what men such as Saul of Tarsus had dreaded. The truth was preached to a whole new audience. Philip, who is later termed "the evangelist", or 'preacher of the gospel' (21:8) preached firstly in Samaria. Many responded to his words (8:6,14). He was then told to travel towards Gaza (verse 26). The plan and purpose of God determined that he would be instrumental in revealing the Gospel message to one more who was desperate to understand and embrace the hope of Israel. This man was an Ethiopian eunuch.

The Ethiopian eunuch

As Philip travelled towards one of the ancient cities of the Philistines (1 Samuel 6:17), he heard a familiar sound. A man was reading his Old Testament:

> "And he arose and went: and, behold, a man of Ethiopia, an eunuch of great authority under Candace queen of the Ethiopians, who had the charge of all her treasure, and had come to Jerusalem for to worship, was returning, and sitting in his chariot read Esaias the prophet." (Acts 8:27,28)

We considered the people of Ethiopia in chapter 27. They were descended from Ham, and often hostile towards God's people. One faithful Ethiopian, who was also a eunuch, saved the prophet Jeremiah (Jeremiah 38:7-13). As Philip expounded the wonderful Gospel message to the eunuch, we can be sure he made reference to this man.

If we were speaking solely of the things which relate to this life, we may well conclude that this man had done very well for himself. He worked for the royal family of his people, being their chief treasurer. He had the freedom to travel great distances, even to the ancient city of Jerusalem. Despite all these things, he was in a quandary. He had been to Jerusalem to worship, yet it seems there were great gaps in his knowledge regarding the God he sought to serve.

He appears to have been a proselyte to the Jewish faith, like those who had heard the truth preached in their own languages on the day of Pentecost (Acts 2:10). Unlike those men who had rejoiced when the word of God was revealed unto them through Peter and the apostles, this man remained in darkness. It is appropriate that he was on the road to Gaza. After being betrayed by Delilah, Samson suffered in this same place:

> "But the Philistines took him, and put out his eyes, and brought him down to Gaza, and bound him with fetters of brass; and he did grind in the prison house." (Judges 16:21)

In due course the eunuch's eyes would be opened. There is, in fact, hidden away in the text, a further reference to this. Philip had been instructed to go "towards the south" (Acts 8:26). This is a somewhat confusing translation of the original Greek, which means (as the RV margin states) "at noon". This same word is translated "about noon" in Acts 22:6. Spiritually, despite the sun being at its highest, the man was in darkness. He wanted to know more of the one of whom he was reading. Deuteronomy 28:29 and Job 5:14 both speak of men "groping" at noonday, being unable to see. This is precisely what took place here. This Gentile man needed to be enlightened, and Philip was the one chosen by God for the task.

Philip's meeting with the eunuch

When Philip saw the chariot, he was instructed to greet the man:

> "Then the Spirit said unto Philip, Go near, and join thyself to this chariot." (Acts 8:29)

The word "join" is particularly apt. The Greek word means exactly what we might expect: to 'glue' or 'stick'. In Acts chapters 8, 9 and 10 we have three different converts to the truth. They are representatives of all mankind:

Acts 8	Acts 9	Acts 10
The Ethiopian Eunuch	Saul of Tarsus	Cornelius the Centurion
A proselyte	A Jew	A Gentile
Descended from Ham	Descended from Shem	Descended from Japheth

In each case this same Greek word, translated "join" in Acts 8:29, is used:

> "And when Saul was come to Jerusalem, he assayed to join himself (same word) to the disciples: but they were all afraid of him, and believed not that he was a disciple." (9:26)

"And he said unto them, Ye know how that it is an unlawful thing for a man that is a Jew to keep company (same word), or come unto one of another nation; but God hath shewed me that I should not call any man common or unclean." (10:28)

What are we being told? That any can come and be "joined" to the one true God, embracing Israel's hope, by grace. In Christ there is "neither Jew nor Greek", for we are "all one" (Galatians 3:28).

"And Philip ran thither to him, and heard him read the prophet Esaias, and said, Understandest thou what thou readest? And he said, How can I, except some man should guide me? And he desired Philip that he would come up and sit with him."

(Acts 8:30,31)

Philip ran to the chariot. This is a minor point, for no man would be able to catch up with a speeding chariot whilst walking! There is, however, a powerful echo of these things in the life of David. The rebellion of Absalom had been crushed, and Joab determined to send news of the victory to the king:

"Then said Joab to Cushi, Go tell the king what thou hast seen. And Cushi bowed himself unto Joab, and ran."

(2 Samuel 18:21)

On the surface "Cushi" appears to be a man's name; however this is not the case. Both the Revised and New King James Versions correctly translate this as "the Cushite" (i.e., a man of Cush). Cush is the Old Testament name for Ethiopia. The same word rendered "Cushi" above is elsewhere translated "Ethiopian" (2 Chronicles 14:9).

What a contrast there is between these two passages. In 2 Samuel 18 a man of Ethiopia ran to David with news of the death of his son, causing much sorrow. In Acts 8 a man of Israel ran to one of Ethiopia, the truth regarding the death of a son of David was expounded, and the result was great joy.

The man had been reading from Isaiah, but was unable to understand what he had read. He asked for Philip to sit with him and explain the prophecy. Like Jehu and Jehonadab

(2 Kings 10:16, see chapter 26), the two men sat in the chariot together. We are reminded of the words of Paul:

"How then shall they call on him in whom they have not believed? and how shall they believe in him of whom they have not heard? and how shall they hear without a preacher?"
(Roman 10:14)

There is powerful exhortation for us in these things. The people of this world are, for the largest part, in "gross darkness" (Isaiah 60:2). Very few know anything of God's word. Just occasionally we may meet someone like this Ethiopian. Such a person may be desperately searching for the truth, but not sure where to turn. Surely the duty of every one of us who are privileged to know the "great and precious promises" (2 Peter 1:4) is to manifest what we believe by the way we act and speak. Just occasionally some might be moved to ask of the hope we have (1 Peter 3:15).

The suffering servant in the prophecy of Isaiah

The section of scripture the eunuch was reading is what we know as Isaiah 53. The record speaks of one who was led as a sheep to the slaughter, being dumb, humiliated and slain (Acts 8:32,33). The eunuch was moved to ask Philip of whom Isaiah was speaking. Why was he so very interested in this particular man? Surely there is one key phrase in the section which he had read which would have hit home more than any other:

"... who shall declare his generation?"   (verse 33)

A eunuch is unable to father children. No wonder he felt a fellow feeling with this one. The man in Isaiah 53 was, naturally, childless. We know that this is the case, for the Master had no natural descendants. He did, however, have a spiritual family, and they are depicted later in Isaiah's prophecy:

"... he shall see his seed, he shall prolong his days, and the pleasure of the LORD shall prosper in his hand."(Isaiah 53:10)

Doubtless this was one of the first things Philip expounded to the eunuch as he "preached unto him Jesus" (Acts 8:36). There are a number of passages that may have been used that day, in

Isaiah and elsewhere in the Old Testament. The most obvious one is found in Isaiah 56:

"… neither let the eunuch say, Behold, I am a dry tree. For thus saith the LORD unto the eunuchs that keep my sabbaths, and choose the things that please me, and take hold of my covenant; even unto them will I give in mine house and within my walls a place and a name better than of sons and of daughters: I will give them an everlasting name, that shall not be cut off. Also the sons of the stranger, that join themselves to the LORD, to serve him … even them will I bring to my holy mountain, and make them joyful in my house of prayer …"
(Isaiah 56:3-7)

This man was both a eunuch and a stranger. How he must have rejoiced at these things. He would, in due course, embrace that "everlasting name", and be made joyful in God's house of prayer. How different from his experiences prior to this when he attended Jerusalem as an outsider and returned home in ignorance.

Perhaps the words of king Solomon, spoken at the consecration of the temple, were also quoted to him:

"Moreover concerning the stranger, which is not of thy people Israel, but is come from a far country for thy great name's sake, and thy mighty hand, and thy stretched out arm; if they come and pray in this house; then hear thou from the heavens …" (2 Chronicles 6:32,33)

How well this describes the clear Bible teaching that Israel's hope would, one day, be extended to a far greater number. This man had indeed been to the temple with a genuine desire to worship the only true and living God, but only when his eyes were opened by Philip was he able to "lay hold on eternal life" (1 Timothy 6:12).

"They came unto a certain water"

As they continued on their journey, they reached water. The eunuch, having been taught the importance of baptism by Philip, expressed his desire to be baptized. The words which appear in

Acts 8:37 of the KJV, where Philip says he must believe with all his heart and the eunuch responds by stating he believes that Jesus is the son of God, may not be part of the original inspired record. The RV and Rotherham's Literal Translation omit them entirely, although the RV margin states that some ancient authorities insert wholly or partly the words which appear in the KJV. What we do know is that the importance of baptism was stressed. We know also that, as both men had been together in the chariot, both descended into the water:

> "And he commanded the chariot to stand still: and they went down both into the water, both Philip and the eunuch; and he baptized him." (verse 38)

There was mental unity between these men. We need not consider in any detail the fact that what took place was obviously total immersion. Drinking water would have been in the chariot. If sprinkling had been acceptable it would not have been necessary for them to have waited until a lake or river came into view.

How long had they been together in the chariot? Probably only a few hours. Does this mean that someone can learn all that is necessary in a few hours today? Almost certainly not. This was different for two key reasons. Firstly, this man had a knowledge of Old Testament scripture. He was not coming to the truth completely 'cold'. Certainly there were gaps in his understanding but, as a proselyte, he must have had a reasonable comprehension of certain aspects of the law and prophets. Secondly, Philip was Spirit-inspired (verse 13). We have no such men amongst us today. The Father, through His Spirit, had directed Philip to preach to this man (verse 26), and then chose to carry him away to Azotus afterwards (verses 39,40).

Much as we pray for the Father's guidance and blessing in all of our efforts to serve Him, believing that He is with us and will lead us, we do not receive such instructions directly from Him in our day. His word has been provided, which is able to make someone wise unto salvation (2 Timothy 3:15). "That which is perfect (or 'entire') is come" (1 Corinthians 13:10). Paul's words regarding prophecies failing and tongues ceasing have come to pass (verse 8). We must do all we can to ensure that the first principles are known and believed before anyone is baptized (Hebrews 5:12; Mark 16:16).

Philip was carried away by the Holy Spirit (Acts 8:39). Like Elijah and Elisha (2 Kings 2:11,12), the power of God had determined that these two should be parted. Indeed, exactly the same phrase is used in relation to the separation of two prophets and Philip and the eunuch:

"… he saw him no more …" (verse 12; Acts 8:39)

In the days of the prophets, communities of believers, termed "the sons of the prophets" (1 Kings 20:35; 2 Kings 2:3; 4:1; 5:22; 6:1) had begun to be established. In the days of the apostles, ecclesias were being set up. Many in Samaria had embraced the truth. A proselyte of Ethiopia had done the same. In due course the word of God would go forth to "the uttermost part of the earth" (Acts 1:8).

Unlike others from Ethiopia, this eunuch was not hostile to those of Israel. In fact the very opposite was true. He knew something of God's law and the message of His prophets. All that was needed was one who would come and expound unto him the way of God more perfectly (18:26).

Having been guided by Philip, he believed the truth and was given a name which speaks of eternity. He was baptized into "the name of the Father, and of the Son, and of the Holy Spirit" (Matthew 28:19), and doubtless he did what so many others have done since that time. He arose from the baptismal waters, determined to "walk in newness of life" (Romans 6:4). And as he did so, he went on his way rejoicing (Acts 8:39) – as we should do.

Cornelius

THE disciples had spent time with their risen Lord. Their doubts, which had persisted even after they had seen him alive (Matthew 28:17), had been dispelled. Would the kingdom be established there and then? Jesus was very clear in his answer to Peter's question: it is not for man to know. In the Father's good time all things will be restored (Acts 1:6,7). Before he departed from the eleven, however, there was a promise of great blessings for them. They would receive the power of the Holy Spirit (verse 8). Jesus would be with them always (Matthew 28:20). And at this time a command was given which, doubtless, provoked a degree of uncertainty in the minds of these men:

"Go ye therefore, and teach all nations, baptizing them in the name of the Father, and of the Son, and of the Holy Spirit …"
(Matthew 28:19)

Similar things are recorded in Acts:

"… and ye shall be witnesses unto me both in Jerusalem, and in all Judaea, and in Samaria, and unto the uttermost part of the earth." (Acts 1:8)

This appears to have been the very last thing that Jesus said to his beloved followers. Immediately after he had delivered this message he was taken up from them (verse 9). So the parting words of the Master implied that the Gospel would be preached to all men. In Acts 1 he spoke of their witnessing in four specific areas. As we read the book of the Acts, we see this prophecy was fulfilled to the letter.

The truth was preached at Jerusalem (2:14), in Judaea (8:1), and Samaria (verse 5). In time the Gospel would go forth to "the uttermost part of the earth". Despite their uncertainty regarding this, the apostles would realise that all, regardless of nationality, can come to serve Israel's God and embrace the glorious promises made in His word. In Acts chapter 10 we read of the first real Gentile convert. The Ethiopian in chapter 8 was almost certainly a proselyte (see chapter 35). He had some contact with Israel. Yet in Acts 10 we meet a man with no direct association with the truth. This was the turning point. Cornelius the centurion was the first man from the Gentile world to be baptized into Jesus Christ.

Simon Peter, lodging at Joppa in the house of a tanner

Peter was chosen as the apostle through whom this conversion would be accomplished. At the end of Acts 9 we read of his raising of Tabitha, also called Dorcas (verses 36-41). At the conclusion of these things he is recorded as lodging in Joppa with Simon a tanner. The city, and the occupation of the man with whom Peter dwelled, are highly appropriate.

Joppa was one of Israel's links with the outside world (see chapters 19 and 24). Items were imported and exported via Joppa. Produce from Israel, then as now, left the land via this port. These events at Joppa would result in something else leaving Israel: the hope of Israel would go forth, ultimately reaching all corners of the earth.

Initially Jonah had refused to preach to Gentiles, attempting to flee from God's presence via Joppa. At the same location Peter was instructed to preach to a faithful Gentile man who would, like the Ninevites, respond to the word of God. During his ministry the Master had promised Peter that he would be given the "keys of the kingdom of heaven" (Matthew 16:19). Similar things were said to all the apostles (18:18). The door of salvation would be unlocked by these men. Did Peter ponder these words of Jesus as he met with Cornelius, and witnessed the Holy Spirit descending upon him?

A tanner is someone who makes leather goods. He takes the carcases of animals and uses their hides to produce all sorts of different items. The life of a tanner would have been a hard one. His work would have been dirty and smelly. Yet what he did in reality, God was about to do in symbol. A dead carcase can be used in a positive way. Cornelius, a Gentile man, was "dead in trespasses and sins" (Ephesians 2:1). He was about to be made alive in Christ (1 Corinthians 15:22).

Cornelius the centurion

We are introduced to this centurion in Acts 10:

> "There was a certain man in Caesarea called Cornelius, a centurion of the band called the Italian band." (Acts 10:1)

There were two cities called Caesarea in the New Testament. In Caesarea Philippi Jesus had asked the twelve what people were saying about him. Peter made his bold declaration regarding the Master being "the Christ, the Son of the living God". Jesus responded by blessing Peter, and speaking of the work he would go on to do (see above, Matthew 16:13-19).

It is very likely that Cornelius lived in the other Caesarea, known as Caesarea Augustus. This was around thirty-five miles north of Joppa on the Mediterranean coast. It was a key location. Smith's Bible Dictionary states:

> "... the city was built by Herod the Great. It was the official residence of the Herodian kings, and of Festus, Felix, and the other Roman procurators of Judaea."

Cornelius is a Latin name. He was a centurion. We considered these men in chapters 32 and 33. He was "of the band [or cohort] called the Italian band".

The word of God is placing emphasis on this man's Gentile origins. He was a Roman, and had a Latin name. He worked for the Romans, leading and commanding other Romans. He lived in a city named after Roman rulers, where Roman leaders lived and reigned. His legion of soldiers was called the Italian band. Everything about this man was Roman. He couldn't possibly have been more Gentile. Yet this man was chosen by God, and became the first Gentile in Acts to embrace the hope of Israel.

There is a vital lesson in these things. It is not for us to decide who might make a good brother or sister in Christ. Some have come to the truth having been, initially, totally opposed to the things we believe. Some of the most faithful people lived very worldly lives prior to their calling by God. Would we have chosen a Roman centurion as a suitable brother? Or Saul of Tarsus? God looks on the heart, and He knows what we can never know (1 Samuel 16:7). Let us seek to sow the seed where we can, praying for God's blessing, and knowing that He alone gives the increase (1 Corinthians 3:7).

What kind of a man was Cornelius? The word of God leaves us in no doubt:

> "A devout man, and one that feared God with all his house, which gave much alms to the people, and prayed to God alway." (Acts 10:2)

He was "devout". This is a very accurate translation of the Greek word. Peter was later inspired to use the same term:

> "The Lord knoweth how to deliver the godly (same word as 'devout') out of temptations, and to reserve the unjust unto the day of judgment to be punished …" (2 Peter 2:9)

We see a classic example of this very principle in the life of Cornelius. He prayed to God. He was spiritually in trouble, for he had no hope. Possibly he wanted to embrace the things of the truth. As in the days of Noah, salvation was at hand.

Interestingly, the divine summary of Cornelius and that of mortal men was precisely the same. God's word states that he was devout and feared God (Acts 10:2). When his servants appeared before Peter they were moved to say exactly the same thing (verse 22). Surely we are being reminded of the Master:

> "And Jesus increased in wisdom and stature, and in favour with God and man." (Luke 2:52)

The record makes a point of telling us that Cornelius "feared God with all his house". All his family shared his high standards. Is this an echo of Abraham?

"For I know him, that he will command his children and his household after him, and they shall keep the way of the LORD, to do justice and judgment; that the LORD may bring upon Abraham that which he hath spoken of him." (Genesis 18:19) Despite his Gentile roots, Cornelius, like others before him (Caleb and the Rechabites, see chapters 9 and 26) was seeking to live as Abraham had lived.

Some have connected Cornelius with the faithful centurion at Capernaum (see chapter 33). Others have suggested that the centurion at the crucifixion, who feared greatly and declared "truly this man was the Son of God" (Mark 15:39), might have been Cornelius. Of course, we cannot possibly know for sure. But there are three centurions in the Bible of whom we know anything, and all were good men!

An angelic visitor

As Cornelius prayed to God, he received an unexpected message:
"He saw in a vision evidently about the ninth hour of the day an angel of God coming in to him, and saying unto him, Cornelius. And when he looked on him, he was afraid, and said, What is it, Lord? And he said unto him, Thy prayers and thine alms are come up for a memorial before God. And now send men to Joppa, and call for one Simon, whose surname is Peter: he lodgeth with one Simon a tanner, whose house is by the sea side: he shall tell thee what thou oughtest to do."

(Acts 10:3-6)

He prayed at the "ninth hour". This was the time that the Master died (Matthew 27:46). How appropriate that one of the beneficiaries of that work – the very first Gentile beneficiary – should be visited by an angel at the same time.

We see that his prayers and alms were accepted by God as a "memorial". God had remembered him. This same word is only used on two other occasions, and both speak of the woman who anointed the Master (26:13; Mark 14:9). On both occasions we read of those who performed good works (see above, "alms").

Also on both occasions there were those who were displeased with what had taken place (Matthew 26:8; Acts 11:1,2).

Peter's vision
The servants of Cornelius journeyed to Joppa to find Peter. At this time the apostle was praying to God, and fell into a trance (10:10). This is the Greek word *ekstasis*, from which we get our English words 'ecstasy' / 'ecstatic'. This was no normal dream. He would be amazed by what he saw, and the meaning of it:

> "… and saw heaven opened, and a certain vessel descending unto him, as it had been a great sheet knit at the four corners, and let down to the earth: wherein were all manner of fourfooted beasts of the earth, and wild beasts, and creeping things, and fowls of the air." (verses 11,12)

Strong says "vessel" means 'a linen cloth, especially a sail'. Perhaps this fisherman, who would become a "fisher of men" (Matthew 4:18,19), was struck by that which resembled a sail being used to contain all sorts of animals. In due course he would "fish" Cornelius from the world, a place which is represented in God's word by the seas (Isaiah 57:20; Revelation 17:15).

In response to the command of God to "kill and eat" (Acts 10:13), Peter quoted the law. In Leviticus 11 we read of creatures which could and could not be eaten. The words of the Father through the angel caused genuine consternation for the apostle (Acts 10:17). Peter regarded the Gentiles as "unclean". Despite the instructions of Jesus (see above), he was still struggling to accept that the Gospel would be preached to all lands. The Father's message to him, repeated three times, was very clear:

> "What God hath cleansed, that call not thou common." (verse 15)

The Greek word translated "cleansed" is *katharizo*, from which we get the English word 'catharsis'.

Peter's meeting with Cornelius
As this vision concluded, the servants of Cornelius arrived at the house. They relayed to Peter how their master had been instructed

by an angel of God to send for him. The next day Peter arrived at the house of the centurion, who had gathered his family and friends together in anticipation of his arrival (verse 24).

> "And as Peter was coming in, Cornelius met him, and fell down at his feet, and worshipped him. But Peter took him up, saying, Stand up; I myself also am a man." (verses 25,26)

There are some in the churches around us who would elevate certain of their number above others. The Roman Catholic church regards Peter as their first "bishop of Rome", or Pope. It is not uncommon to see people bowing before the one who holds this office today. Peter, however, refused to permit such a practice. All are of one rank in Christ Jesus. We call none by any special title. Jesus is our Master. The Lord God is our gracious, loving Heavenly Father (Matthew 23:8-10). We are, by grace, His servants.

Peter described the vision he had seen, and quoted the words of God regarding not calling any man common or unclean (Acts 10:28). He then asked why he had been called. Cornelius outlined what had taken place. Some of this may have been already relayed by his servants (see verse 22); however he described in detail how, when he was fasting, he saw a man "in bright clothing". He explained how the angel had said his prayers were heard and his alms accepted by God. Peter's response was both beautiful and powerful:

> "Then Peter opened his mouth, and said, Of a truth I perceive that God is no respecter of persons: but in every nation he that feareth him, and worketh righteousness, is accepted with him." (verses 34,35)

"God is no respecter of persons." Unlike many in the world, God does not respect someone based on his or her ancestry (see John's words to the leaders, chapter 32). Certainly the Jews are God's chosen race, for He has not "cast away his people" (Romans 11:1,2). However, respecting a man because of his family tree is worldly in the extreme. In every nation those who seek to serve the Father are accepted. Just like those faithful Gentiles in Old Testament times, Cornelius was accepted by Israel's God.

This is confirmed by the speech of Peter which follows. He referred to Jesus as being "Lord of all" (Acts 10:36). He also said that "... whosoever believeth in him shall receive remission of sins" (verse 43). This was an acknowledgment of the might of Jesus over all nations and that forgiveness was not solely the preserve of Abraham's natural descendants.

As if to prove that Israel's God had indeed accepted Cornelius, a most unusual thing took place:

"While Peter yet spake these words, the Holy Spirit fell on all them which heard the word." (verse 44)

This is not unique, but is most certainly untypical. Normally the gifts of the Holy Spirit were passed on by the laying on of hands (as in Samaria, 8:17). Here the power was given directly from God, as if to prove that these faithful Gentiles had been accepted by Him. Peter responded by asking a (rhetorical) question:

"Can any man forbid water, that these should not be baptized, which have received the Holy Spirit as well as we?" (10:47)

Peter had finally accepted what the Master had said to him prior to his ascension. The Jews were God's people; they always have been and they always will be. But Gentiles would also be free to embrace those things which had, until then, been the preserve only of the children of Israel. From this point on, minor hiccoughs not withstanding (Galatians 2:11-16), Gentiles would be welcomed into the household of faith. Through the work of men like Paul (termed "the apostle of the Gentiles" in Romans 11:13), Silas, Barnabas, Timothy, Titus, Apollos and John Mark, great numbers of Gentiles would learn the truth and put on Jesus Christ through baptism. In time ecclesias would be established throughout the Roman world.

Later still the word of God would be accepted many miles from the places described in the pages of God's word. In 1832 an English doctor called John Thomas embarked on a voyage to America on board a ship called the Marquis of Wellesley. Events transpired during that journey which would have far-reaching effects for him and many others. In time many more Gentiles would come to know the truth. Ecclesias were established in almost every country of the world. To this day the word of God still sounds forth, calling all to come to Him in faith.

How honoured we are to know of these things. No matter what our nationality, gender or social standing, we have been permitted to embrace the hope of Israel and become sons and daughters of the Living God. Some of the best known and most oft-quoted verses in our Bible talks reflect this truth so powerfully:

"For as many of you as have been baptized into Christ have put on Christ. There is neither Jew nor Greek, there is neither bond nor free, there is neither male nor female: for ye are all one in Christ Jesus. And if ye be Christ's, then are ye Abraham's seed, and heirs according to the promise."

(Galatians 3:27-29)

Surely in the lives of these faithful Gentiles we are being shown a small representation of those who were to come after them. We are now, just like Cornelius, part of Abraham's seed, and heirs according to God's promises – and we wait for the time when, by grace, we shall play our part in manifesting these things to those who will be permitted to survive the "time of trouble such as never was" (Daniel 12:1). In that great day, those with whom the Father is pleased will be clothed with the "garments of salvation" (Isaiah 61:10), even immortality and incorruptibility (1 Corinthians 15:53). How fitting it is that, when the darkness of this age will be swept away, and the world will be filled with the glorious light of God's power, mercy and love, those immortal saints are portrayed as shining like lights in the darkness:

"And they that be wise shall shine as the brightness of the firmament; and they that turn many to righteousness as the stars for ever and ever." (Daniel 12:3)

Scripture index

Genesis

1 248
2 :14 192
3 :6 115
:6,7 13
:15 .... 94, 261
:24 13
4 :25 94
6 :2 13
:11 13
7 :4,12 195
9 :25 80
10 :6 214
:6,16 129
:6,17 76
:7 155
:8 214
:11 191
:15 161
:28 155
11 :10,11,16,17 9
12 :1 251
:1-3 .... vii, 7
:3 .... 17, 54, 110, 213, 234, 251, 258
:5 8
:7 .... 8, 251
:10 22

13 :7 8
:15 8
:18 62
14 10
:13 .... 9, 10
:13,24 59
:18 12
:23 174
:24 10
15 201
:13 40
:13,14 56
:14 40
:18 .... 10, 77, 79, 149, 154, 201, 207
:18-21 8
:19 .... 53, 58, 88, 207
:19-21 201
:20 113
:21 .... 76, 129
16 :11 239
17 :11 .... 45, 69
:12 31
:14 45
:19 239
18 :6 163
:19 .... 205, 292
19 :11 180
:31-38 124

:37,38 .... 96, 106
20 :12 13
:17 140
21 :19 180
22 163
:1 22
:2 132
:12 .... 131, 135
:17,18 140
:18 .... 7, 110
23 133
:6 .... 9, 103
:10 113
:10-15 134
:15 9
:19 62
24 :15,67 13
25 :1,2 41
:2 41
:3 155
:7 9
:9 62
:20 169
:27 46
:30-34 139
27 18
28 :5 13
:20 189
29 :8 42
:10 42

:16,23-28 13
:23 43
30 :24 27
:27 43
:30 140
31 :7 43
:38-41 169
:52 12
32 :2 122
:24-29 12
:28 .... 1, 12, 42
33 :1 42
:4 12
:17 12
:18 12
34 12
:1 13
35 :21 42
37 :2 21
:27 14
:28 .... 21, 41
:28,36 41
:35 .... 12, 14
:36 21
38 :1,2 13
:3-5 14
:6 14
:7 15
:8 119
:9 15
:10 15
:11 16
:12 17
:14 17
:17,18 18
:20,21 18
:23 18
:24 19
:26 19
:27-30 20
39 :1-5 21
:1-6 220
:3 23

:5 140
:9 22
:14 187
:20,21 21
40 22
:15 23
:23 22
41 :1 24
:8 249
:9-14 24
:16 24
:25,28,32 24
:37,38 25
:39-41 25
:45 .... 26, 27, 42
43 19
:23 28
44 :18-34 .... 14, 19
45 :8 26
:26,27 158
46 :6 22
:12 .... 16, 20
:32 12
47 :30 99
48 :5 27
:22 76
49 :18 70
:31 62
50 :13 62
:25 99

Exodus

1 :5 .... 29, 131
:12 29
:16 29
:22 .... 29, 31
2 :1,2 29
:2 .... 29, 31
:6 30
:7-9 31
:10 31
:11-15 40

:16 42
:17 42
:18 42
:21 43
:22 43
3 43
:1 42
:8 .... 76, 113, 129
:14,15 155
4 :4 18
:18 43
:22,23 44
:24-26 44
5 :2 35
6 :3 155
:4 274
:20 29
7 :1 36
:7 .... 31, 41
:11 249
:11,12 35
:17 34
:22 35
8 :2 34
:7 35
:16 .... 34, 35
:19 35
:22,23 34
9 :16 54
:18 83
:20,21 36
10 :7 36
:23 .... 23, 37
12 :7 71
:12 .... 24, 36
:13 .... 71, 131
:22 71
:23 .... 71, 131
:29 71
:37 34
:38 37
:41 71
13 :5 129

Scripture index

:19 32
14 :10 37
:13 39
:19,20 .... 37, 252
:20 90
:21,22 37
15 :15 97
:24 .... 39, 81
16 :1 45
:8 161
:21 60
17 :16 231
18 :2,3,5,7 46
:4 43
:9,10 46
:11 47
:12 47
:13 48
:18 48
:23 48
:27 48
20 :12 205
:24 174
21 :2 139
22 :31 276
23 :23 129
:27 235
:29 164
25 :4 92
:8 116
:11 253
:17 253
:18-20 102
:22 116
27 :20 163
28 :28 18
30 253
:23 254
:34 253
32 :4-6 39
34 :5-7 155

:6 .... 78, 182, 259
:7 102
:24 262
40 :38 49

Leviticus
1 :4 47
:10 92
11 293
:13,15 162
13 .... 67, 169
16 :27 93
18 :21 125
:24 246
19 :9,10 100
20 :10 118
21 :9 19
25 :23 150

Numbers
1 :50 116
:50,51 142
6 189
:25 23
9 :1 56
10 :29 .... 42, 49, 53
:29-31 149
:31,32 49
11 :4 39
:4-6 39
13 82
:1-3 57
:4-15 57
:6 .... 57, 142
:8,16 57
:20 59
:23 59
:25 195
:28 63
:29 .... 76, 113
:30 60

:32 60
:33 60
14 :4 60
:8 57
:9 60
:10 61
:24 61
:34 195
15 :38 18
16 :48-50 135
21 :13 97
:21-31 77
:24,35 75
:26,29 97
:28 97
22 :1 97
:1-6 97
:4,5 106
:7 41
:31 180
24 :17 252
25 66
:1 .... 66, 98
:1,6 41
:1-8 106
:8 135
:17,18 41
28 :4 161
30 189
31 :1,2 41
:7 41
32 :9 59
:12 .... 57, 142
35 177

Deuteronomy
1 :36 61
2 :9 97
:14 65
:19 124
4 :39 254
6 :4 25

7 :1 129	:4,5 78	:6 82
:6-8 1	:6 67	:8 83
10 :10 195	:7 69	:10 83
11 :11 76	:9-11 .... 68, 75	:11 83
:16,17 160	:11 .... 61, 72	:12-14 83
12 :7 47	:12 71	**11** :3 76
:10-31 vii	:12,13 69	:19 .... 76, 79
:18 47	:16 69	**13** :8,25 124
12,14-18 135	:18 .... 70, 71	:26 122
13 :6-11 vii	**4** 99	:32 122
14 :23 47	:3,8,20 262	**14** 58
:26 47	:9 262	:10,11 63
15 :20 47	**5** :2-5 45	:12 62
17 :6 204	**6** 15	:13 62
18 :9 246	:19 72	**15** :14 63
:15,18 133	:21 71	:63 130
19 :10-13 188	:22 71	**18** :25 76
21 :8,9 188	:23 .... 71, 73	**19** :13 .... 185, 194
:10-13 73	**7** 175	:29 146
:17 27	:1 72	**20** :7 .... 62, 88
23 :3 .... 98, 107	:4,5 72	**21** :17 76
:3,4 124	:5 72	:38 122
:7 52	:7 77	**24** :32 32
:21-23 189	:24 72	
24 :19 101	:24,25 72	**Judges**
25 :5,6 .... 15, 119	**9** :1,2 130	**1** :10 63
:18 52	:3-6 78	:16 ...... 50, 200, 201
27 :7 47	:4 .... 79, 85	:20 63
28 :28 204	:6 79	:21 130
:29 282	:7 .... 76, 79	:27-33 62
29 :4 47	:9 79	:34 63
:5 79	:11 80	**3** :3 76
32 :39 172	:12,13 79	:12,14 97
34 :3 15	:14,15 81	**4** 50, 53, 89
:7 .... 41, 221	:16 81	:2 90
	:17 .... 76, 138	:6,9,10 89
Joshua	:18 81	:11 .... 42, 88
1 :4 113	:21 82	:11,17 201
2 70	:22 81	:14-16 87
:1 66	:24 82	:15,16 90
	:27 82	:17 90
	10 :2 76	:18,19 92
	:3-5 82	
	:5 77	

Scripture index

:21 93
5 :6 91
:6,7 91
:7 91
:8 87
:15 87
:20,21 90
:24 95
:26 95
6 41
7 41
:24 262
9 :4,5 123
:54 93
13 :25 221
14 :1-6 17
:6 221
:12-19 156
16 :6 221
:21 281
19 :12 130

Ruth

1 :1-5 98
:12 70
:14 98
:15 99
:16,17 .... 99, 108
:20 169
2 100
:8-10,14-16 73
:10,13 101
:11 102
:12 102
:15,16 277
:22 103
3 100
:2 132
:9 .... 68, 102
:10 102
:11 102
4 :1-11 15

:6 103
:11,12 103
:12 20
:13 111
:15 104
:17 111
:21,22 96

1 Samuel

1 :11,24-28 .... 135, 163
:17 44
:19-28 31
2 :5 104
:12-17 137
4 :3,4 137
:4 84
:9-18 137
:22 137
5 .... 137, 159
6 :7-12 137
:17 281
:17,18 108
:19 137
:21 138
7 :2 138
9 :2 109
10 :1 254
11 :1 125
:1,2 107
:2 124
:11 .... 107, 125
13 :8,9 51
:9-13 189
:13,14 51
:14 .... 114, 139
14 :11 187
15 :2 .... 52, 53
:3 51
:6 .... 53, 201
:8 231
:9 54

16 :7 .... 81, 291
:18 153
17 :4 .... 108, 109, 138
:43,49 108
:51,54 95
20 :41,42 46
:42 44
21 :10 139
22 :2 121
:3,4 97
26 :6 114
:8 112
:20 121
27 :2 121
29 :3 187
30 :9 127
31 :2,3 109
:4,5 109

2 Samuel

2 :1 62
:8 122
:8-10 128
:16 76
4 :5-8 128
5 :3 128
:6,7 128
:11 146
6 159
:1,2,10 137
:3 137
:7 137
:9 138
:10 138
:11 139
:12 141
7 :1-3 145
:12,29 140
:13 242
:19 257
8 :2 106

:6 169	:27,28 126	**3** :4 84
:18 112	:28,29 126	:5 84
9 :4,7 123	:29 127	:5-12 152
10 125	**18** 283	:7 153
:1,2 .... 107, 125	:2 .... 108, 122	:9 153
:1-4 107	:21 283	:13 152
:2 126	**19** :9 121	:14 152
:3,4 .... 125, 126	:21,22 112	:16-27 153
:7 105	:31-39 123	:28 153
:13-19 ..... 107, 125	:32 122	**4** :20,21 135
11 114	**20** :6,7 109	:21 154
:1 .... 107, 115	:7 105	:24 154
:3 114	**21** :1-9 84	:25 154
:6-8 116	:2 .... 76, 77	:34 155
:9,10 117	:14 84	**5** :1 146
:11 116	:19 138	:7 .... 148, 158
:13 .... 117, 118	**22** :17 32	:12 149
:14 118	**23** 105	:13-18 149
:14,15 117	:1 115	**6** :12 152
:15 118	:15 212	**7** :13,14 149
:27 16	:18 112	:15,40,45 149
12 :13 .... 117, 119	:19 106	**8** :35 160
:25 42	:20 107	**9** :4-9 152
:26,29,30 126	:20-23 112	:10,11 150
13 20	:34 114	:12,13 150
15 :6 121	:39 .... 105, 112	:20,21 130
:7-12 121	**24** :15 131	:26 149
:12 121	:16 131	:27 149
:13 121	:17 131	:28 149
:18 .... 108, 127, 138	:18 .... 133, 134	**10** :1 .... 155, 156
:18,19 108	:20 134	:2 156
:19-21 122	:20,21 133	:3 157
:20 108	:22 133	:5-9 158
:21 108	:23 .... 133, 134	:10 158
:31 114	:24 134	:13 158
16 :6 105	:25 135	**11** 153, 159
:9,10 112	**1 Kings**	:1 .... 101, 113
:10 166	**1** :5 109	:1-8 160
:23 .... 114, 121	:8 105	:7 .... 97, 125
17 :24,27 122	:12 123	:14,23,26 154
:27 .... 122, 125, 126	:38 .... 109, 112	:23-25 170
	2 :35 112	:42 153
		13 :2 239

15:29 123
16:25 160
:30 160
:31 160
17:1 160
:4 162
:4-6 .... 161, 275
:9 .... 161, 162
:10 .... 162, 165
:11 162
:12 163
:13 165
:13,14 163
:15 166
:15,16 164
:18 166
:24 .... 165, 166
18:5 162
19:2 166
:6 165
:15 170
:19-21 175
20:27 162
:35 287
:42,43 170
21 161
:1,2 115
:8 18
:23 276

2 Kings

2:3 287
:9 166
:11,12 287
:11-13 179
:12 287
3:13 166
4:1 287
:32-35 166
:38 182
5 177
:1 169
:2 173

:3 170
:5,6 171
:7 171
:8 172
:12 172
:13 173
:14 173
:15 174
:15,16 174
:15,20 115
:17 174
:19 44
:20 175
:22 .... 175, 287
:23 175
:25 175
:27 175
6:1 287
:8 177
:8-10 255
:8-23 170
:9,10 177
:11 178
:12,13 178
:13 178
:15 178
:16 179
:17 179
:18 180
:19 180
:20 181
:22 182
:23 182
:24 182
:25 182
7:6,7 179
8:13 170
9:1-3 203
:20 204
:24 203
:27 203
:33 203
:34 205
:35,36 276

10 .... 203, 206
:7 203
:14 203
:15,16 203
:16 284
:23 204
:29-31 205
:32 170
11:1 .... 30, 123
:3 140
:21 27
13:3 170
:17 170
:21 166
14:23 184
:24 184
:25 .... 184, 194
15:19,20 192
:29 .... 192, 194
16:7 192
:8,9 192
17:1 193
:4-6 193
:6 249
:23 .... 193, 194
18:13,14 193
:15,16 193
:19 193
19:14 193
:35 193
:36 192
:36,37 193
20:1 193
21:16 188
22:1 27
23:30,34 211
24:1 226
:2 .... 107, 124
:6 211
:8-12 226
:17 211
25 238

:1-12 226
:11 249
:27-30 239

1 Chronicles

2 :55 200
6 :76 88
11 105
:5 128
:6-8 130
:9 105
:26-47 106
:39 106
:41 106
:46 106
13 :14 143
14 :1 146
15 :18 .... 141, 142
:21 142
:24 142
:25 .... 141, 142
16 :4 142
:37,39 83
21 :5 105
:20 133
:27 135
22 145
:3 145
:4 145
:8,9 145
:9 239
:14 145
23 :14-17 48
26 :4,5 140
:4,5,8 143
:5 143
:15 143

2 Chronicles

1 :13 84
2 :11 148
:12 148
:16 148
3 :1 .... 132, 135
6 :32,33 285
8 :1,2 151
:3 154
14 :9 .... 105, 283
16 :7-9 170
17 :14-19 105
20 :1 .... 107, 124
25 :24 143
28 :15 15
32 :7 179
33 :9-13 239
35 :24,25 211
36 :15 30
:22,23 241

Ezra

1 :1-3 241
2 :1,2 249
5 :1,2 242
:3 242
:6-17 242
6 :1-7 242
:8 242
:9 242
:11 242
:21 246
7 242
:1 242
:6 249
:7 243
:12,13 243
:14 243
:15 243
:16 243
:17,22 243
:19 243
:20 243
:23 .... 243, 244
:24 243
:25 243
:26 243

Nehemiah

1 :11 244
2 :5-8 244
:6 244
:8 244
:10 245
:11 249
:19 245
3 85
:7 85
:14 208
4 :1-3 245
:7 245
5 :17 246
6 :1,2 245
:4 245
:5-7 245
:10-12 245
:15 246
7 :25 85
13 :3 38
:7,8 245
:23 107
:26 160
:28 245

Esther

1 231
:1 214
:13 249
2 .... 231, 233
:7 232
3 231
:1 231
:2 232
:2-4 232
:12,13 234
:15 232

4:16.................... 233
6:6-11 234
　:12.................... 234
　:13.............54, 234
7:9..................... 235
　:10................... 242
8:9..................... 214
　:11................... 236
　:16..................... 90
　:17................... 236
9:5,10 236

Job

1:15.................... 156
5:14.................... 282
6:19.................... 156
11:6..................... 158
29:15................... 181

Psalms

2:6..................... 134
　:9..................... 240
5:8...................... 92
22 118
　:16................... 276
　:25................... 189
36:9......................... 3
40:2..................... 212
　:4..................... 212
　:8..................... 212
41:8.................... 122
　:9.................... 114
45:10....................... 5
　:12...........149, 278
48:2...............86, 123
　:12..................... 86
49:4..................... 156
　:14,19 3
51:2.................... 119
　:13.................... 119
　:18..................... 86
57:1..................... 133
59:6,14 276
68:29................... 240
69:8..................... 101
71:18................... 208
72:6..................... 164
　:10,15 156
　:11................... 154
　:11,17 110
　:13................... 123
74:21................... 123
76:2..................... 12
78:2..................... 156
80:15,17 134
82:4..................... 123
84:4..................... 140
91:16..................... 63
92:12..................... 15
102:16................... 240
103:12................... 119
104:18..................... 92
105:17-19 21
　:21,22 25
　:37..................... 34
107:20................... 269
　:23,25,28,29,31
　................ 190
118:19................... 240
　:22................... 277
119:5..................... 170
　:9..................... 171
125:5..................... 92
137:1,4-6 220
　:1-6 238
141:2..................... 254
146:7-9 182
149:6-9 110
　:7-9 63

Proverbs

1:6..................... 156
8:5....................... 79
　:12..................... 79
12:22..................... 78
14:1..................... 154
15:1..................... 173
24:12................... 157
26:27................... 235
28:10................... 235
　:13..........119, 269
31:10................... 103

Ecclesiastes

5:5..................... 189
9:10................... 144
10:8..................... 235

Song of Solomon

3 253

Isaiah

1:18..................... 70
2:5..................... 180
5 263
　:1,2................... 262
　:7................... 262
9:6..................... 60
11:3..................... 81
　:9..................... 155
　:10............... 2, 218
　:11................... 214
15 97
16 97
　:14..................... 97
19:24,25 198
20:3-5 214
30:21................... 255

:24 132	:6 156	:19 217
35 :5 182	**61** 168	**39** :1-10 216
38 :8 83	:10 296	:3 249
40 258	**62** 129	:11-14 ..... 216, 226
:3,4 92	**63** :11 42	:15-18 216
:31 221		**41** :12,16 85
41 :13 240	**Jeremiah**	**43** :7 246
:17 123	**13** :23 214	**48** 97
42 :1 80	**14** :8 50	**50** :5 275
:1-3 181	**17** :9 .... 61, 115	:6 275
:6 3	:13 50	**51** :33 132
:6,7 215	**18** :11 210	**52** :11 238
:6,7,16 181	**20** :9 212	
:16 92	**28** :1 85	**Lamentations**
43 :6 241	**29** :1-7 219	**3** :48 212
:10,12 .... 7, 146	:10 238	:53,54 212
:23 253	**33** :20 7	:55 212
44 241	**34** 202–206	
:5 113	:2 202	**Ezekiel**
:8 146	:8-10 202	**1** :1 250
:28 .... 239, 240	:11 202	:2 226
45 :1 .... 239, 240	:18 202	**4** :6 195
:2 92	:19-22 202	**16** :3 113
49 3	**35** 199–206	**17** :18 204
:6 3	:1 202	**20** :8 39
50 :4 20	:6-8 203	**25** :16 109
52 :4 192	:7 .... 200, 205	**26** :7 147
53 .... 118, 284	:10 46	:8,9 147
:3 .... 35, 123	:11 170	:12 147
:5 94	:13,14 206	**27** :17 147
:10 284	:18,19 207	:22 156
:11 80	**37** 215	**33** :7 228
54 :17 235	:5 211	:11 44
55 :1 28	:13-16 211	**37** :11 70
56 :3-5 214	:21 211	**38** 57
:3-7 285	**38** 215	:5 214
:7 247	:5 211	:8 169
57 :20 293	:6 212	:13 156
59 :15 .... 16, 232	:7-9 213	:22 83
60 :1-3 viii	:7-13 281	**39** 57
:2 284	:13 215	

:2 169
40:2 250
43:1,2 250
:3 250
44:23 220

Daniel
1 .... 223, 249
:1,6 226
:7 220
:8 220
:9 221
:15,16 221
:20 249
:21 239
2 223–224
:2 249
:5 242
:20-23 222
:27,28 222
:38 222
:47 222
3 232
:15 223
:16-18 223
:25 224
:29 .... 224, 242
4 .... 224, 227
:6 249
:24 225
:24-27 224
:27 225
:33 225
:34,37 225
5:3 227
:5 227
:7 249
:8 227
:13 227
:14 230
:22,23 227
:25 227
6:3 228

:7 228
:10 .... 219, 228, 250
:14,15 30
:15 229
:16 229
:20 229
:21,22 229
:28 239
7:13 250
9 219
:2 .... 244, 250
10:1 239
11:41 124
:43 214
12:1 296
:2 167
:3 296

Hosea
2:15 72

Joel
3:4-6 147

Amos
1:9 147
:13 125
2 97
:10 77

Jonah
1 196
:3 186
:4 186
:5 186
:9 187
:10 .... 187, 188
:13 187
:14 188
:16 188
2:9 191

3:1 191
:3 194
:4 195
:5,6 195
4:11 197

Micah
3:6 248
4:2 136
:3 198
5:2 252
6:5 66

Habakkuk
2:1 228
:6 156
:14 155
3:12 132

Zephaniah
2 97
:5 109
:8,9 124
3:9 197
:10 214

Zechariah
2:8 142
8:23 237
12:4 204
13:7 240
14:1 217
:9 197
:16 197

Malachi
1:2,3 6
:13 100
3:16 250
:17 .... 54, 253

4:2 255

Matthew

1:3 .... 20, 104
:5 .... 73, 99, 111
:6 119
:21 239

2 252
:1,2 248
:1-6 150
:4 252
:8 252
:9 251
:9-11 252
:12 255
:14 22
:15 253
:16 255
:16-18 29
:19,22 255

3:5,6 .... 172, 258
:5,6,13 262
:7 .... 94, 259, 261
:11 263
:14 263
:17 240

4:2 195
:13 265
:15,16 185
:18,19 293
:19 181

5:14 .... 4, 129, 218, 274
:14-16 .... 13, 183
:15 .... 25, 230
:16 ...... 28, 55, 141, 155
:35 123
:44 182
:44,46 268
:45 153

6:2,5,16 78
:3 101
:11 211
:19-21 176
:24 39
:33 278

7:7 157
:13,14 70
:24-27 72

8:1 264
:4 264
:6 267
:20 118
:22 .... 181, 255

9:4 197
:9 181
:10 277
:29 278

10:16 55
:36,39 vii

11:11 257
:23 265

12:18 80
:18-20 181
:38,39 196
:40,41 196
:42 159

14:6-10 30
:20 277

15:1,2 272
:8,9 272
:13,14 272
:21 .... 272, 273
:22 .... 274, 275
:23 275
:24 275
:25 276
:28 278
:37 277

16:13-19 290
:18 42
:19 289
:21 167
:24 181

17:21 233
:24 265

18:3 173
:18 289

19:21 181
:28 49

21:23 270
:32 258
:42 277

23:8-10 294
:23 156
:33 94
:37 102

25 39
:21 271
:31-46 93
:33,34,41 18
:35,36 127
:36 216

26:8 293
:13 292
:42 134
:53 180
:71 150
:73 89

27:4 188
:23,24 211
:46 292
:54 266

28:13 167
:17 288
:19 .... 287, 288
:20 288

Mark

1:21 264

4:41 189

5:7 166

6:6 271

7:24 .... 165, 273, 274
:25 276
:26 .... 165, 274
:27 276

Scripture index 309

:28.................... 277
:29.................... 278
:30.................... 279
9 :33.................... 264
12 :40.................... 165
:42.................... 165
:44.................... 165
13 :14.................... 211
14 :8...................... 100
:9...................... 292
:50.................... 118
15 :39.................... 292
:46..................... 68
16 :16.......... 173, 287

Luke

1 :13.................... 239
:27..................... 74
:28..................... 95
:31.................... 239
:32..... 60, 124, 159
:32,33 6
:34,35 251
:42..................... 95
2 :2...................... 170
:32................. 3, 248
:35.................... 164
:52.................... 291
3 :4,5.................. 258
:5..................... 258
:6..................... 258
:7..................... 259
:7,8.................. 261
:10.................... 259
:12.................... 259
:14.................... 259
4 :16,29 265
:21.................... 168
:24.................... 168
:25,26 168
:27.......... 168, 171, 177
:31.................... 265

7 :2,3.................. 267
:4...................... 268
:4,5................... 268
:6...................... 268
:7,8................... 269
:9...................... 270
:12.................... 165
:14.................... 166
:16.................... 165
:28.................... 257
8 :54,55 166
9 :62.................... 175
14 :31.................... 105
16 :31.................... 167
17 :10.................... 269
:18.................... 173
19 :40.................... 263
:41.................... 212
20 :6..................... 258
22 :31..................... 42
23 :2..................... 211
24 :32.................... 157

John

1 :14.................... 163
:28.................... 262
:29,36 257
:42..................... 42
:47................. 4, 62
2 :17.................... 101
:20.................... 136
:25.................... 165
3 :21.................... 224
:23.................... 262
4 :10..................... 42
:21-24 174
:22..................... 1
:46-54 265
:48.................... 269
5 :26,27 270
:35.................... 258

6 :16-21 264
:59.................... 264
7 :37.................... 172
:41,52 150
:49.................... 258
:52............ 89, 186
8 :12...... 4, 183, 202, 248
:41.................... 186
:56............ 11, 257
9 :5......... 4, 183, 248
:7..................... 172
:25.................... 183
:32.................... 182
:39.................... 182
:40.................... 182
10 :11..................... 42
:11,15 131
:31..................... 61
11 :16..................... 42
:43,44 166
12 :10,11 167
13 :30.................... 178
:35.................... 247
15 :13.................... 118
18 :3.................... 178
:10,11 135
19 :25.................... 164
20 :25.................... 269

Acts

1 288
:6,7.................. 288
:8........ 2, 168, 263, 287, 288
:9..................... 288
2 :7..................... 89
:10.................... 281
:14.................... 289
:24.................... 167
5 175
:29............. 33, 228

:40.................... 167	:34,35 .... 2, 111, 294	**6**:4...................... 287
6:3,8.................. 280	:36.................... 295	:12.................. 118
7:22................ 32, 40	:43.................... 295	:22.................. 119
:23...................... 41	:44.................... 295	**7**:14.................... 162
:25...................... 40	:47.................... 295	:17.................... 64
:58-60 280	**11**:1,2................... 293	:21............. 52, 114
8 ...... 280, 282–283, 289	:18....................... 2	:24,25 269
:1.............. 280, 289	**12**:21-23............. 225	**8**:3........................ 64
:5...................... 289	**13**:6...................... 249	:13............... 52, 95
:6,14 280	:11.................. 180	:31-39............. 218
:12................... 204	:22.................. 114	**9**:7.......................... 6
:13................... 286	:47....................... 3	:13................... 139
:17.................... 295	**14**:8,21 91	:17..................... 54
:26.......... 280, 282, 286	:19.................... 91	**10**:1.................. 1, 194
:26-39 213	:22............... 35, 91	:12.................... 274
:27,28 281	**15**:14...................... 80	:14.................... 284
:29.................... 282	**16**:1...................... 28	**11**:1................. 1, 158
:30,31 283	:29....................... 3	:1,2................. 294
:32,33 284	**17**:31........... 124, 167	:13.................... 295
:33.................... 284	**18**:26.................. 287	**12**:1,2.................. 256
:36.................... 284	**20**:32................. 271	:2........................ 55
:37.................... 286	**21**:8...................... 280	:20.................. 182
:38.................... 286	**22**:6...................... 282	**13**:12.................. 183
:39.................... 287	:16..................... 78	**14**:10.................. 271
:39,40 286	**23**:6...................... 182	**15**:4........................ 39
9 282	**26**:23....................... 3	:12.................. 151
:9............. 180, 182	**28**:20................. 1, 50	
:26.................... 282		**1 Corinthians**
:36-41 289	**Romans**	**3**:7...................... 291
10 .... 282, 289	**1**:16....................... 7	**5**:7....................... 71
:1..................... 290	:31.................... 30	:11..................... 48
:2..................... 291	**2**:9,10 7	**10** 38
:3-6 292	:28,29 144	:5....................... 39
:10................... 293	:29..................... 62	:6,11 .... 23, 38
:11,12 293	**3**:23........... 114, 269	:13..................... 34
:13................... 293	**4**:3,5.................. 253	**13**:8...................... 287
:15........... 148, 293	:12.................... 251	:10.................... 286
:17................... 293	:16....................... 7	**15**:22.................. 290
:22.......... 291, 294	**5**:8,9................... 74	:53............. 68, 296
:24.................... 294		:58............. 24, 228
:25,26 294		
:28........... 283, 294		

Scripture index

2 Corinthians
- **3**:14-16 8
- **4**:4 180
- **6**:14-18 220
- :17,18 55
- **8**:9 134
- **11**:2 154

Galatians
- **1**:8,9 38
- **2**:9 204
- :11-16 295
- **3**:14 50
- :16 56
- :16,29 140
- :27 68
- :27-29 .... 8, 50, 296
- :28 .... 274, 283
- **4**:28 6
- **6**:1 115
- :7 179
- :9 24

Ephesians
- **2**:1 .... 67, 290
- :8 .... 153, 217
- :9 173
- **4**:8 .... 124, 171
- :24 61
- **5**:8 37
- :23-27 96
- :25-27 159
- **6**:7 143
- :11 79
- :17 64

Philippians
- **2**:7 118
- :8 134

Colossians
- **1**:10 218
- **2**:15 64
- **3**:1 .... 69, 117
- :5 52
- **4**:5 .... 55, 79

2 Thessalonians
- **1**:7-10 197

1 Timothy
- **1**:15,16 38
- :18 .... 64, 118
- **2**:14 51
- **3**:16 116
- **4**:2 14
- **6**:6 260
- :12 ..... 64, 115, 285
- :13 146

2 Timothy
- **2**:3 49
- :11 271
- :24 .... 54, 63
- **3**:3 30
- :15 286
- **4**:8 49

Hebrews
- **1**:9 134
- **2**:14 94
- **3**:13 157
- :17 39
- **4**:9-11 23
- **5**:12 287
- **6**:20 51
- **7**:3 51
- :14 .... 6, 19
- **9**:7 116

- :28 278
- **10**:25 115
- **11** 73
- :1 69
- :4 119
- :6 153
- :8 8
- :8-16 56
- :9 .... 11, 12, 46, 205
- :10 86
- :13 9
- :19 .... 133, 163
- :22 99
- :23 29
- :25 117
- :27 32
- :30 73
- :31 73
- :32 87
- :36,37 210
- :38 210
- **12**:2 180
- :4 114
- :16 139
- **13**:14 209

James
- **1**:8 .... 39, 175
- :13-15 116
- **2** 73
- :14-26 164
- :25 70
- **4**:4 .... 14, 17, 162
- :7 114
- :8 39
- **5**:17 166

1 Peter
- **1**:7 253
- **2**:5 261
- :6 267

:7.................... 277
:9......................... 5
:11....................... 9
3:15................ 4, 10, 20, 141, 183, 230, 284
:21.................. 172
4:4................ 55, 232
5:8.................... 229

2 Peter

1:4.... 153, 221, 284
2:5...................... 10
:9.................... 291

:22.................... 16
3:11.................. 271

1 John

1:7.................... 180
2:19.................... 19
3:2................ 8, 271
:3.................... 247
4:4.................... 179

Revelation

2:8.................... 254
:14........ 41, 66, 98, 106

3:15,16 78
5:5...................... 19
7:9.................. 8, 15
14:6.................... 110
17:1.................... 154
:1,16 19
:15.................. 293
19:7............. 104, 118
:7,8.................. 67
20:2...................... 94
21:23.................... 39
:25.................. 240
22:15.................. 276
:16.................. 252